TRESE 1

MURDER ON BALETE DRIVE

Budjette **Tan**   KaJo **Baldisimo**

ABLAZE

WRITER

BUDJETTE TAN

ARTIST

KAJO BALDISIMO

FOR ABLAZE

MANAGING EDITOR

RICH YOUNG

DESIGNER

RODOLFO MURAGUCHI

Publisher's Cataloging-in-Publication Data

Names: Tan, Budjette, author. | Baldisimo, Kajo, illustrator.
Title: Trese: Volume 1 , Murder on Balete Drive / Budjette Tan; Kajo Baldisimo.
Series: Trese
Description: Portland, OR: Ablaze Publishing, 2020
Identifiers: ISBN 978-1-950912-19-3
Subjects: LCSH Manila (Philippines)—Fiction. | Philippines—Fiction. | Crime—Fiction. | Mystery fiction. | Noir fiction. Graphic Novels. | Detective and mystery comic books, strips, etc. | BISAC COMICS & GRAPHIC NOVELS / Crime & Mystery
Classification: LCC PN6790.P53 .T36 2020 | DDC 741.5—dc23

Trese Volume 1: Murder on Balete Drive. First printing. Published by Ablaze Publishing, 11222 SE Main St. #22906 Portland, OR 97269.

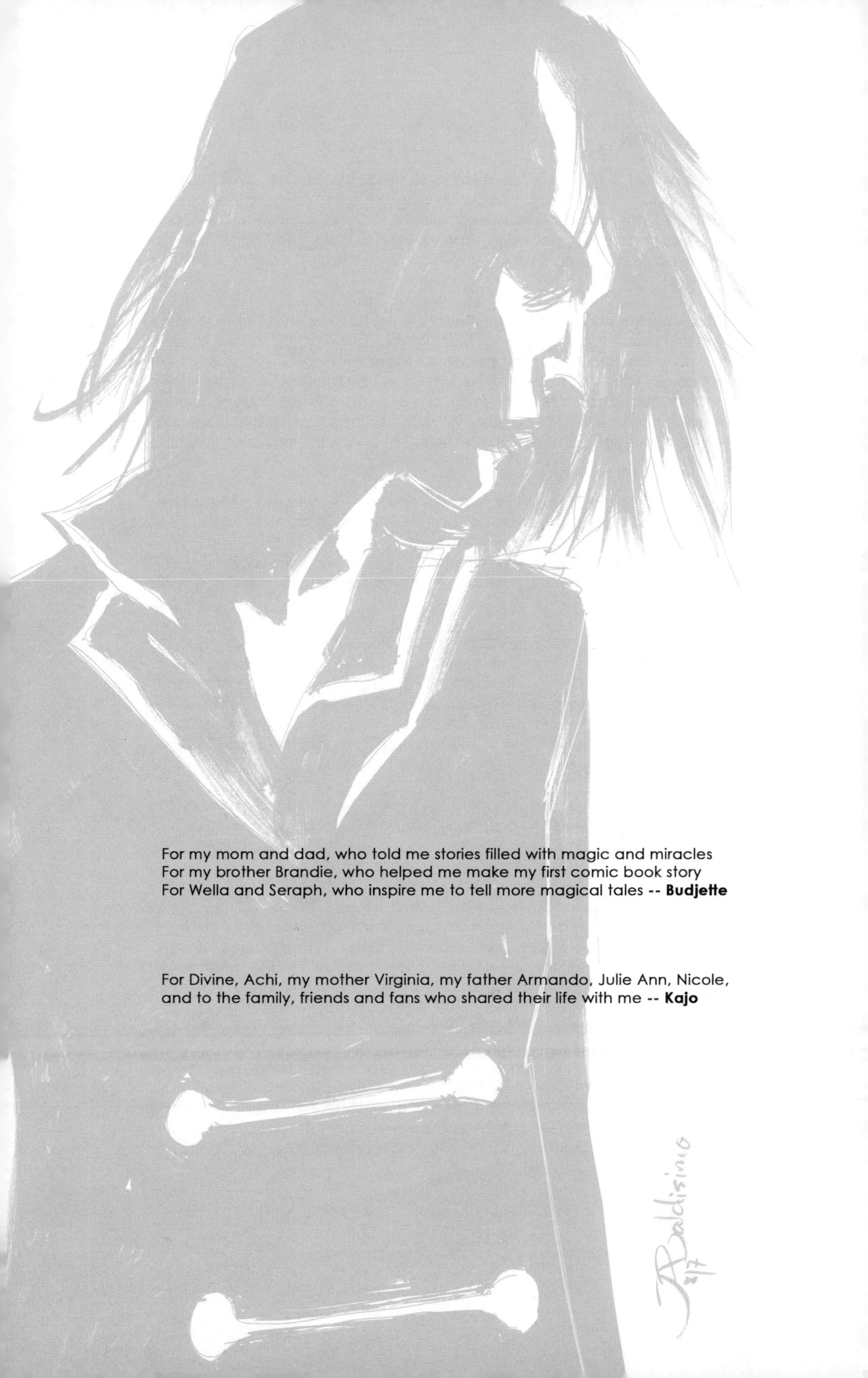

For my mom and dad, who told me stories filled with magic and miracles
For my brother Brandie, who helped me make my first comic book story
For Wella and Seraph, who inspire me to tell more magical tales -- **Budjette**

For Divine, Achi, my mother Virginia, my father Armando, Julie Ann, Nicole,
and to the family, friends and fans who shared their life with me -- **Kajo**

INTRODUCTION

The Philippines is a country that loves comics. The Filipinos love to read them, and love to create them. It's an indelible part of Filipino history and culture. We have produced some of the most talented, most remarkable, and most internationally recognized illustrators. For decades, the Philippines was considered as a country that produces some of the best comics illustrators worldwide.

Writers, well, not very much. Definitely we have had our share of legendary writers like Francisco V. Coching, Mars Ravelo and Pablo Gomez, but we have never had a truly significant comics writer in the last 20 years or more. As much as I am exhilarated and bowled over by the artistic output of our young comic book creators from a new industry of independently produced comics since the early 1990's, I can count with the fingers of just one hand the notable contemporary writers that have crossed this field.

There's Carlo Vergara, David Hontiveros, Arnold Arre, and the one that has impressed me most of all: Budjette Tan.

Budjette's TRESE came out like lightning from the blue, catching me unawares, electrifying me, throwing me clear across my room and flattening me on my back.

Of course, I had already been familiar with Budjette's writing with Comics 101, Batch 72, and a variety of short stories. I thought they were good of course, but they didn't seem too exceptional. It's an observation that prompted me, with far less tact than I would have wanted, to tell Budjette at 2006's Komikon, "Hey Budj, Trese is AMAZING. Why are you all of a sudden THIS GOOD??", with the implication that he wasn't so hot before.

I want to extend a million apologies to Budjette, my old buddy, my old pal. It's just one friend talking to another friend, and you know how it is when friends talk. Sometimes they just want to put down the other as playfully as you can. This time it was completely unintentional.

Budjette's brilliance has always been there, I am sure. It was just looking for the perfect story, the perfect comic book, and the perfect artist before it made itself known. And yes, I do believe TRESE is a brilliant piece of work. It takes an age old theme of Philippine comics: Filipino Mythology, something that's been done to death a hundred times before, and does something completely fresh, completely original and completely exhilarating with it.

Familiar characters are transformed and presented in the most clever and unexpected of ways. They're all here: tiyanak, kapre, duwende, tikbalang, multo, aswang, and even the staple of the genre: the superhero. They're all here but in circumstances and situations that are so maddeningly imaginative that you want to wring Budjette's neck for thinking of it before you did.

But of course, I could have never ever have thought of it. The ideas are so simple in hindsight, but it takes a brilliant mind like Budjette to come up with them in the first place.

This, of course, would not be a comic book without an artist, and Kajo Baldisimo is a great match for TRESE. Kajo is still a young man, and he has the potential to be one of the greatest we have ever had. Here in the early issues of Trese, he is still an artist learning his craft. But the talent is so apparent that it's tantalizing to imagine what he could be doing some years from now. Sparse, stark, with drop dead blacks, the artwork captures Budjette's stories well. Personally, I believe this series would look far better with color, but the artwork can stand well without it.

Originally published as photocopied mini comics, I thought that the comic book could be better served being printed, published, and distributed by a big publisher so it can find the audience that it truly deserves. I'm exceptionally glad that this has now finally come true.

You who are holding this first volume of Trese right now, getting ready to read it from the beginning, I assure you, you have NO idea what you're in for. And you have NO idea how excited I am for you.

Gerry Alanguilan
January 2, 2008
San Pablo City

Gerry Alanguilan (1968 – 2019) was the creator of the award-winning comic book Elmer. His other well-known works were Wasted, Crest Hut Butt Shop, Johnny Balbona, Humanis Rex!, Timawa, Darna Lives!, Where Bold Stars Go to Die, Rodski Patotski, and Bakokak. He was the inker for numerous popular American comics books like Wetworks, Uncanny X-Men, Superman:Birthright, Wolverine, Fantastic Four, and Stone. He was the founder and curator of the Komikero Komiks Museum in San Pablo, Laguna, Philippines. His contribution, guidance, and support to the Philippine comic book industry will be sorely missed.

TRESE created by Budjette Tan and Kajo Baldisimo

BLOG: www.tresecomics.com
TWITTER: https://twitter.com/AlexandraTrese
FACEBOOK:https://www.facebook.com/TreseComics

Budjette Tan has been writing comic books since the 90s and has been working in advertising during the 2000s. He currently works for the LEGO Agency. Aside from TRESE, he is the writer and co-creator of the award-winning comic book "The Dark Colony: Mikey Recio and the Secret of the Demon Dungeon". He co-wrote two books about the creatures of Philippines myth and folklore: "The Lost Journal of Alejandro Pardo" and "The Black Bestiary". He now lives in Denmark with his wife and son, where there no aswang – or so they think.

Kajo Baldisimo is a fan and avid reader of Filipino komiks from the 80s and 90s. He is a storyboard artist by day and comic book creator by night working on TRESE and his self-published bi-weekly zine called WKWKMDNK. After living in Manila for forty years, he is now permanently residing in Davao City, south of the Philippines, where he, together with his wife and son, are beginning to establish an animal shelter.

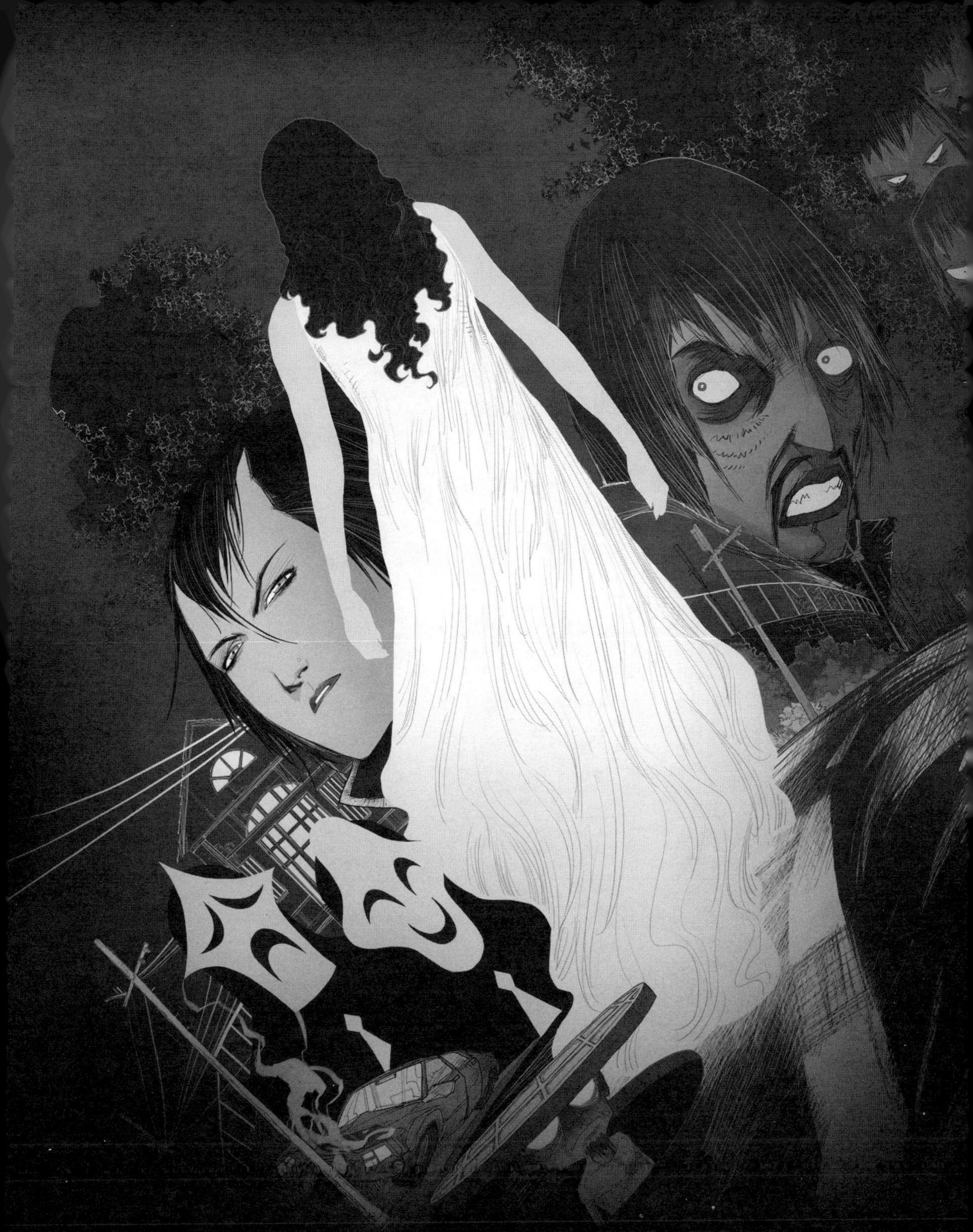

At the Intersection of Balete and 13th Street

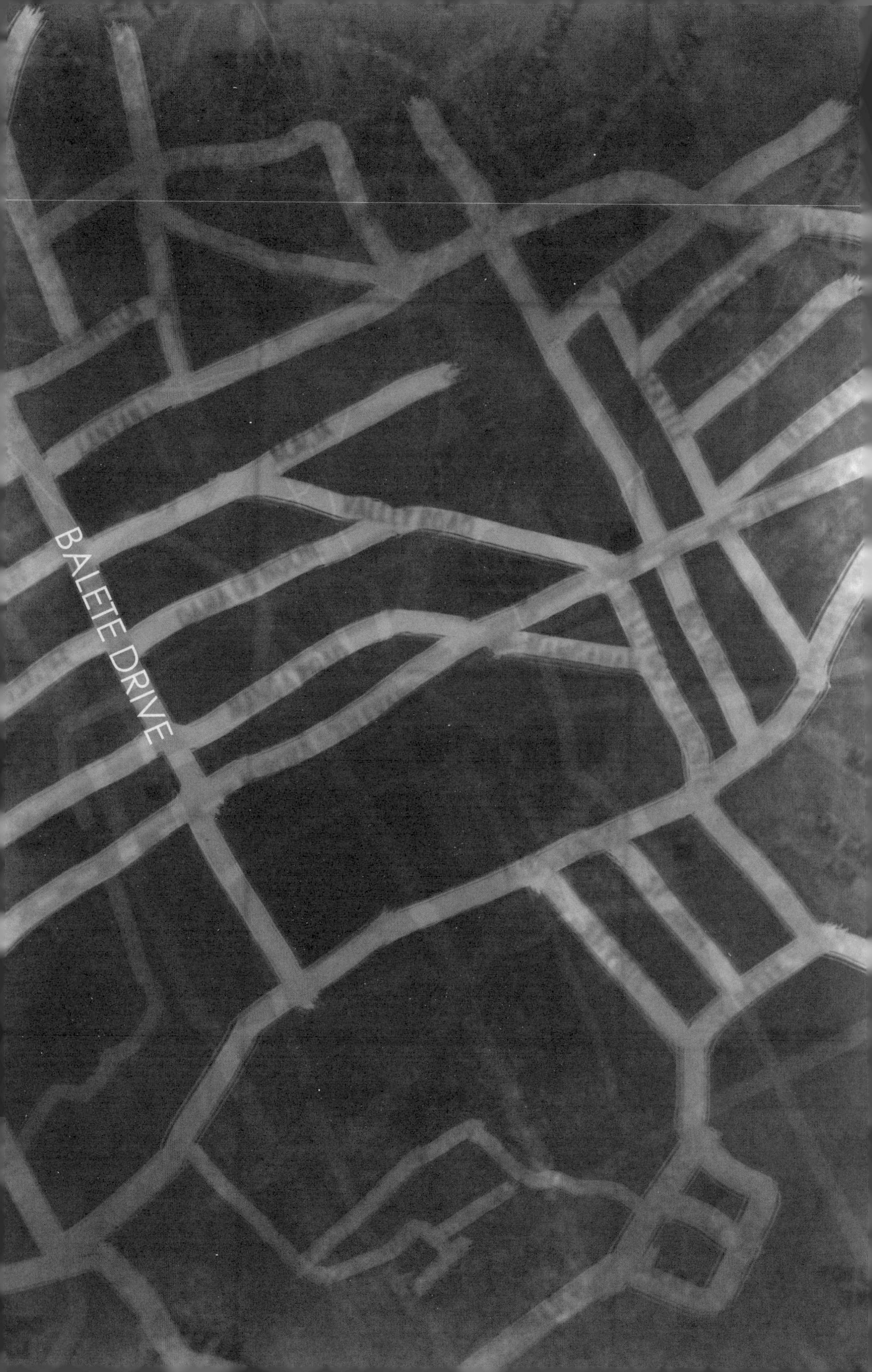
BALETE DRIVE

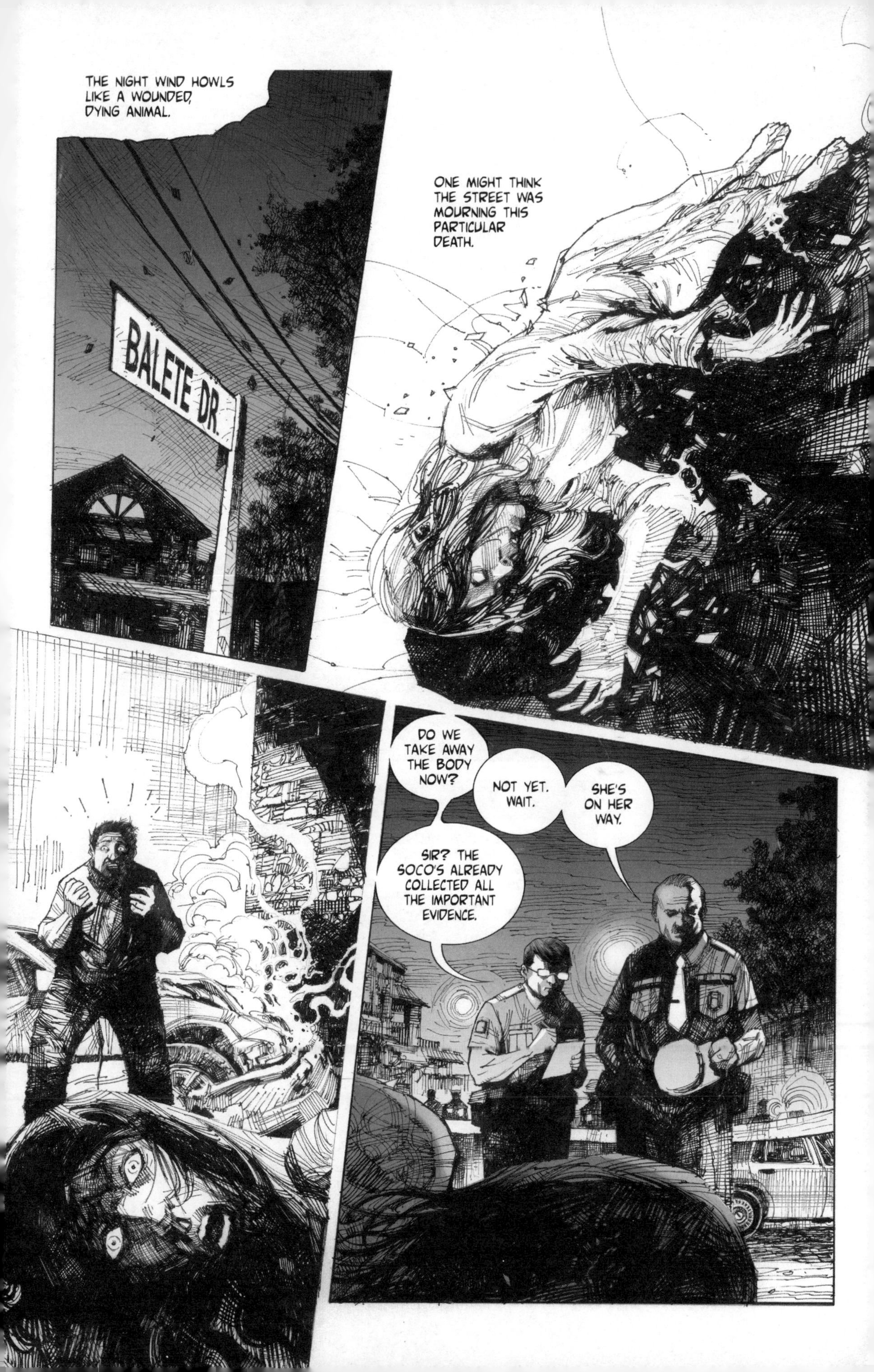
THE NIGHT WIND HOWLS LIKE A WOUNDED, DYING ANIMAL.
BALETE DR.
ONE MIGHT THINK THE STREET WAS MOURNING THIS PARTICULAR DEATH.
DO WE TAKE AWAY THE BODY NOW?
SIR? THE SOCO'S ALREADY COLLECTED ALL THE IMPORTANT EVIDENCE.
NOT YET. WAIT.
SHE'S ON HER WAY.

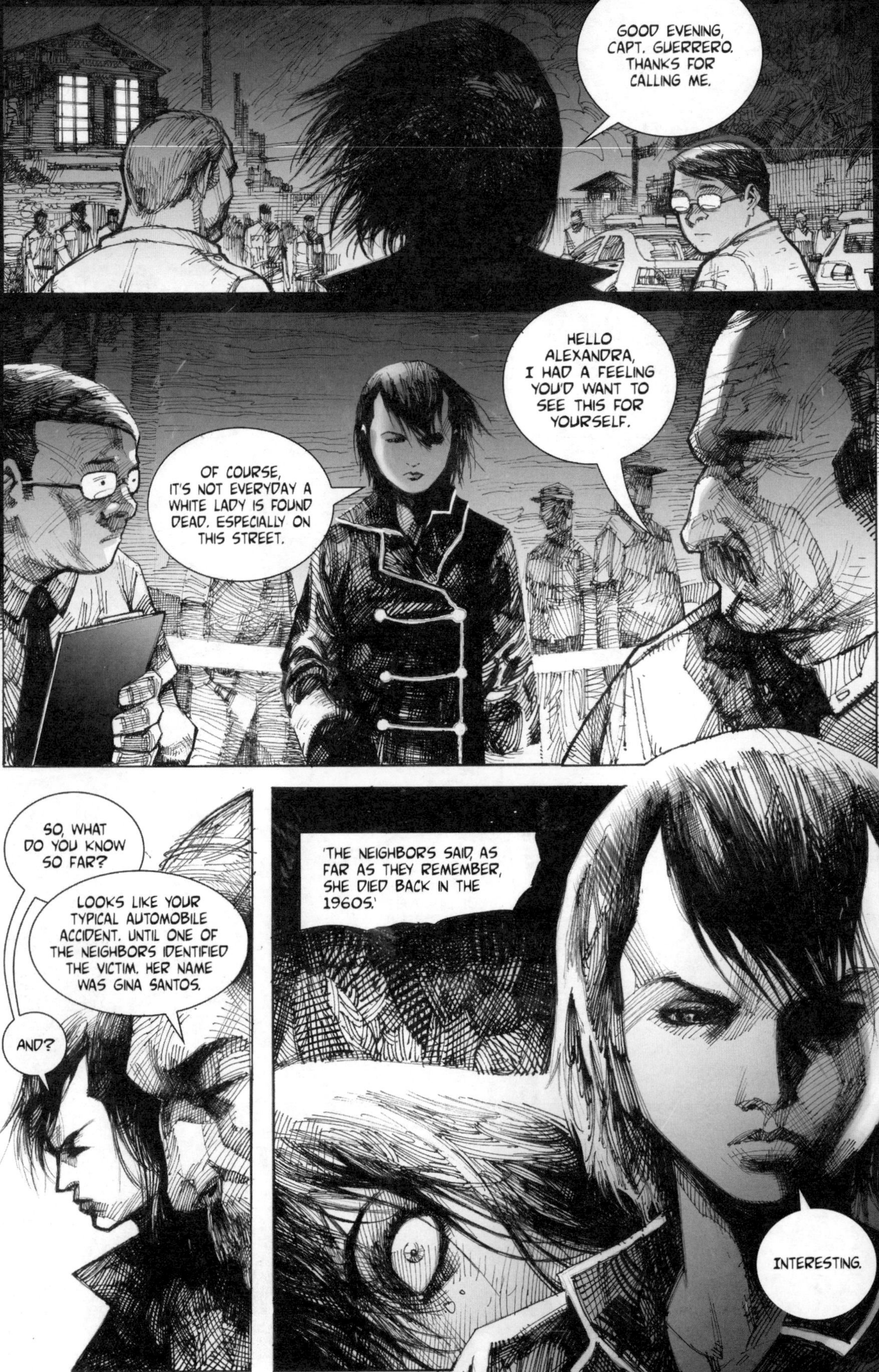
GOOD EVENING, CAPT. GUERRERO. THANKS FOR CALLING ME.
HELLO ALEXANDRA, I HAD A FEELING YOU'D WANT TO SEE THIS FOR YOURSELF.
OF COURSE, IT'S NOT EVERYDAY A WHITE LADY IS FOUND DEAD. ESPECIALLY ON THIS STREET.
SO, WHAT DO YOU KNOW SO FAR?
LOOKS LIKE YOUR TYPICAL AUTOMOBILE ACCIDENT. UNTIL ONE OF THE NEIGHBORS IDENTIFIED THE VICTIM. HER NAME WAS GINA SANTOS.
AND?
'THE NEIGHBORS SAID, AS FAR AS THEY REMEMBER, SHE DIED BACK IN THE 1960S.'
INTERESTING.

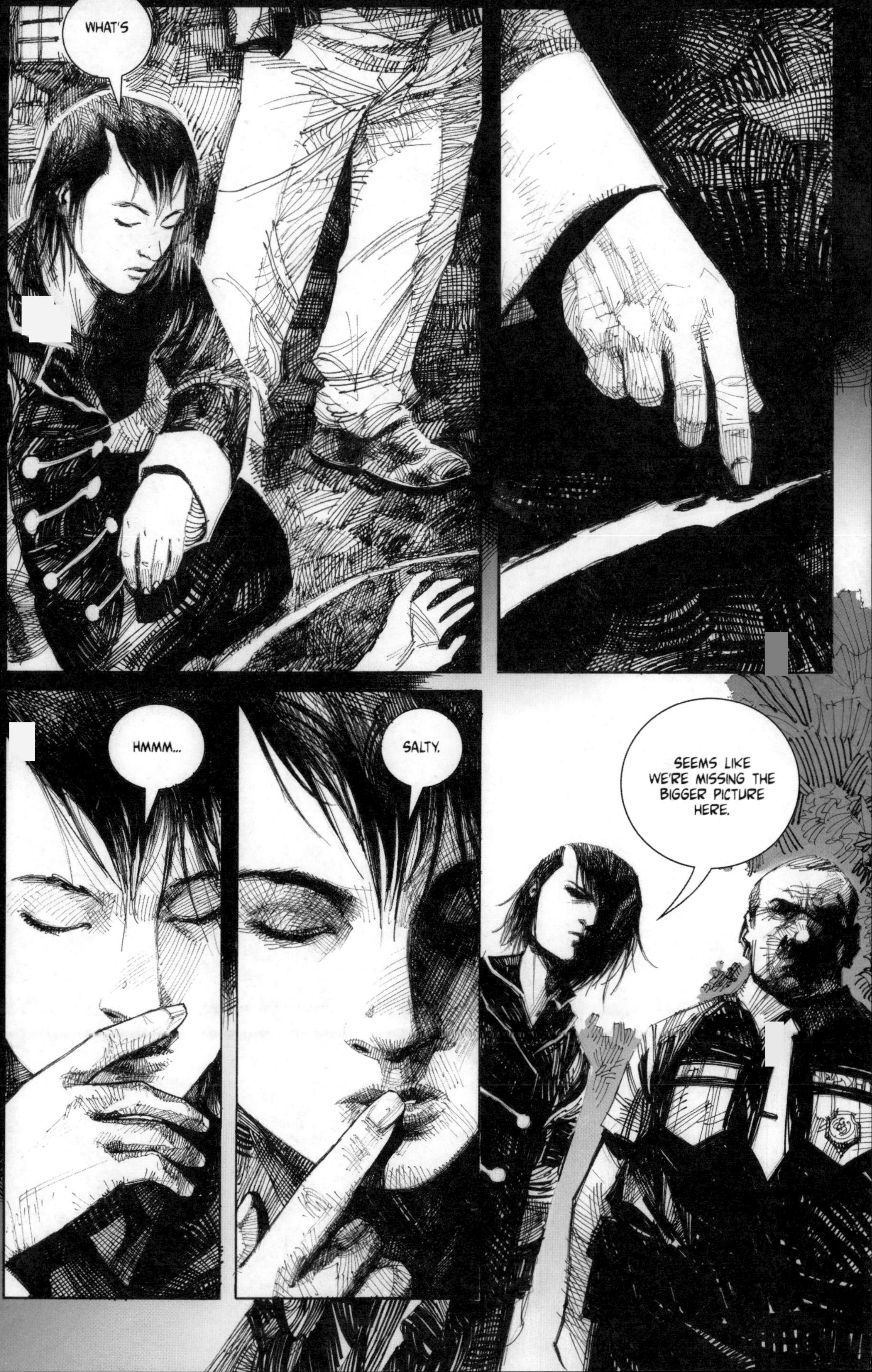
WHAT'S
HMMM...
SALTY.
SEEMS LIKE WE'RE MISSING THE BIGGER PICTURE HERE.

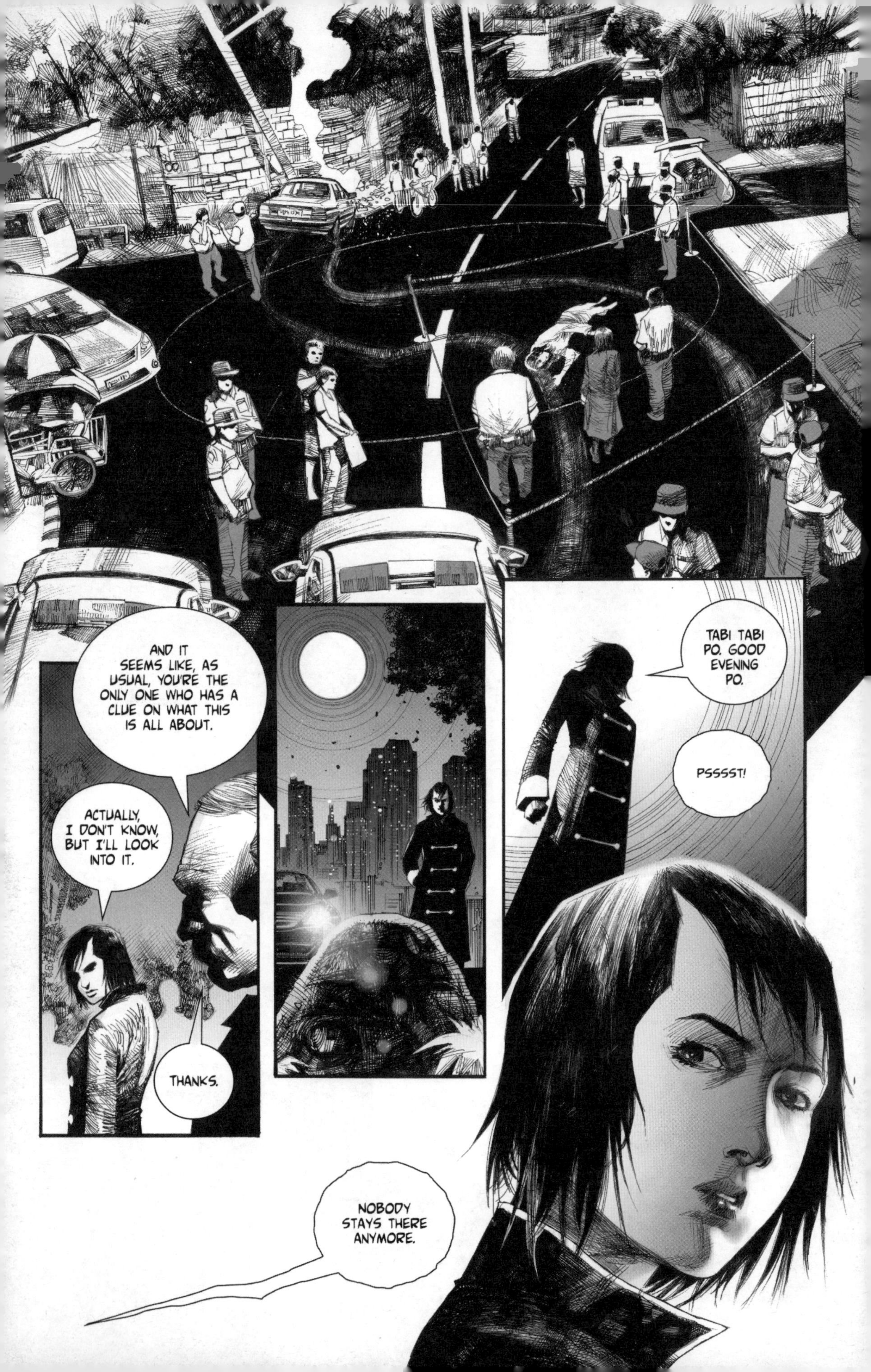
AND IT SEEMS LIKE, AS USUAL, YOU'RE THE ONLY ONE WHO HAS A CLUE ON WHAT THIS IS ALL ABOUT.
ACTUALLY, I DON'T KNOW, BUT I'LL LOOK INTO IT.
THANKS.
TABI TABI PO. GOOD EVENING PO.
PSSSST!
NOBODY STAYS THERE ANYMORE.

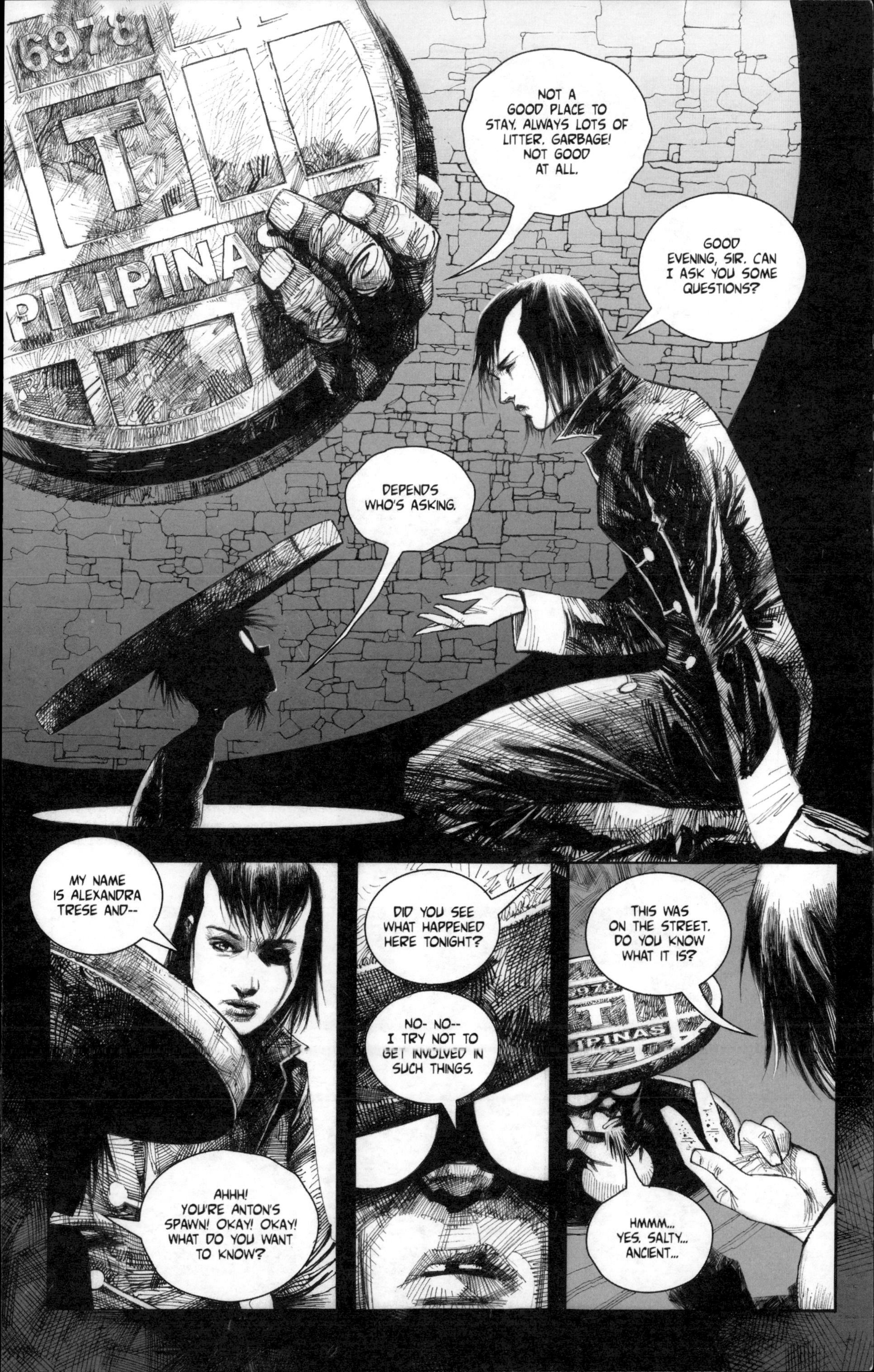
6978
T
PILIPINAS
NOT A GOOD PLACE TO STAY. ALWAYS LOTS OF LITTER. GARBAGE! NOT GOOD AT ALL.
GOOD EVENING, SIR. CAN I ASK YOU SOME QUESTIONS?
DEPENDS WHO'S ASKING.
MY NAME IS ALEXANDRA TRESE AND--
AHHH! YOU'RE ANTON'S SPAWN! OKAY! OKAY! WHAT DO YOU WANT TO KNOW?
DID YOU SEE WHAT HAPPENED HERE TONIGHT?
NO- NO-- I TRY NOT TO GET INVOLVED IN SUCH THINGS.
THIS WAS ON THE STREET. DO YOU KNOW WHAT IT IS?
HMMM... YES. SALTY... ANCIENT...

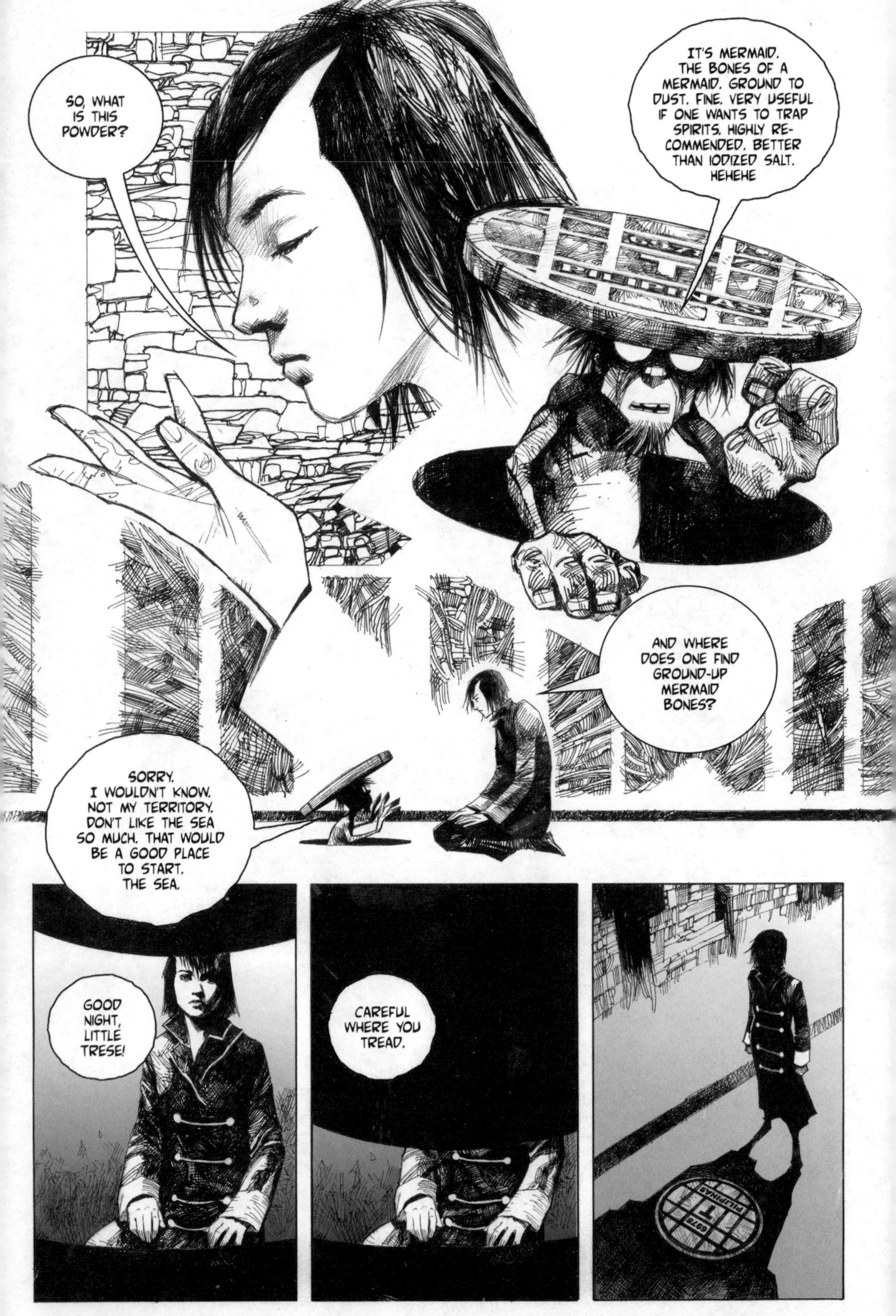
SO, WHAT IS THIS POWDER?
IT'S MERMAID. THE BONES OF A MERMAID. GROUND TO DUST. FINE. VERY USEFUL IF ONE WANTS TO TRAP SPIRITS. HIGHLY RE-COMMENDED. BETTER THAN IODIZED SALT. HEHEHE
AND WHERE DOES ONE FIND GROUND-UP MERMAID BONES?
SORRY. I WOULDN'T KNOW. NOT MY TERRITORY. DON'T LIKE THE SEA SO MUCH. THAT WOULD BE A GOOD PLACE TO START. THE SEA.
GOOD NIGHT, LITTLE TRESE!
CAREFUL WHERE YOU TREAD.

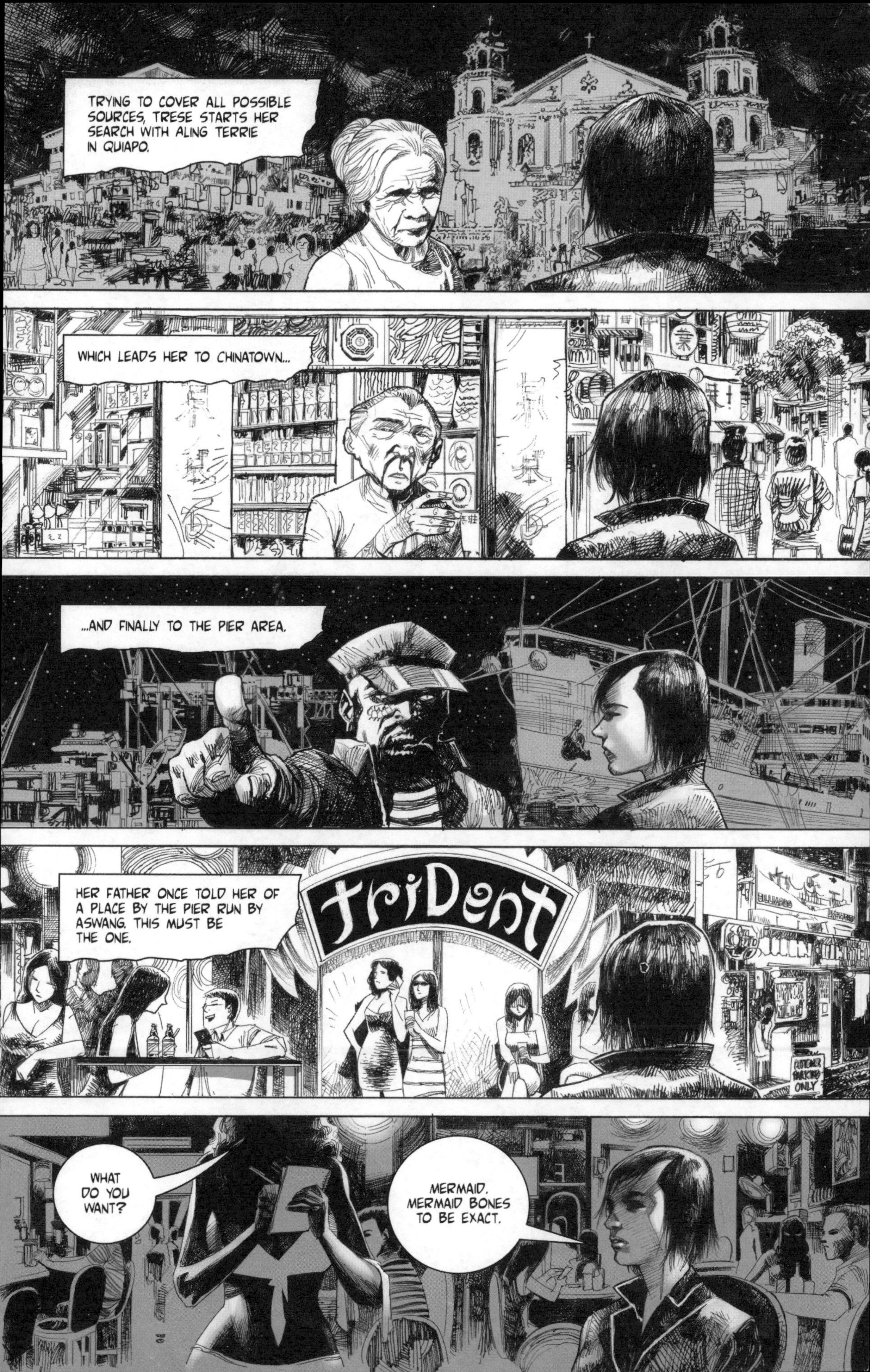
TRYING TO COVER ALL POSSIBLE SOURCES, TRESE STARTS HER SEARCH WITH ALING TERRIE IN QUIAPO.
WHICH LEADS HER TO CHINATOWN...
...AND FINALLY TO THE PIER AREA.
HER FATHER ONCE TOLD HER OF A PLACE BY THE PIER RUN BY ASWANG. THIS MUST BE THE ONE.
triDent
BILLIARDS
CUSTOMER PARKING ONLY
WHAT DO YOU WANT?
MERMAID. MERMAID BONES TO BE EXACT.

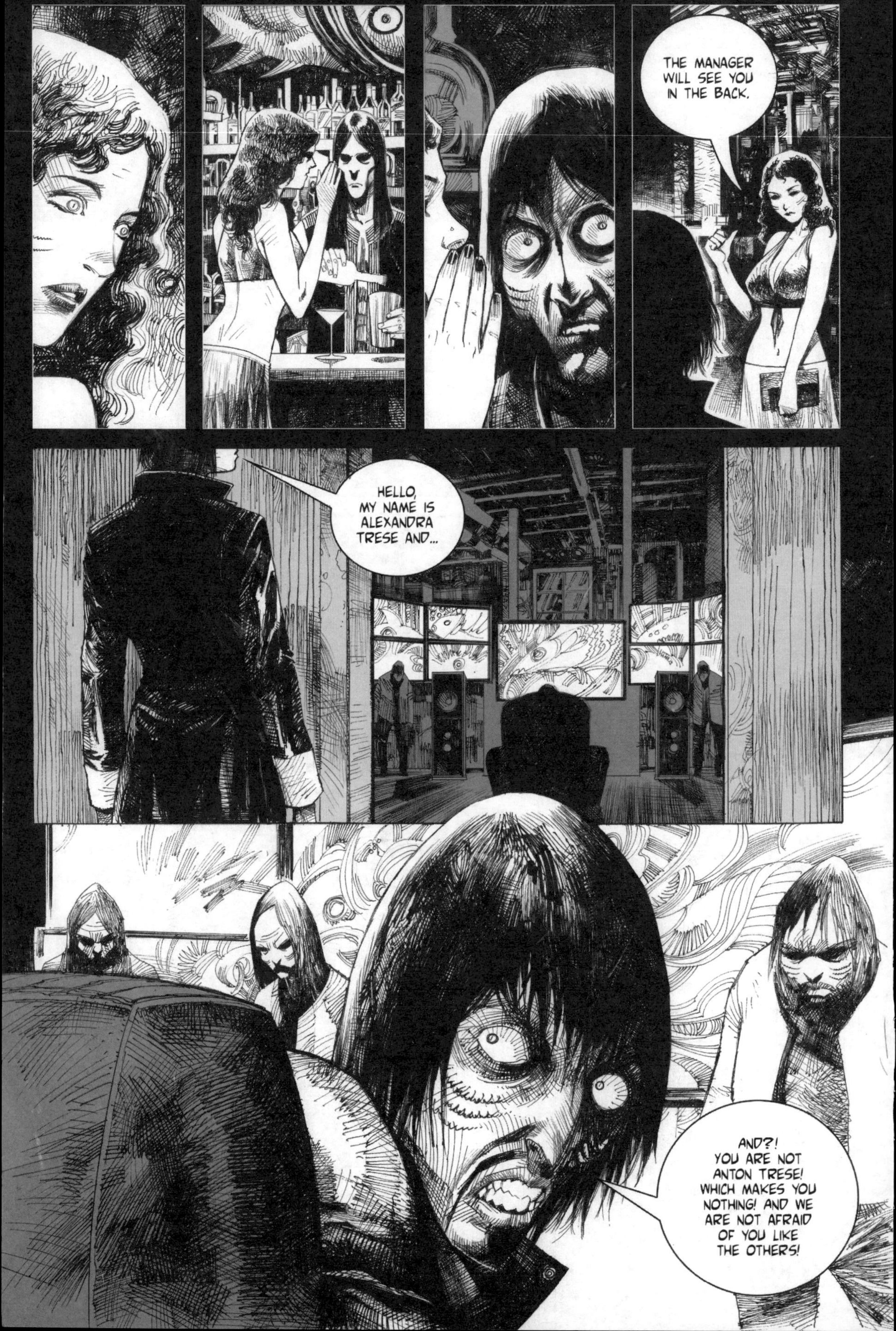
THE MANAGER WILL SEE YOU IN THE BACK.
HELLO, MY NAME IS ALEXANDRA TRESE AND...
AND?! YOU ARE NOT ANTON TRESE! WHICH MAKES YOU NOTHING! AND WE ARE NOT AFRAID OF YOU LIKE THE OTHERS!

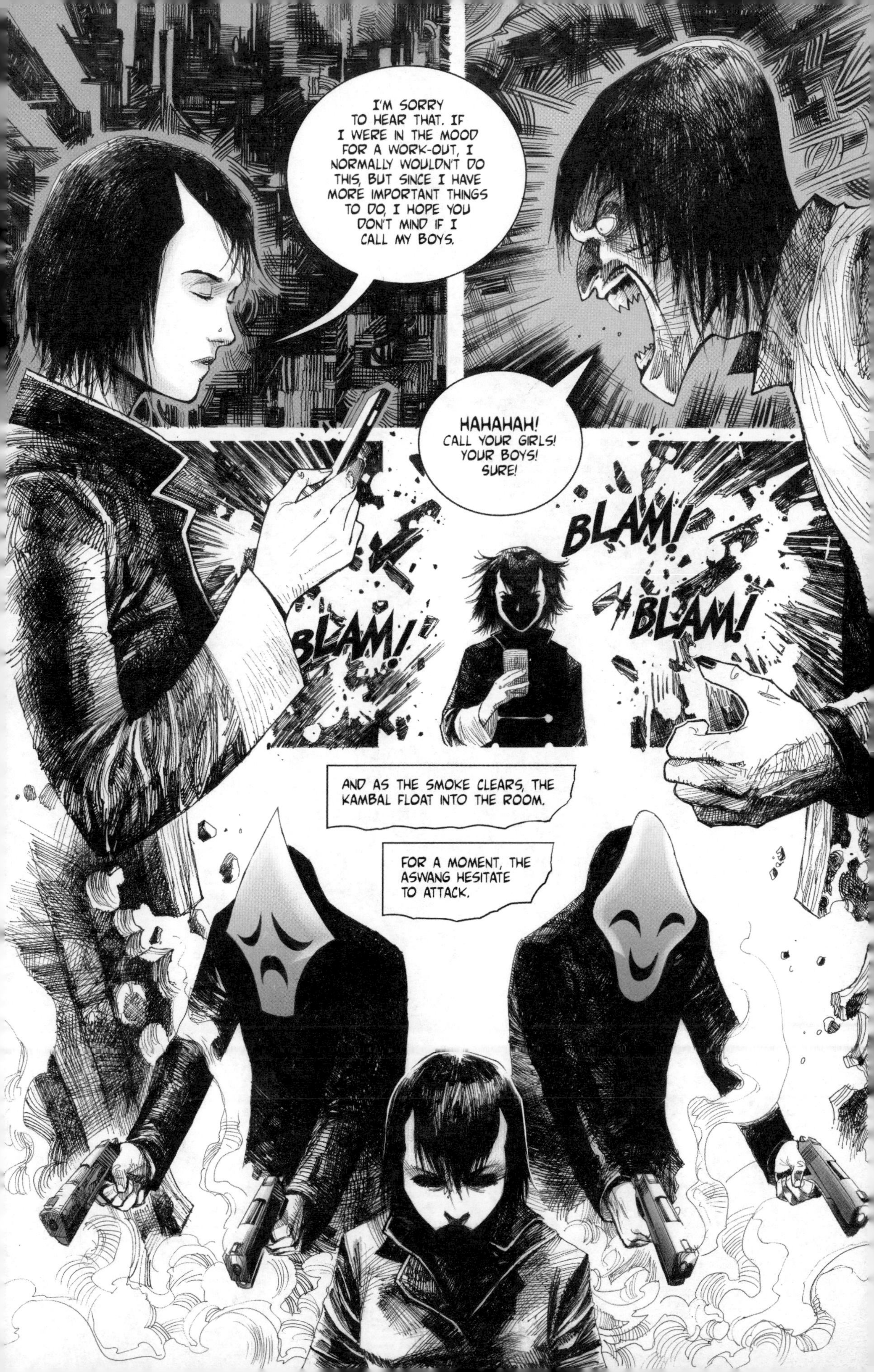
I'M SORRY TO HEAR THAT. IF I WERE IN THE MOOD FOR A WORK-OUT, I NORMALLY WOULDN'T DO THIS, BUT SINCE I HAVE MORE IMPORTANT THINGS TO DO, I HOPE YOU DON'T MIND IF I CALL MY BOYS.
HAHAHAH! CALL YOUR GIRLS! YOUR BOYS! SURE!
BLAM!
BLAM!
BLAM!
AND AS THE SMOKE CLEARS, THE KAMBAL FLOAT INTO THE ROOM.
FOR A MOMENT, THE ASWANG HESITATE TO ATTACK.

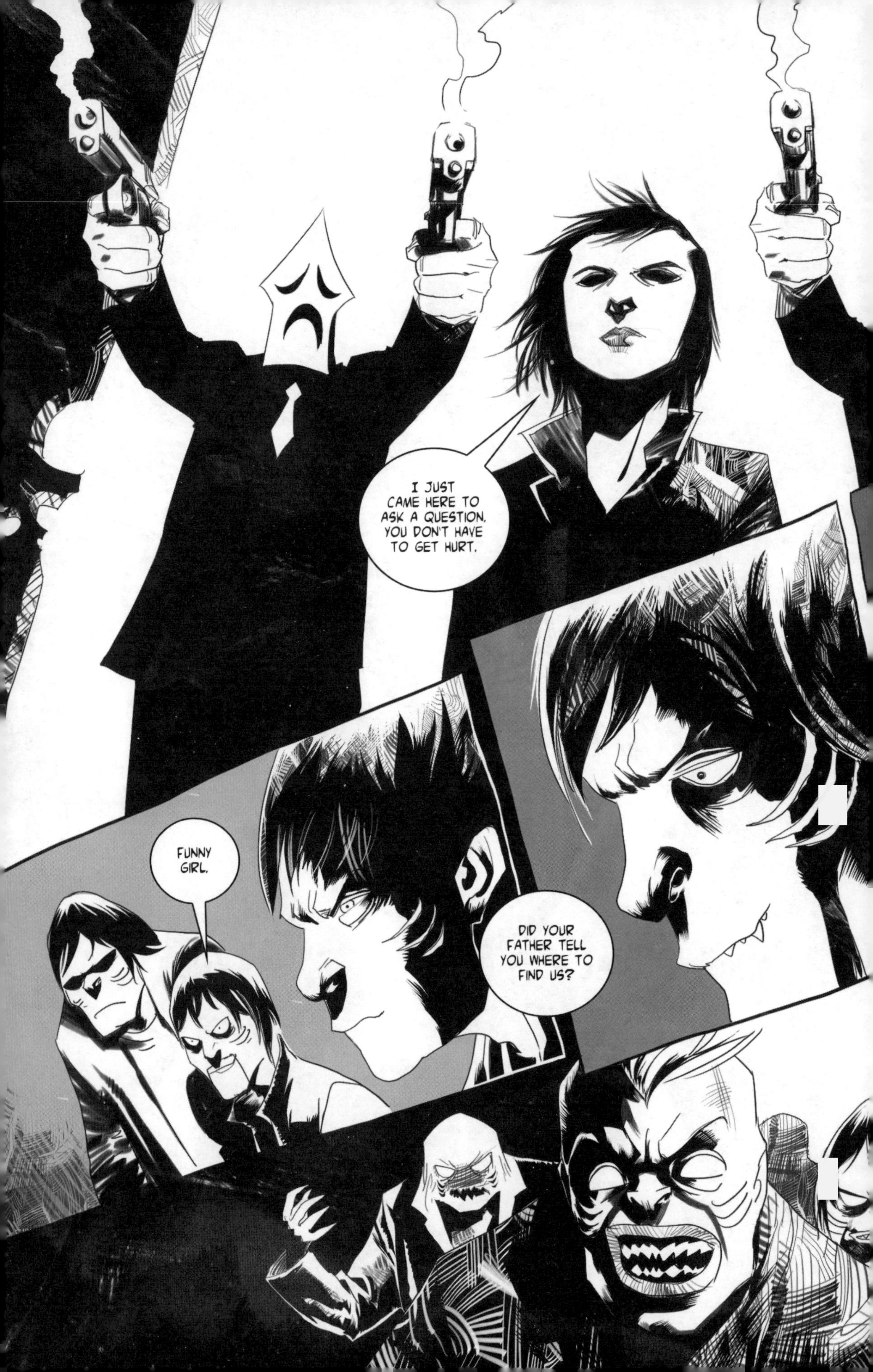
I JUST CAME HERE TO ASK A QUESTION. YOU DON'T HAVE TO GET HURT.
FUNNY GIRL.
DID YOUR FATHER TELL YOU WHERE TO FIND US?

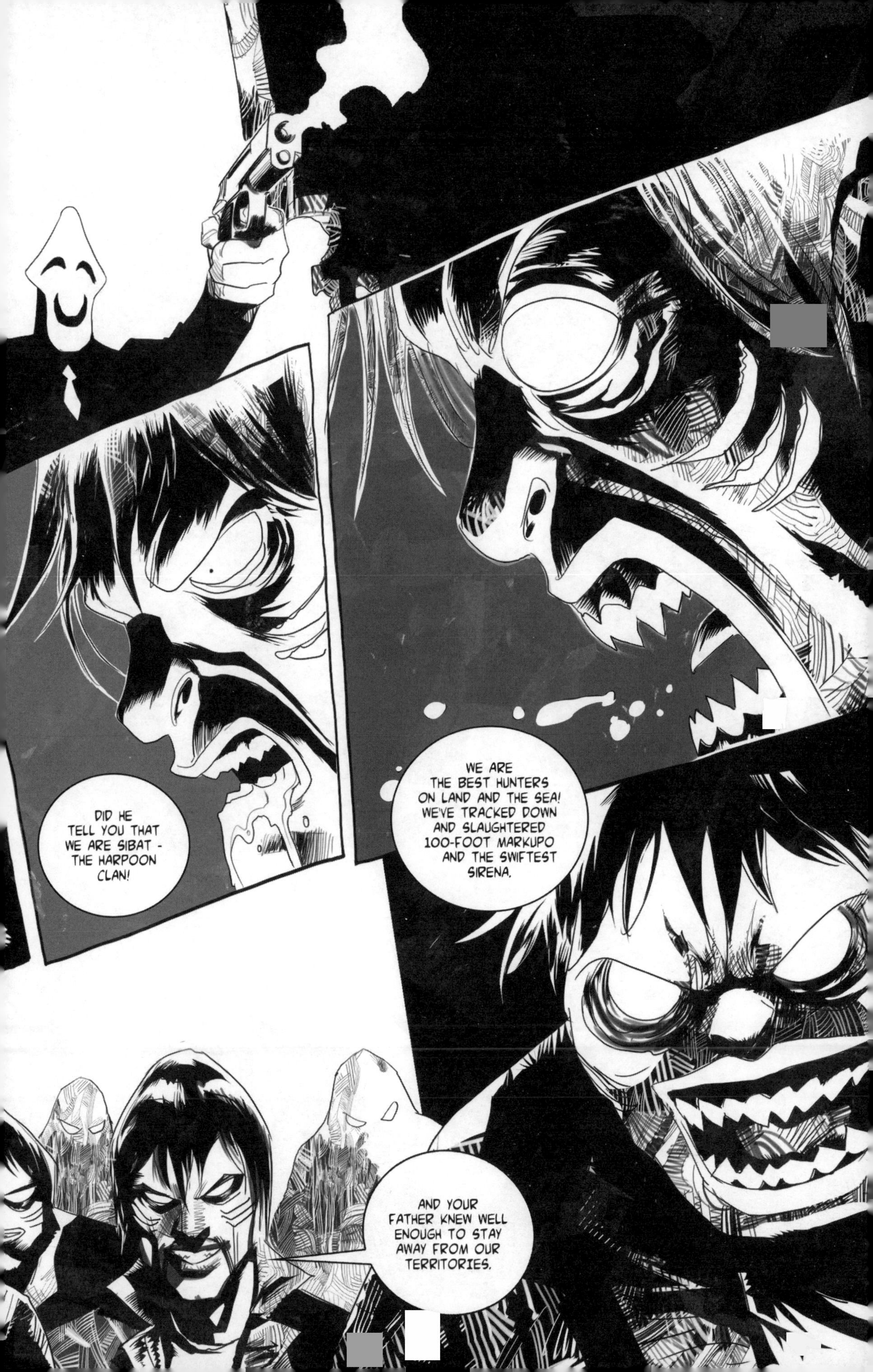
DID HE TELL YOU THAT WE ARE SIBAT - THE HARPOON CLAN!
WE ARE THE BEST HUNTERS ON LAND AND THE SEA! WE'VE TRACKED DOWN AND SLAUGHTERED 100-FOOT MARKUPO AND THE SWIFTEST SIRENA.
AND YOUR FATHER KNEW WELL ENOUGH TO STAY AWAY FROM OUR TERRITORIES.

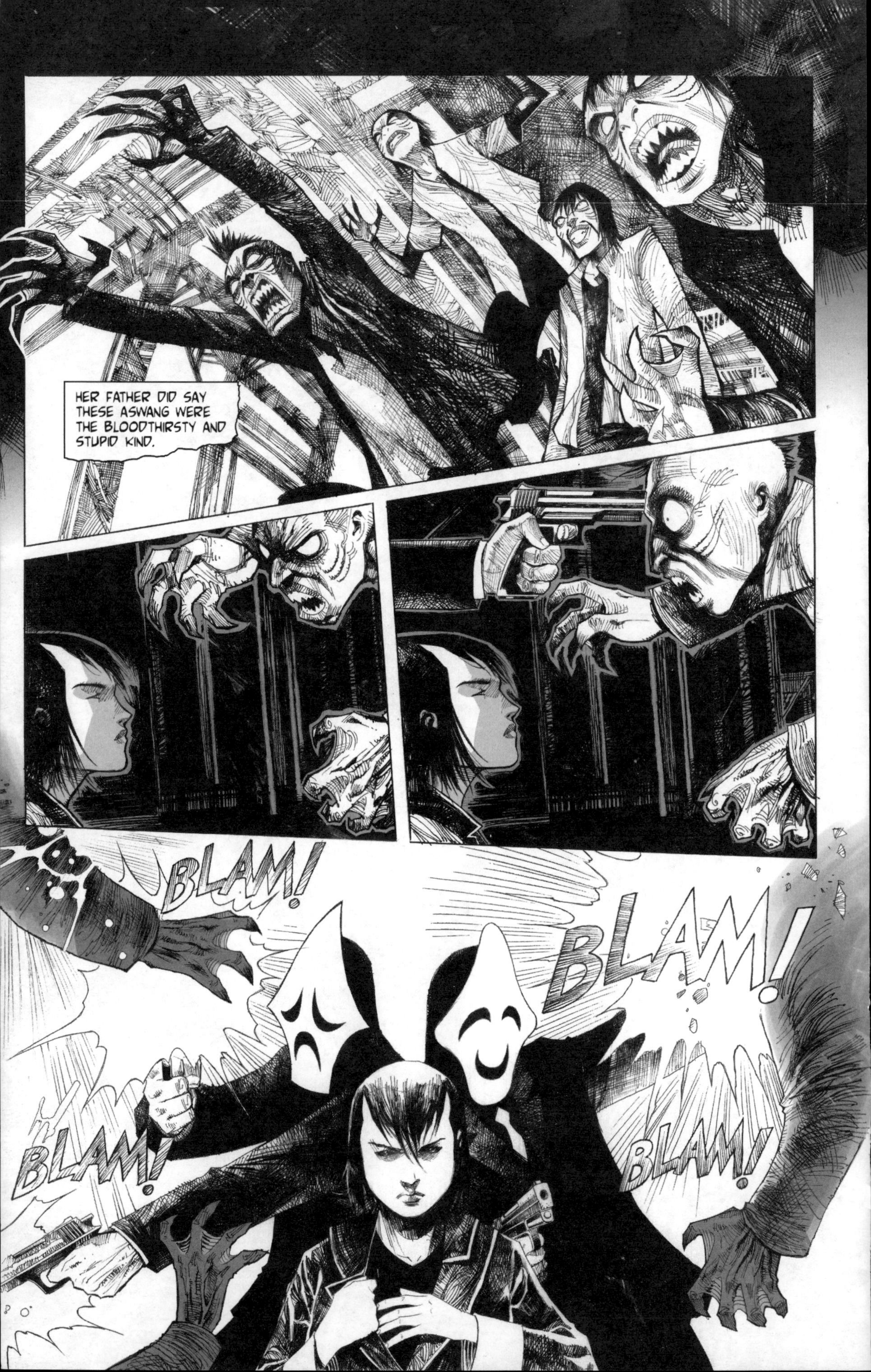
HER FATHER DID SAY THESE ASWANG WERE THE BLOODTHIRSTY AND STUPID KIND.
BLAM!
BLAM!
BLAM!
BLAM!

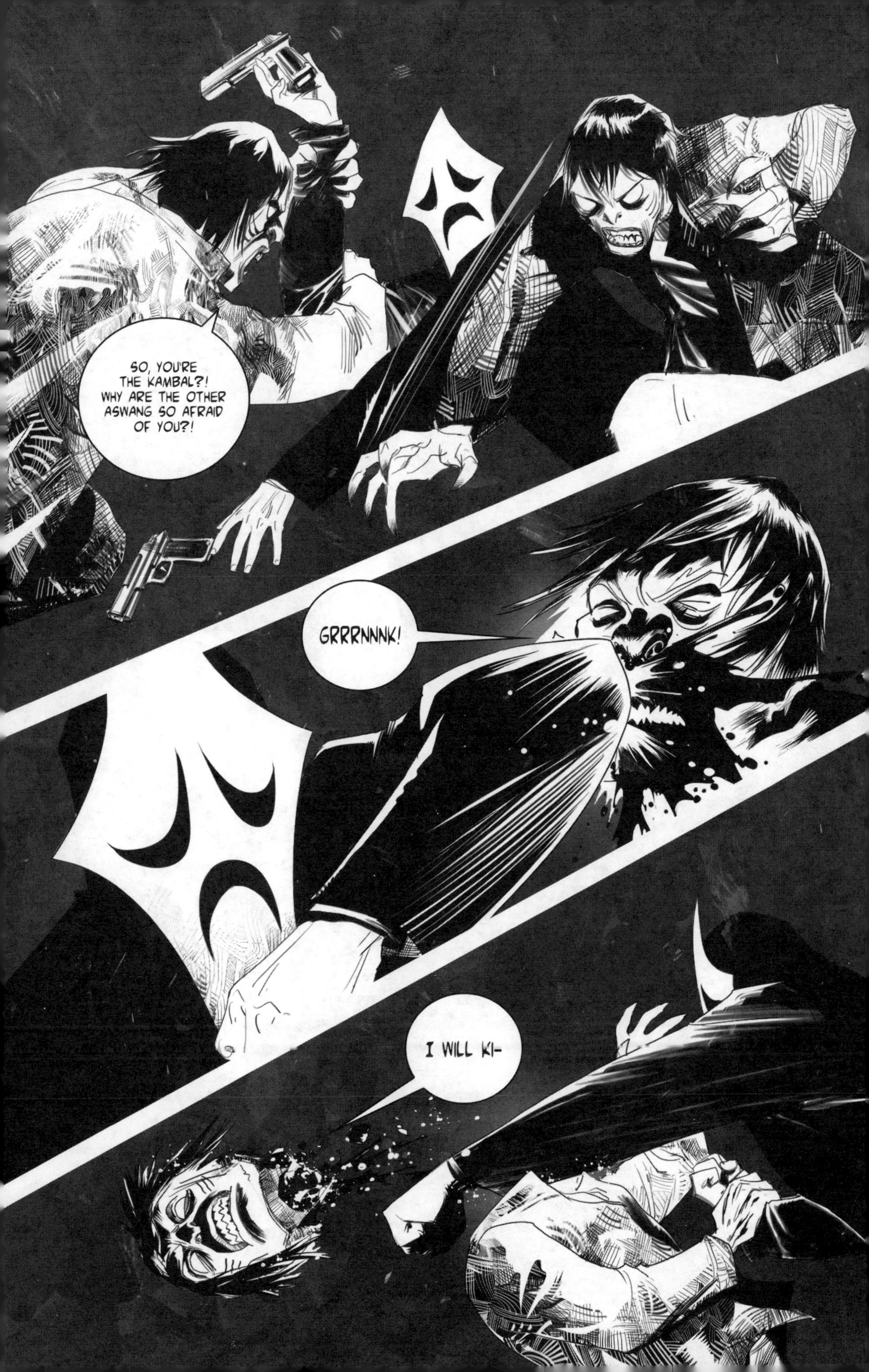
SO, YOU'RE THE KAMBAL?! WHY ARE THE OTHER ASWANG SO AFRAID OF YOU?!
GRRRNNNK!
I WILL KI-

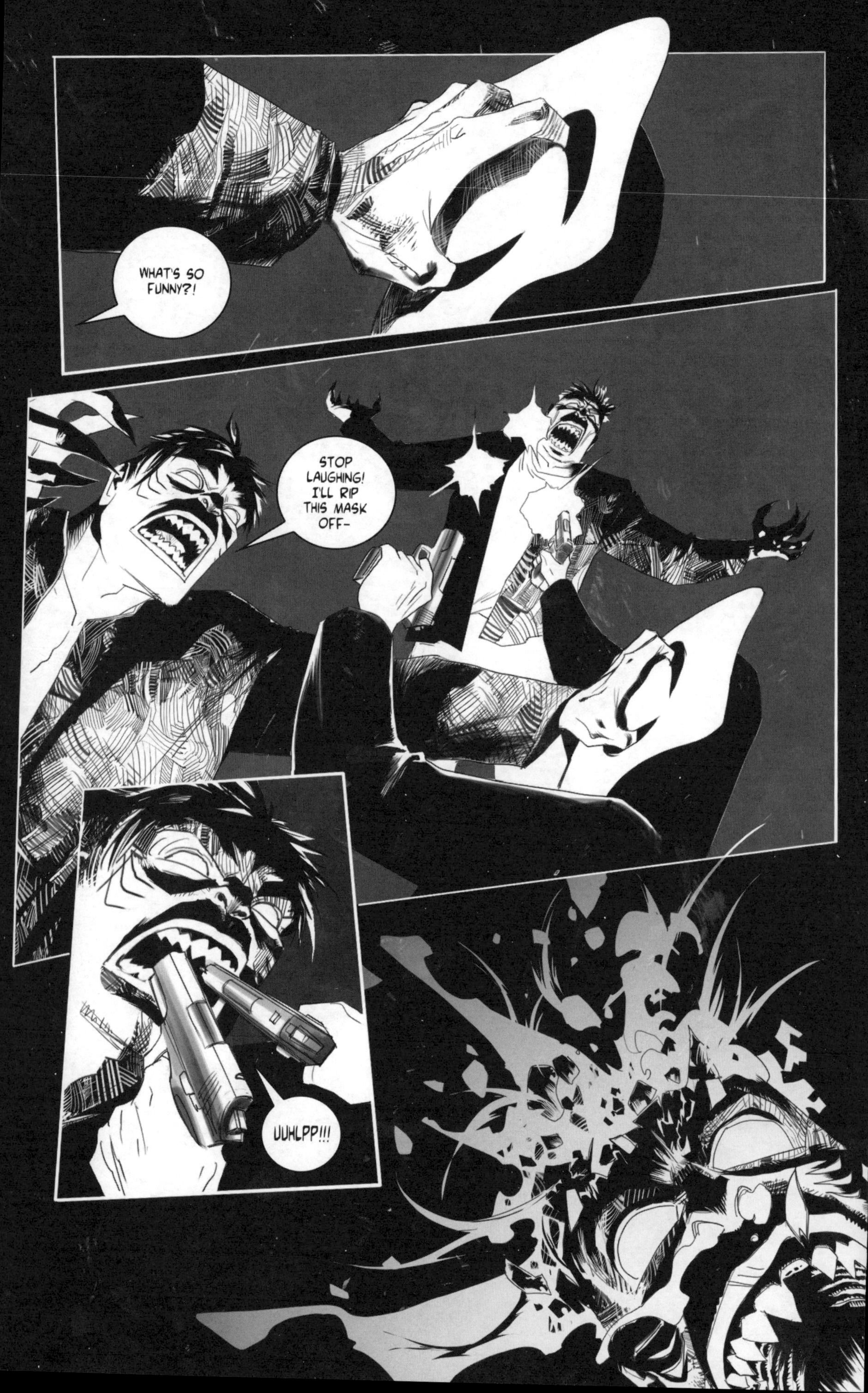
WHAT'S SO FUNNY?!
STOP LAUGHING! I'LL RIP THIS MASK OFF-
UUHLPP!!!

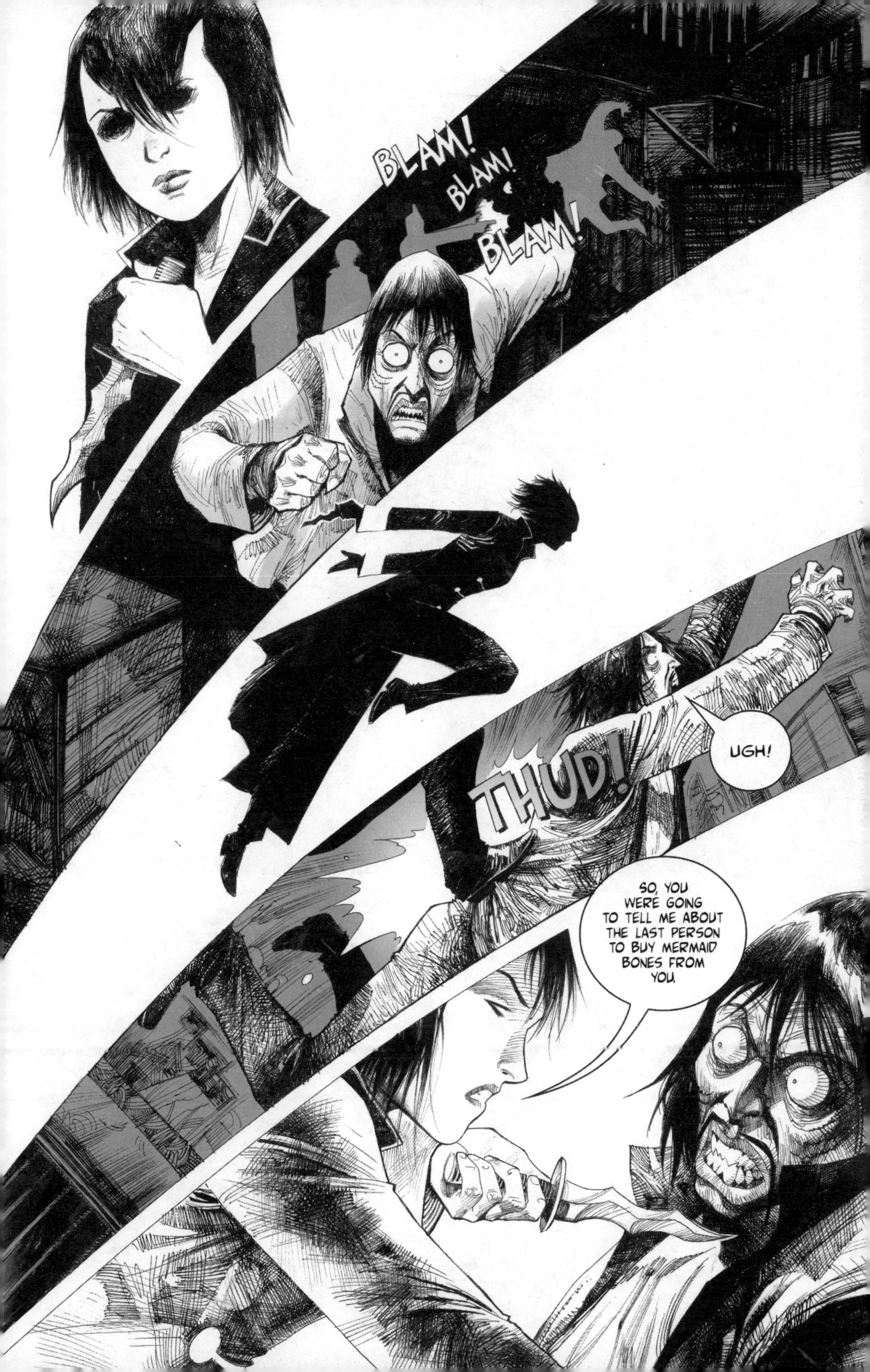
BLAM!
BLAM!
BLAM!
THUD!
UGH!
SO, YOU WERE GOING TO TELL ME ABOUT THE LAST PERSON TO BUY MERMAID BONES FROM YOU.

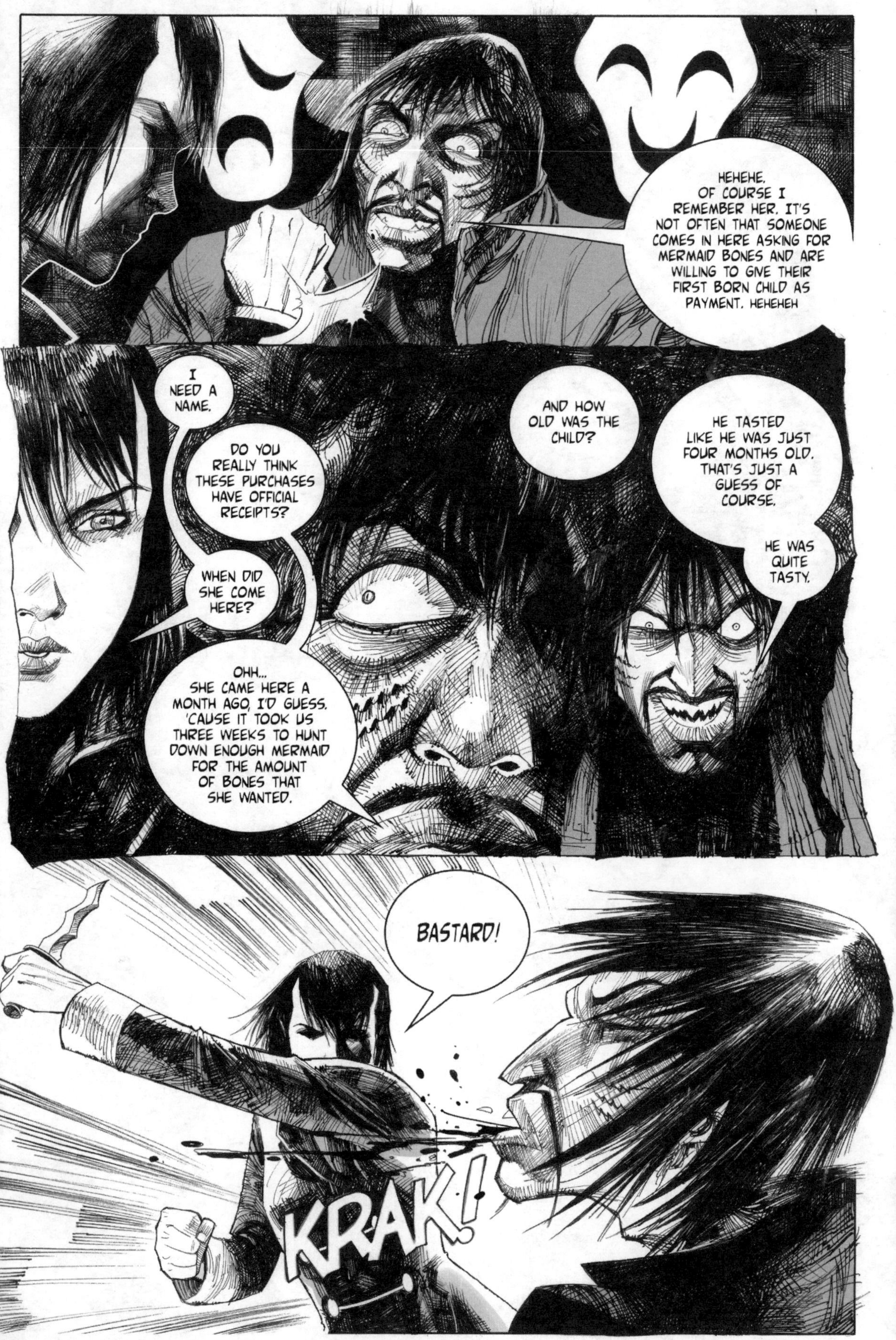
HEHEHE. OF COURSE I REMEMBER HER. IT'S NOT OFTEN THAT SOMEONE COMES IN HERE ASKING FOR MERMAID BONES AND ARE WILLING TO GIVE THEIR FIRST BORN CHILD AS PAYMENT. HEHEHEH
I NEED A NAME.
DO YOU REALLY THINK THESE PURCHASES HAVE OFFICIAL RECEIPTS?
WHEN DID SHE COME HERE?
OHH... SHE CAME HERE A MONTH AGO, I'D GUESS. 'CAUSE IT TOOK US THREE WEEKS TO HUNT DOWN ENOUGH MERMAID FOR THE AMOUNT OF BONES THAT SHE WANTED.
AND HOW OLD WAS THE CHILD?
HE TASTED LIKE HE WAS JUST FOUR MONTHS OLD. THAT'S JUST A GUESS OF COURSE.
HE WAS QUITE TASTY.
BASTARD!
KRAK!

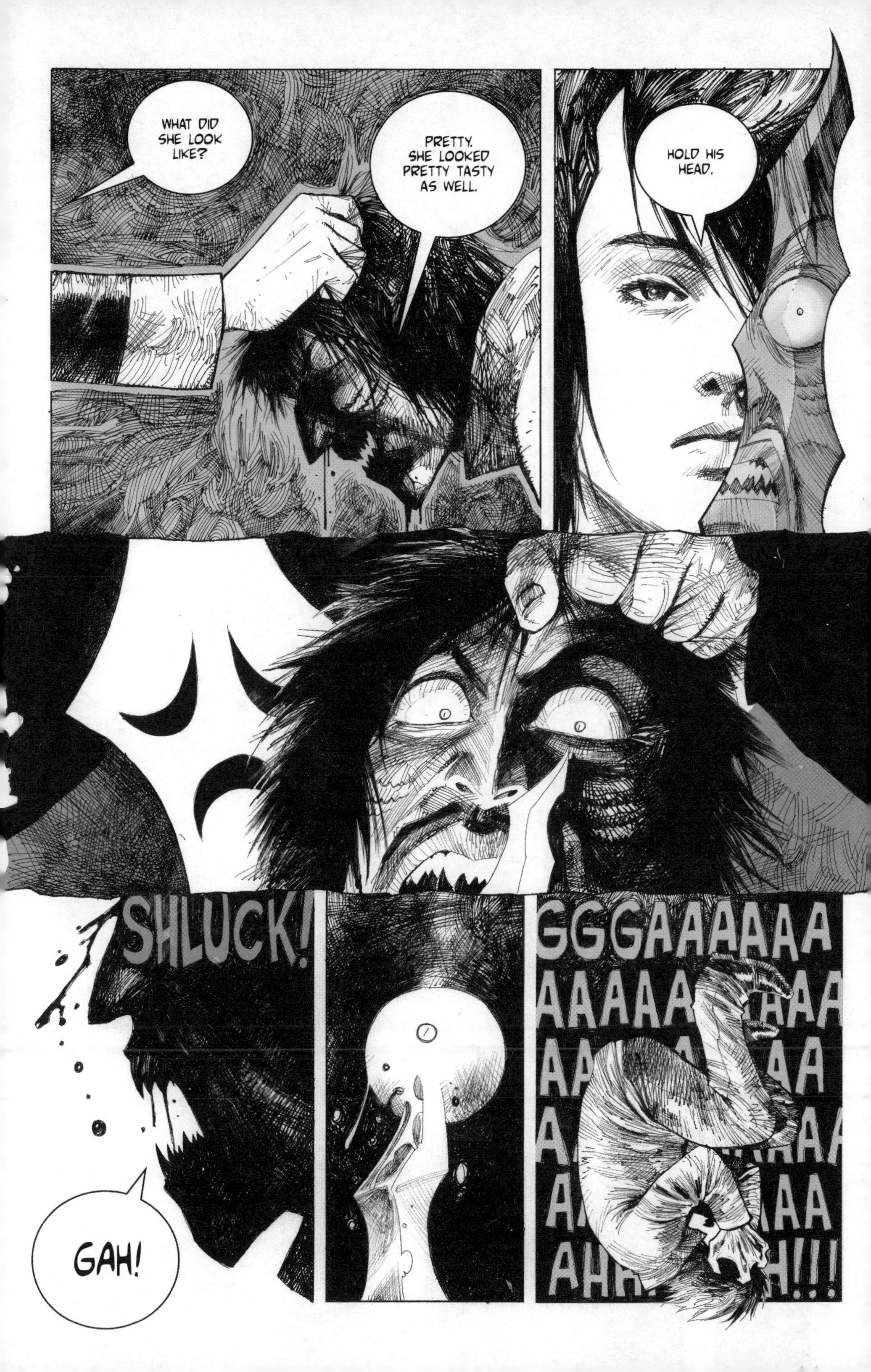
WHAT DID SHE LOOK LIKE?
PRETTY. SHE LOOKED PRETTY TASTY AS WELL.
HOLD HIS HEAD.
SHLUCK!
GAH!
GGGAAAAAA

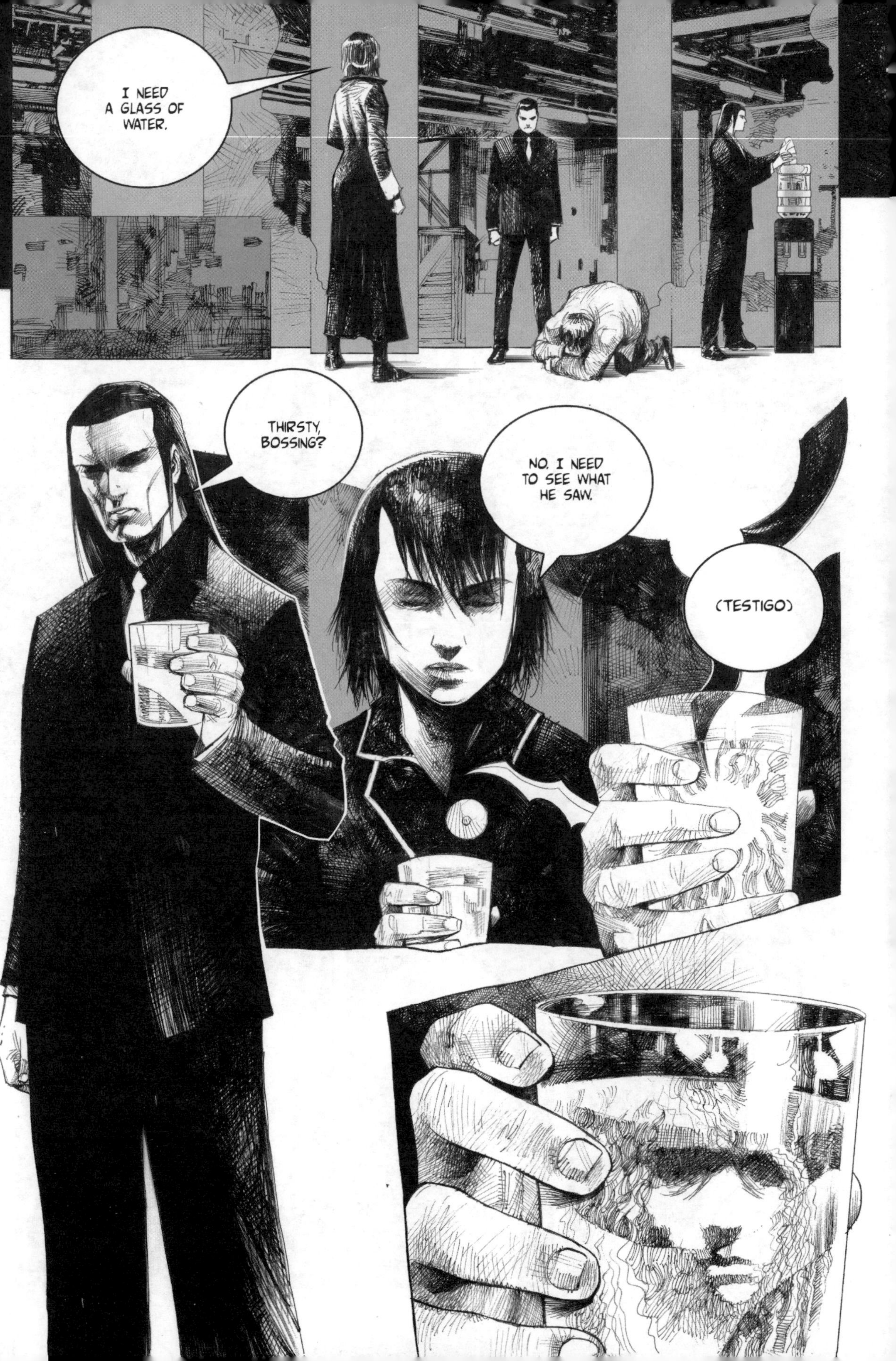
I NEED A GLASS OF WATER.
THIRSTY, BOSSING?
NO. I NEED TO SEE WHAT HE SAW.
(TESTIGO)

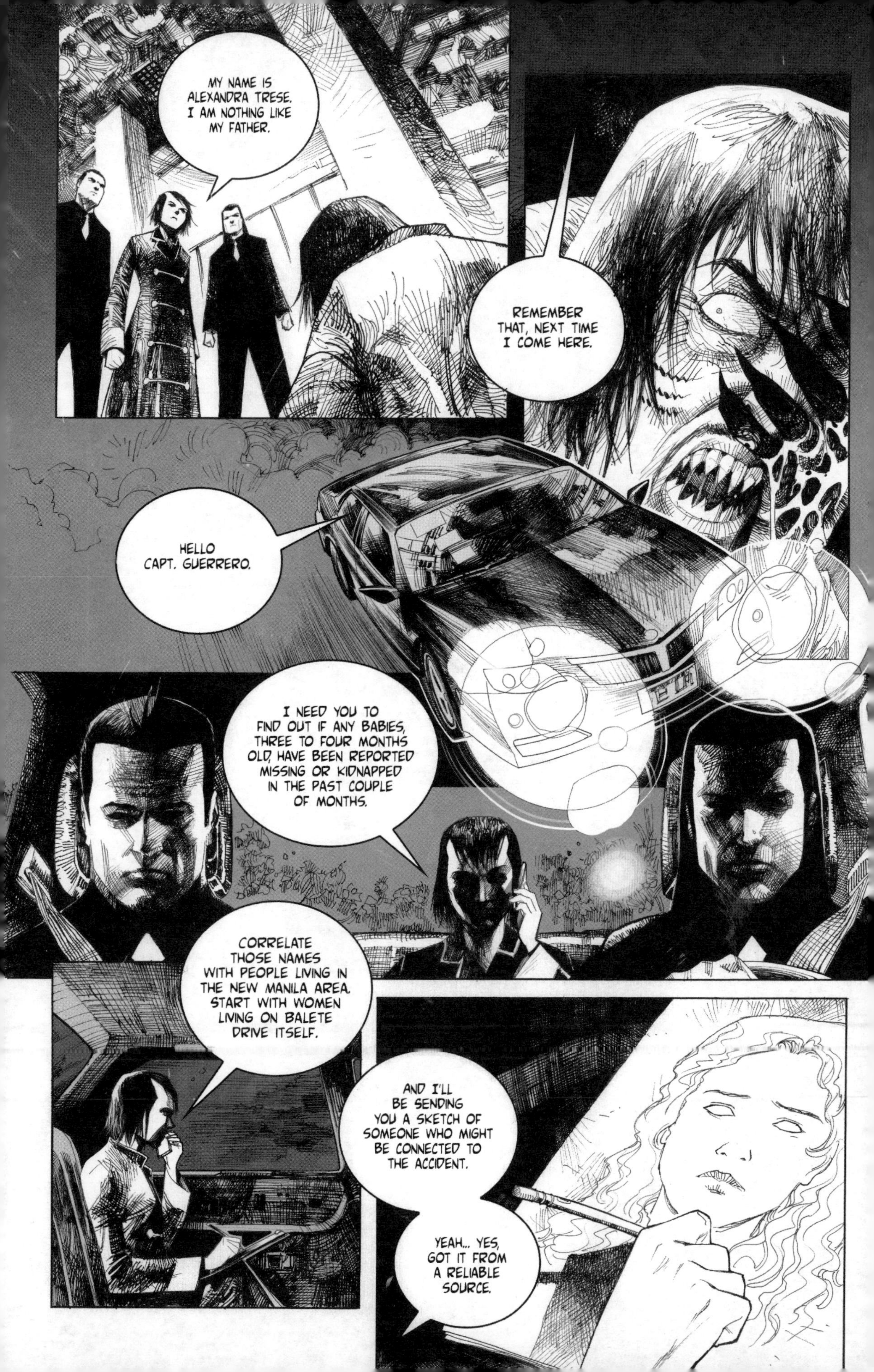
MY NAME IS ALEXANDRA TRESE. I AM NOTHING LIKE MY FATHER.
REMEMBER THAT, NEXT TIME I COME HERE.
HELLO CAPT. GUERRERO.
I NEED YOU TO FIND OUT IF ANY BABIES, THREE TO FOUR MONTHS OLD, HAVE BEEN REPORTED MISSING OR KIDNAPPED IN THE PAST COUPLE OF MONTHS.
CORRELATE THOSE NAMES WITH PEOPLE LIVING IN THE NEW MANILA AREA. START WITH WOMEN LIVING ON BALETE DRIVE ITSELF.
AND I'LL BE SENDING YOU A SKETCH OF SOMEONE WHO MIGHT BE CONNECTED TO THE ACCIDENT.
YEAH... YES, GOT IT FROM A RELIABLE SOURCE.

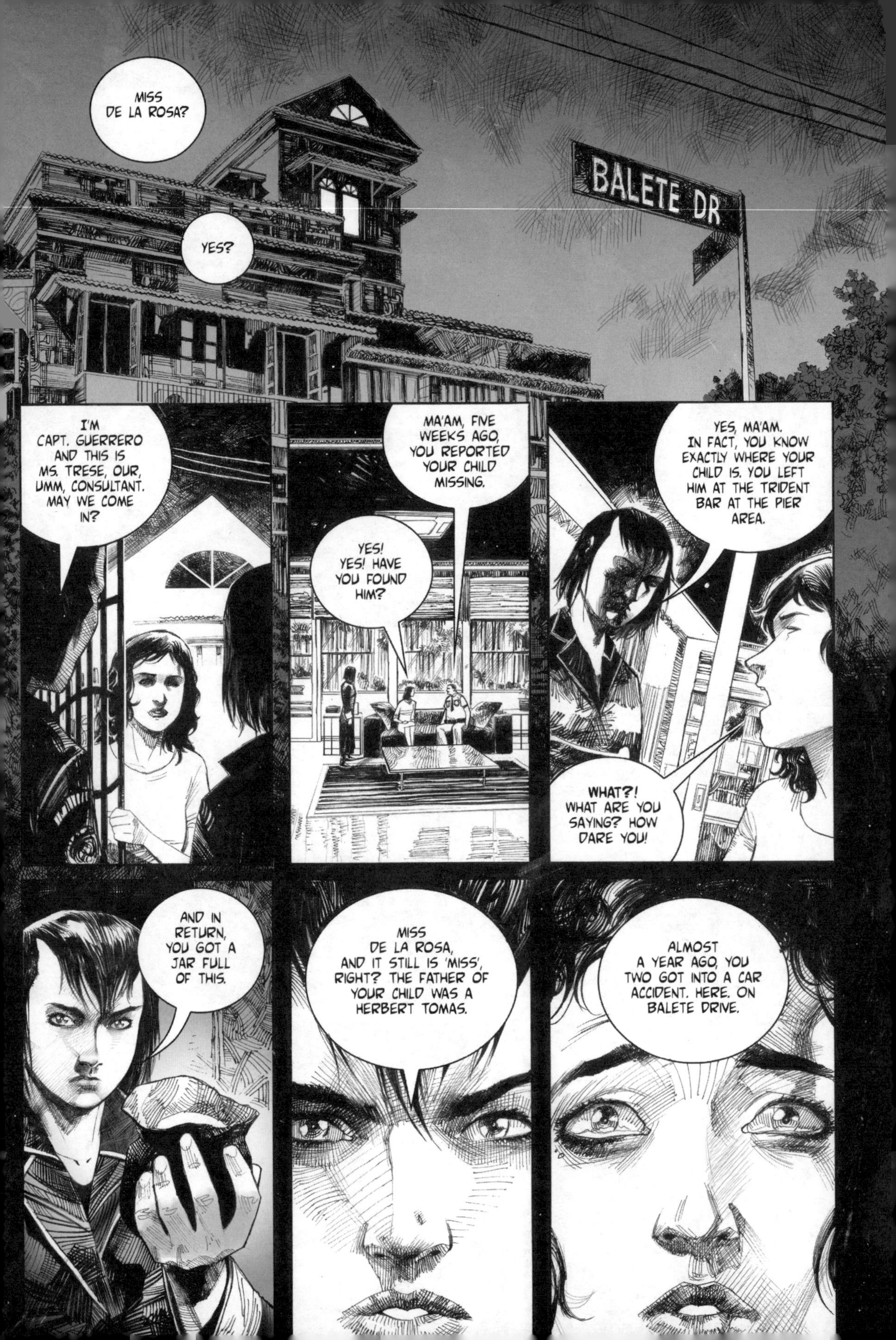
MISS DE LA ROSA?
BALETE DR
YES?
I'M CAPT. GUERRERO AND THIS IS MS. TRESE, OUR, UMM, CONSULTANT. MAY WE COME IN?
MA'AM, FIVE WEEKS AGO, YOU REPORTED YOUR CHILD MISSING.
YES! YES! HAVE YOU FOUND HIM?
YES, MA'AM. IN FACT, YOU KNOW EXACTLY WHERE YOUR CHILD IS. YOU LEFT HIM AT THE TRIDENT BAR AT THE PIER AREA.
WHAT?! WHAT ARE YOU SAYING? HOW DARE YOU!
AND IN RETURN, YOU GOT A JAR FULL OF THIS.
MISS DE LA ROSA, AND IT STILL IS 'MISS', RIGHT? THE FATHER OF YOUR CHILD WAS A HERBERT TOMAS.
ALMOST A YEAR AGO, YOU TWO GOT INTO A CAR ACCIDENT. HERE. ON BALETE DRIVE.

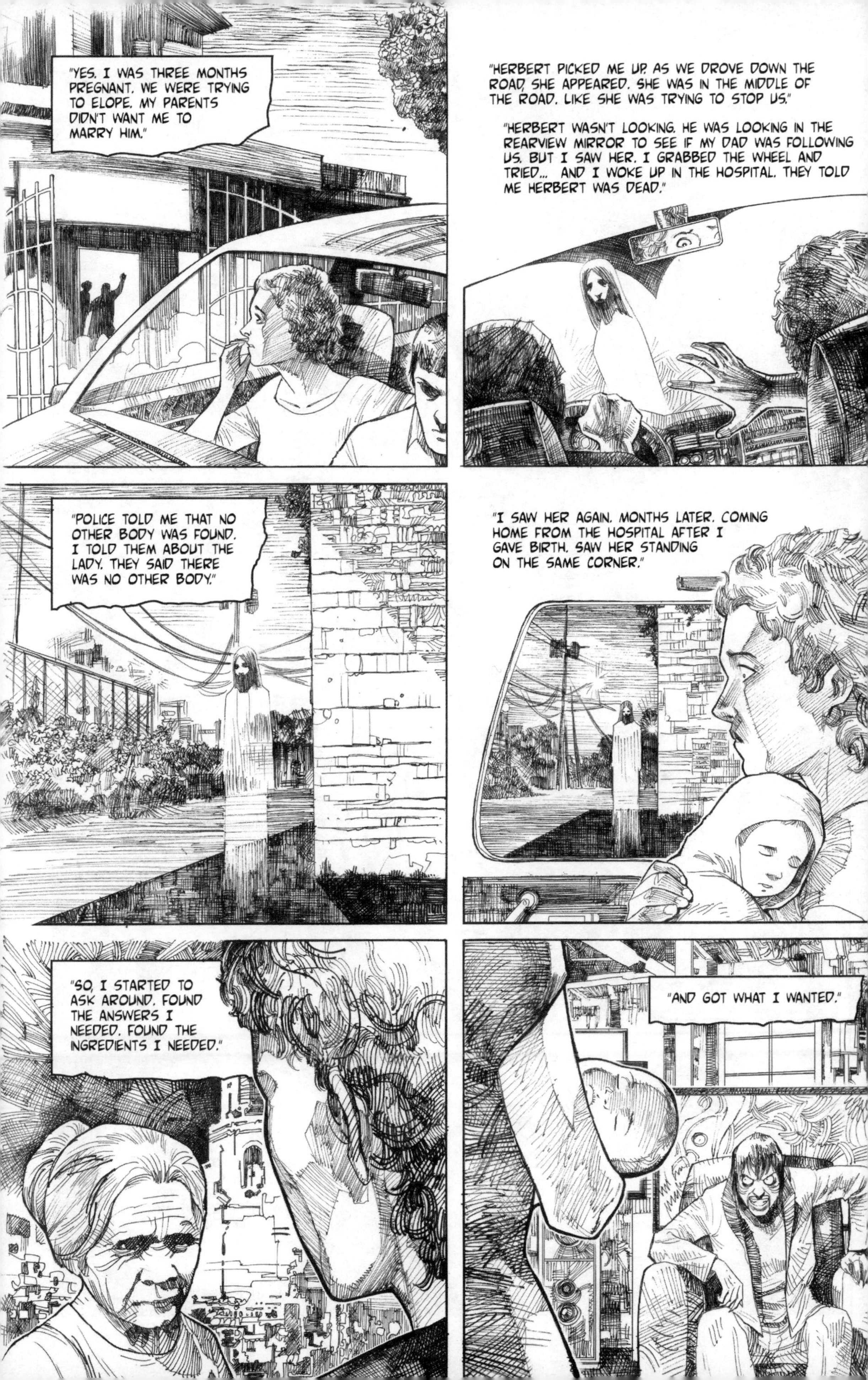
"YES. I WAS THREE MONTHS PREGNANT. WE WERE TRYING TO ELOPE. MY PARENTS DIDN'T WANT ME TO MARRY HIM."
"HERBERT PICKED ME UP. AS WE DROVE DOWN THE ROAD, SHE APPEARED. SHE WAS IN THE MIDDLE OF THE ROAD. LIKE SHE WAS TRYING TO STOP US."
"HERBERT WASN'T LOOKING. HE WAS LOOKING IN THE REARVIEW MIRROR TO SEE IF MY DAD WAS FOLLOWING US. BUT I SAW HER. I GRABBED THE WHEEL AND TRIED... AND I WOKE UP IN THE HOSPITAL. THEY TOLD ME HERBERT WAS DEAD."
"POLICE TOLD ME THAT NO OTHER BODY WAS FOUND. I TOLD THEM ABOUT THE LADY. THEY SAID THERE WAS NO OTHER BODY."
"I SAW HER AGAIN. MONTHS LATER. COMING HOME FROM THE HOSPITAL AFTER I GAVE BIRTH. SAW HER STANDING ON THE SAME CORNER."
"SO, I STARTED TO ASK AROUND. FOUND THE ANSWERS I NEEDED. FOUND THE INGREDIENTS I NEEDED."
"AND GOT WHAT I WANTED."

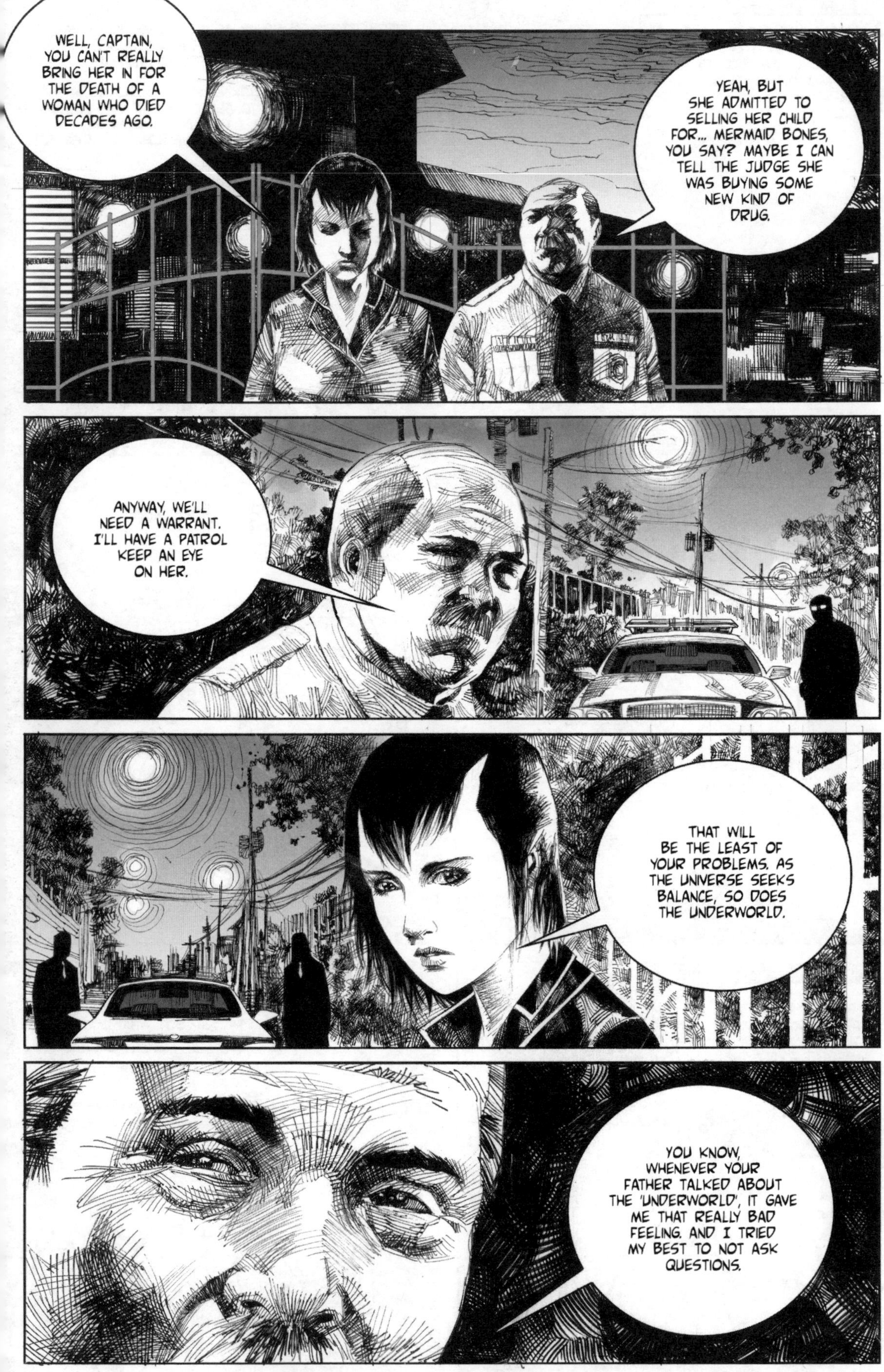
WELL, CAPTAIN, YOU CAN'T REALLY BRING HER IN FOR THE DEATH OF A WOMAN WHO DIED DECADES AGO.
YEAH, BUT SHE ADMITTED TO SELLING HER CHILD FOR... MERMAID BONES, YOU SAY? MAYBE I CAN TELL THE JUDGE SHE WAS BUYING SOME NEW KIND OF DRUG.
ANYWAY, WE'LL NEED A WARRANT. I'LL HAVE A PATROL KEEP AN EYE ON HER.
THAT WILL BE THE LEAST OF YOUR PROBLEMS. AS THE UNIVERSE SEEKS BALANCE, SO DOES THE UNDERWORLD.
YOU KNOW, WHENEVER YOUR FATHER TALKED ABOUT THE 'UNDERWORLD', IT GAVE ME THAT REALLY BAD FEELING. AND I TRIED MY BEST TO NOT ASK QUESTIONS.

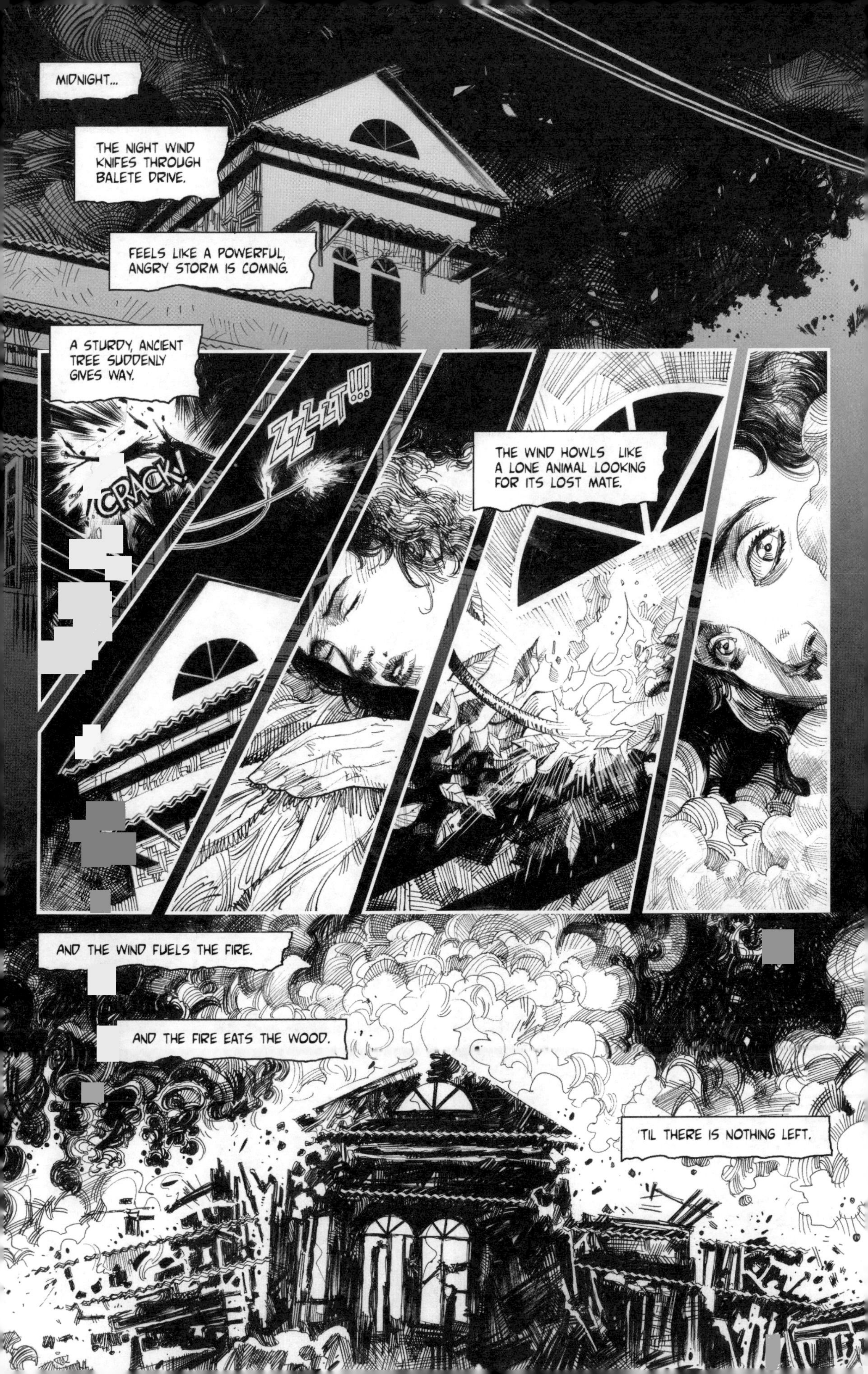
MIDNIGHT...
THE NIGHT WIND KNIFES THROUGH BALETE DRIVE.
FEELS LIKE A POWERFUL, ANGRY STORM IS COMING.
A STURDY, ANCIENT TREE SUDDENLY GIVES WAY.
CRACK!
ZZZT!!!
THE WIND HOWLS LIKE A LONE ANIMAL LOOKING FOR ITS LOST MATE.
AND THE WIND FUELS THE FIRE.
AND THE FIRE EATS THE WOOD.
'TIL THERE IS NOTHING LEFT.

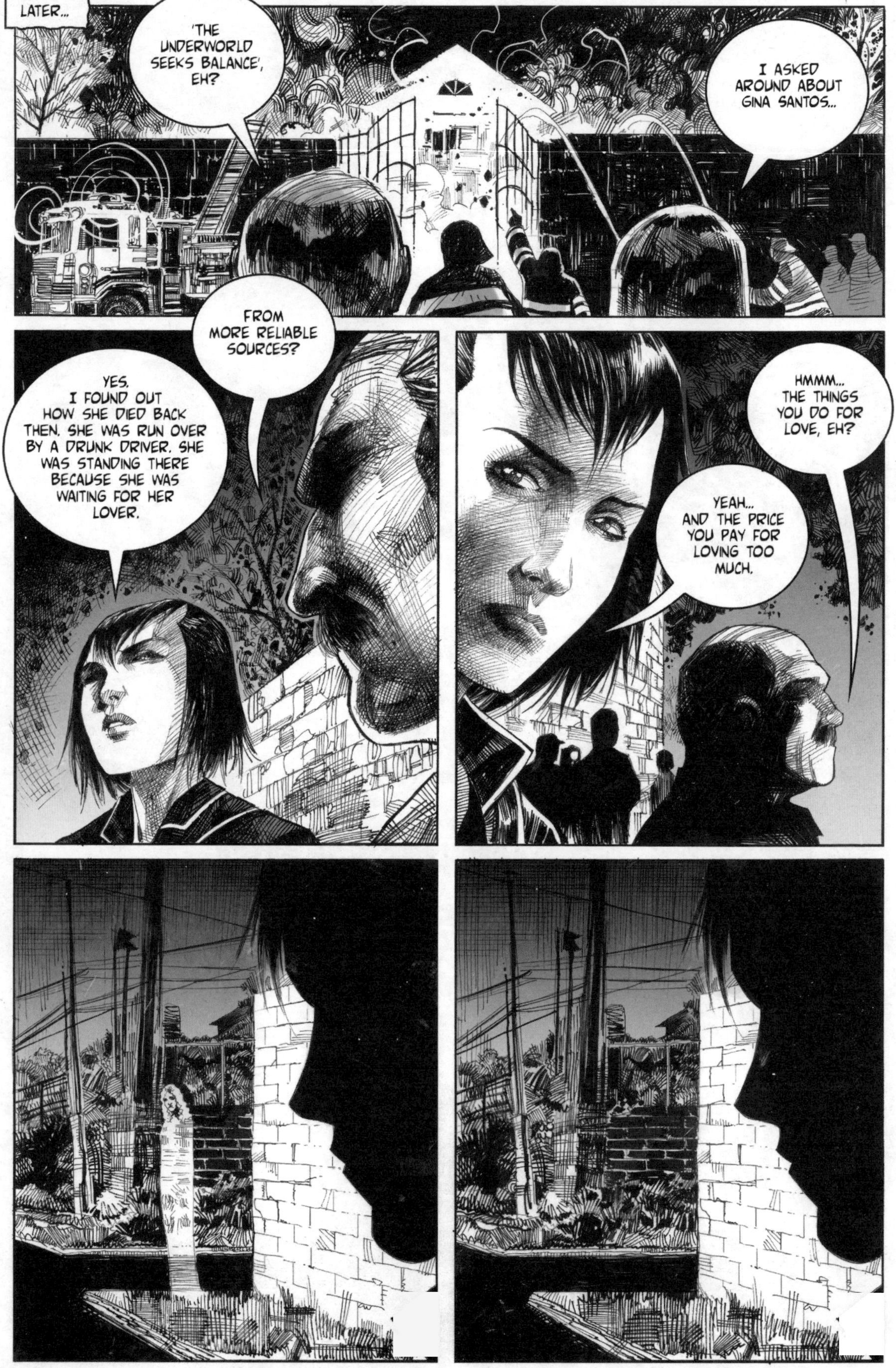
LATER...
'THE UNDERWORLD SEEKS BALANCE', EH?
I ASKED AROUND ABOUT GINA SANTOS...
FROM MORE RELIABLE SOURCES?
YES. I FOUND OUT HOW SHE DIED BACK THEN. SHE WAS RUN OVER BY A DRUNK DRIVER. SHE WAS STANDING THERE BECAUSE SHE WAS WAITING FOR HER LOVER.
HMMM... THE THINGS YOU DO FOR LOVE, EH?
YEAH... AND THE PRICE YOU PAY FOR LOVING TOO MUCH.

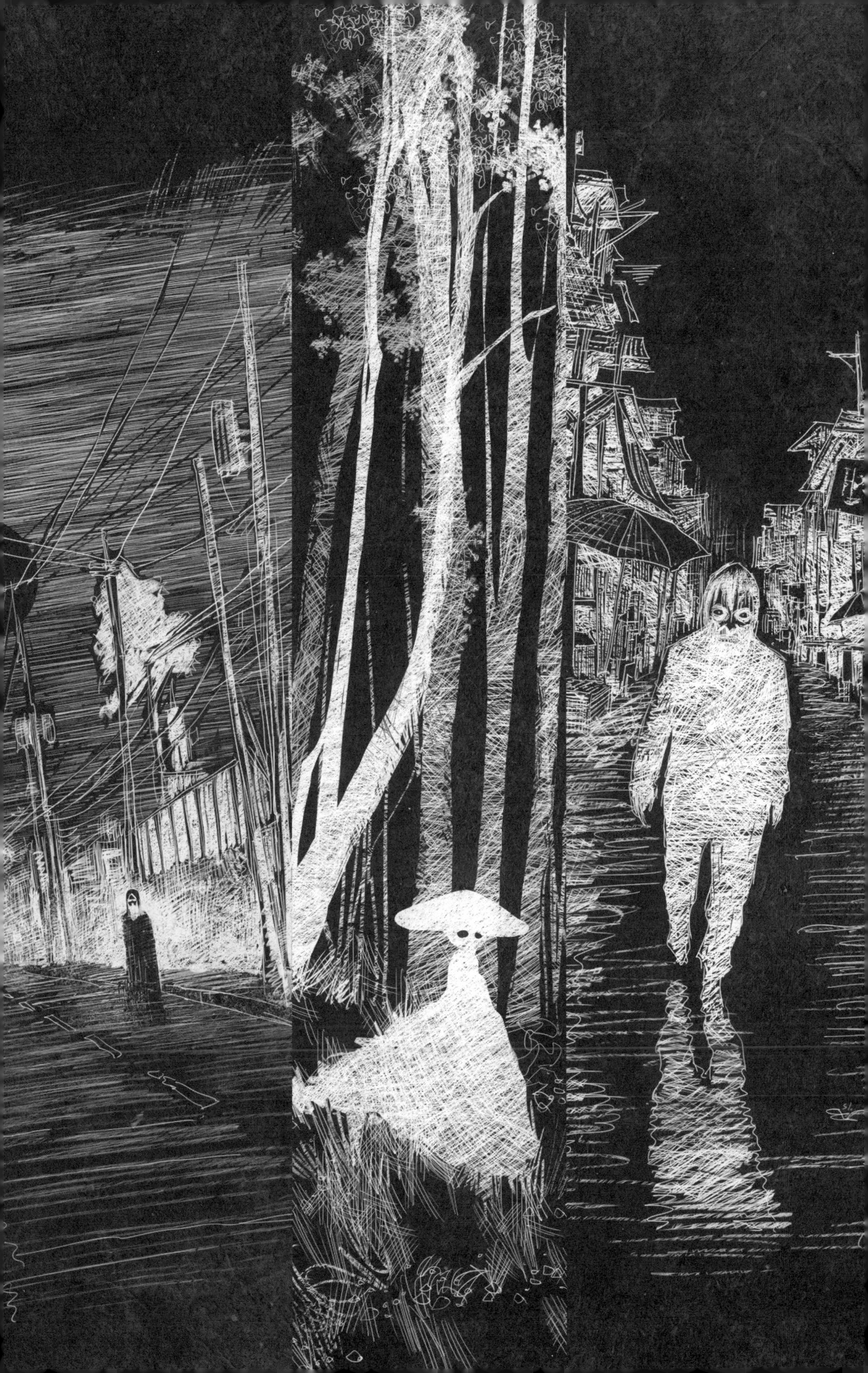

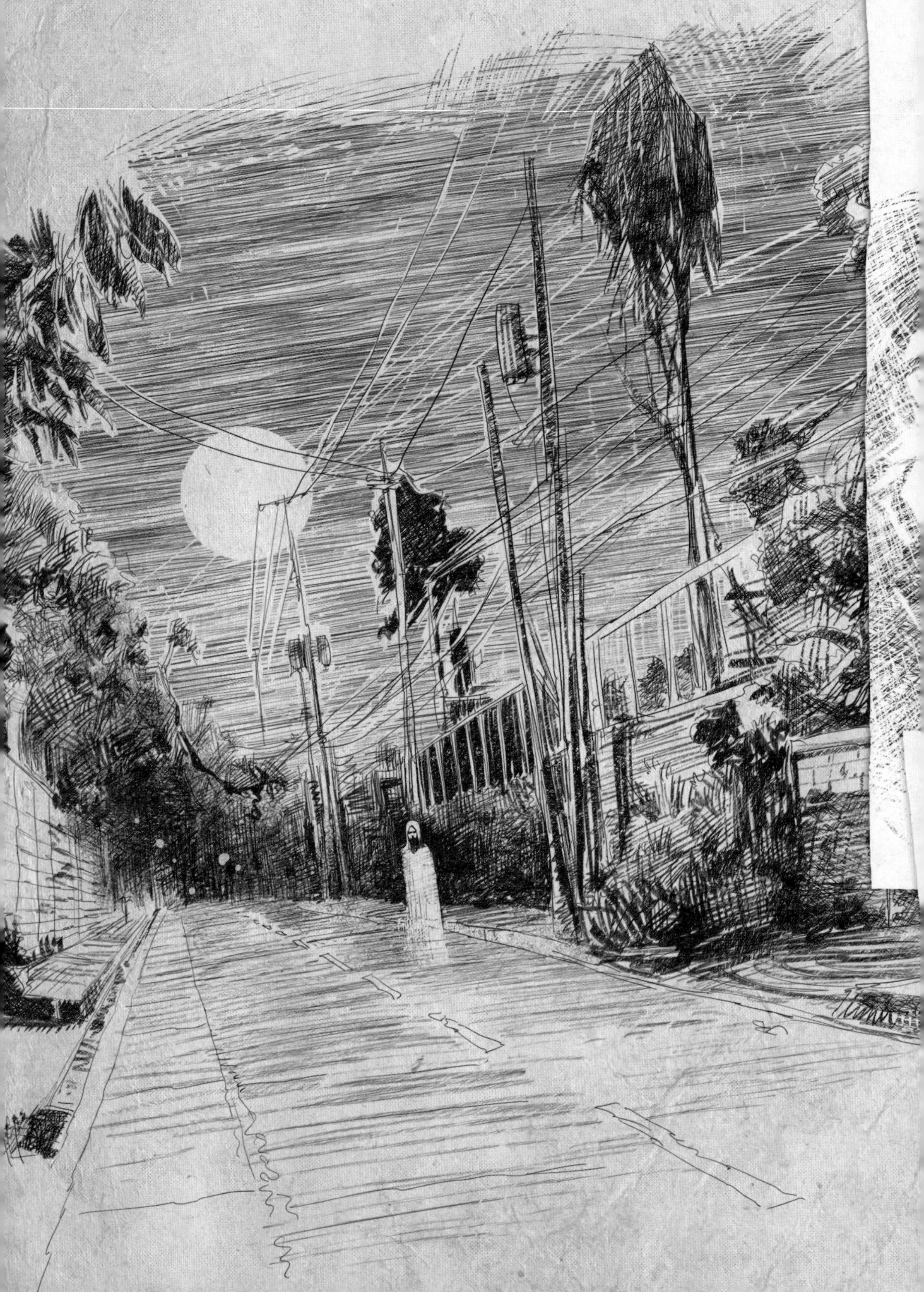

FROM THE JOURNAL OF PROF. ALEXANDER TRESE

June 13

The White Lady of Balete Drive

The story of the lady in white seen along that stretch of road in Quezon City is a tragic tale that has been told and retold as far as I can remember.

There are many versions and variations concerning her origins and fate, but they all share a common conclusion, usually resulting to a death or two.

As the story goes, she would normally be seen after midnight, standing at one of the corners, trying to flag down a passing car. More often than not, one of the taxi cabs would stop for her.

She would give instructions that she just lived down the road. When they arrive at that particular house, the driver would look at his rear-view mirror, ask for payment and discover that his passenger has already disappeared.

The few drivers who were brave enough to get out of the car and ring the doorbell of the house, would usually be greeted by an angry owner roused from their slumber. And when the driver describes his vanishing passenger, the angry owner would suddenly fall silent. He would shiver and slowly close the door, telling the cab driver that the woman he just described died many years ago.

The White Lady's appearance on the road has caused numerous accidents. When drivers do no stop for her, she would suddenly appear in the backseat of their car, surprising the driver and making them swerve into a lamp post or a nearby wall.

We attempted to communicate with the spirit of the White Lady and accidentally summoned a diwata, a spirit of the forest, who resided in one of the Balete trees. The diwata mentioned that they've tried to pacify the restless spirit, but the lady has remained elusive.

The White Lady seems to have a psychic link to the street. The Balete trees that line the road serve as a connection to the underworld and to realms beyond.

We will continue to observe and find other ways to reach out to the Lady in White.

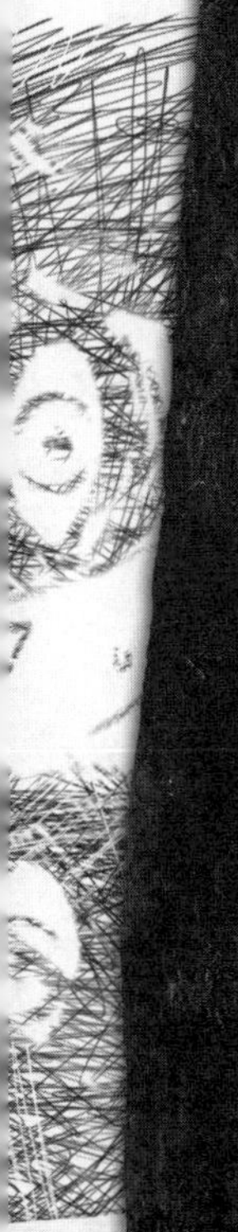

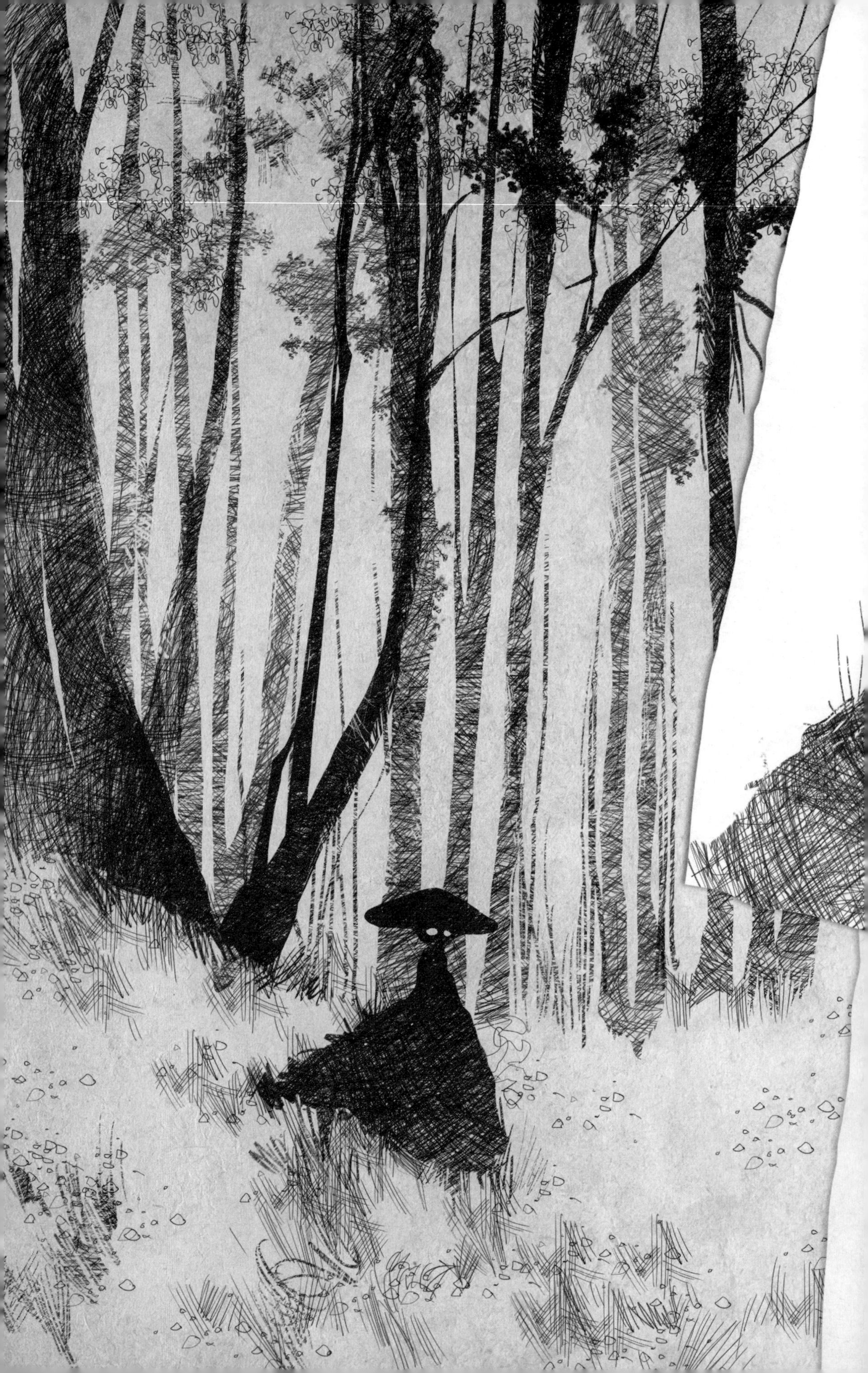

FROM THE JOURNAL OF PROF. ALEXANDER TRESE

May 19

Nuno sa Punso

The *nuno* seems to be related to the *duwende*. They are creatures of the earth, with a close affinity to other "earth elementals".

The *nuno* typically lives alone, choosing to reside near the roots of a Balete Tree or a Mango Tree. When they do appear to humans, they are seen squatting on a termite mound.

If you happen to offend a *nuno*, by accidently stepping on his home (or worse, by urinating on his termite mound) they have been known to cast a spell and give the offending person a minor ailment.

The only way to be healed from the *nuno*'s curse is to return to the *nuno*'s home and ask for forgiveness. A tribute of food is usually enough to pacify the ancient creature.

To avoid accidentally harming a *nuno*, it has become a custom in certain provinces, while traveling through the forest or tree-lined roads, to announce your presence to the nuno and say, "*Tabi-tabi po!*" and ask for permission to pass through his home.

The *nuno* tend to lead solitary lives, as opposed to the *duwende*, who live in tribes and are more social.

Some *nuno* find mates, and if they do, that will be their mate for life.

We've discovered that if treated properly, the *nuno* will be cooperative and will gladly share information about the underworld, like a nosy neighbor.

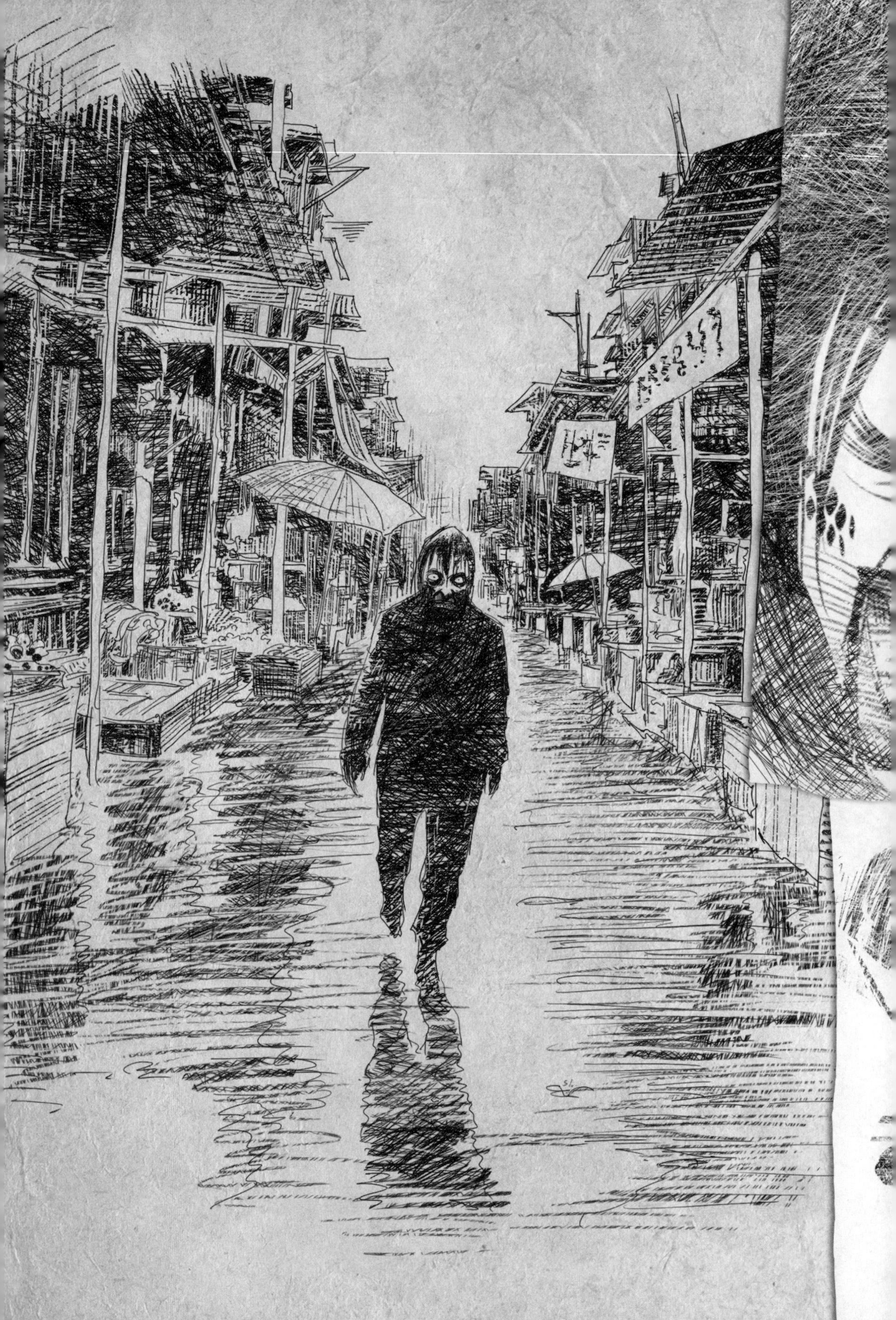

FROM THE JOURNAL OF PROF. ALEXANDER TRESE

October 3

Aswang

These predators maintain a human form during the daytime, but when they crave for flesh and blood, they undergo a transformation and become these horrible beasts. In this form, they are stronger than the average man and can attack at a speed that would surprise most of their prey.

When they scout for food, they can take on the shape of a feral dog, a wild pig, a bat, or a black crow-like bird.

We have witnessed a ritual that transforms an ordinary person into an aswang and involves swallowing a black chick. The ebony avian is somehow swallowed whole by the person. The bird, which is still alive, submits to the ritual and freely enters the mouth of the subject.

We have yet to determine the origins of the black chick and believe it to be an entity in disguise, some sort of parasite looking for a host.

Other reports have been received that a person that tastes aswang blood or saliva can also be transformed into an aswang.

The clan of aswang in the Trident Bar have developed the ability to change into sea creatures, allowing them to hunt down sirena and other taga-dagat.

While most aswangs in the city now feast on a daily supply of cows and pigs, some still hunger for human blood and flesh. Those are the ones that we need to track down and stop.

The aswang have also organized themselves as gangs and now run some of the metro's kidnapping rings and drug rings. We continue to monitor their activities with help from the police and our other contacts in the underworld.

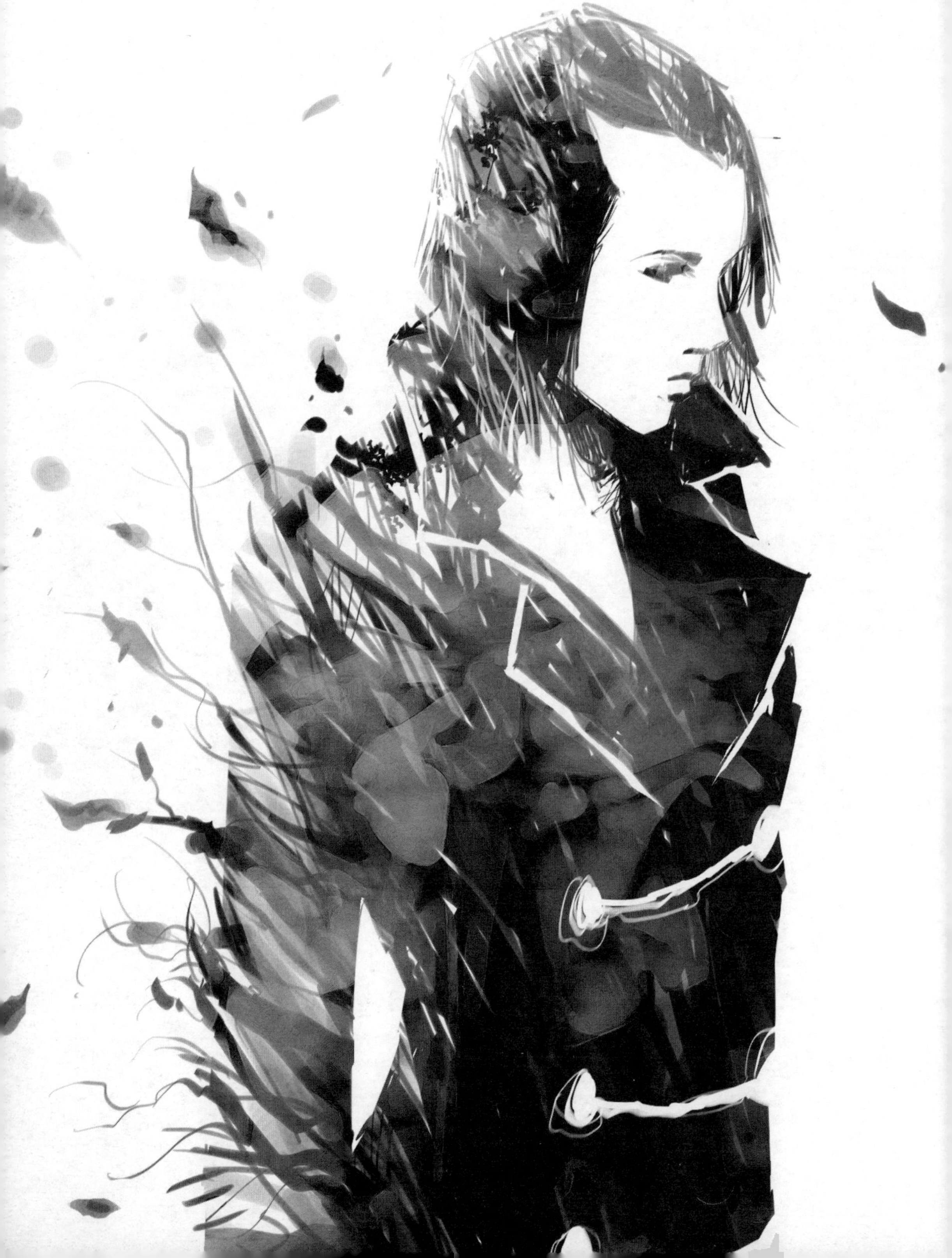

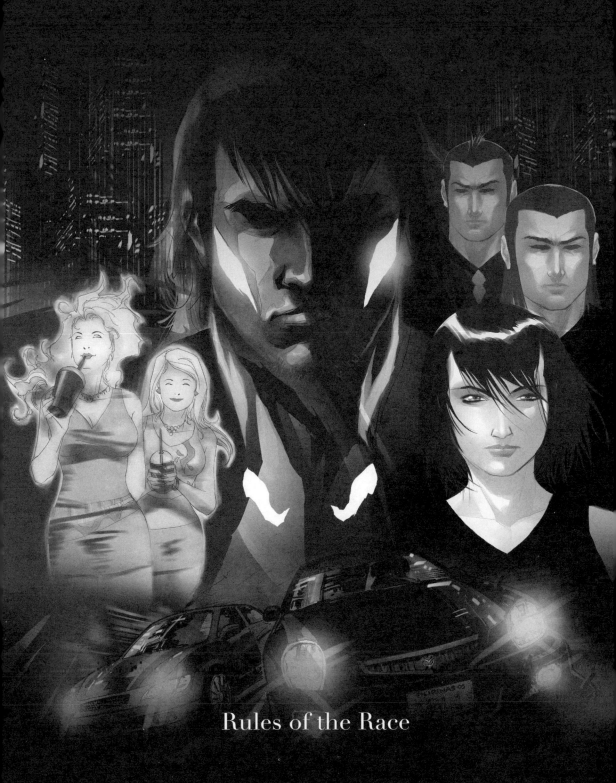

Rules of the Race

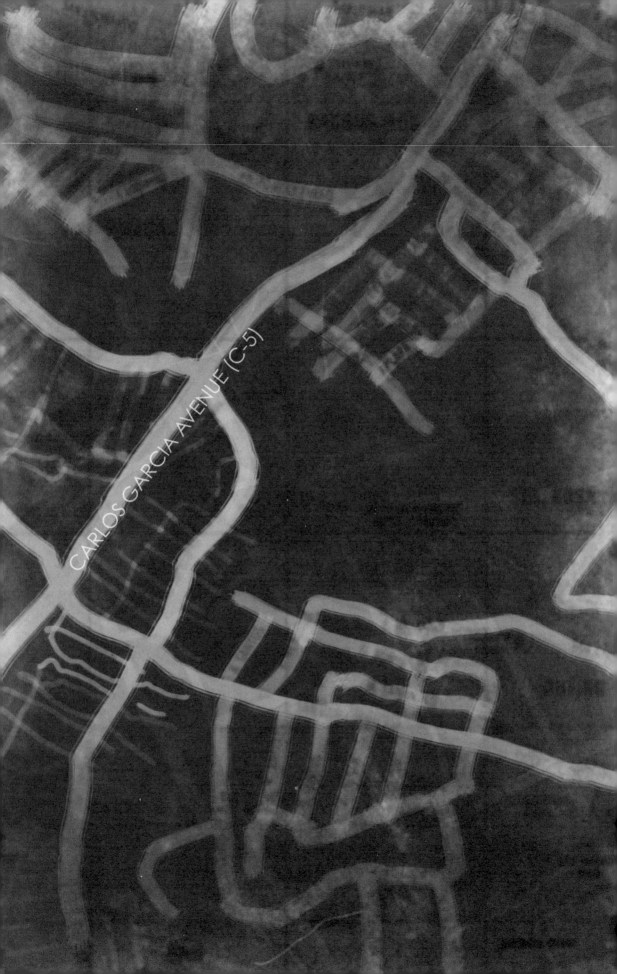
CARLOS GARCIA AVENUE (C-5)

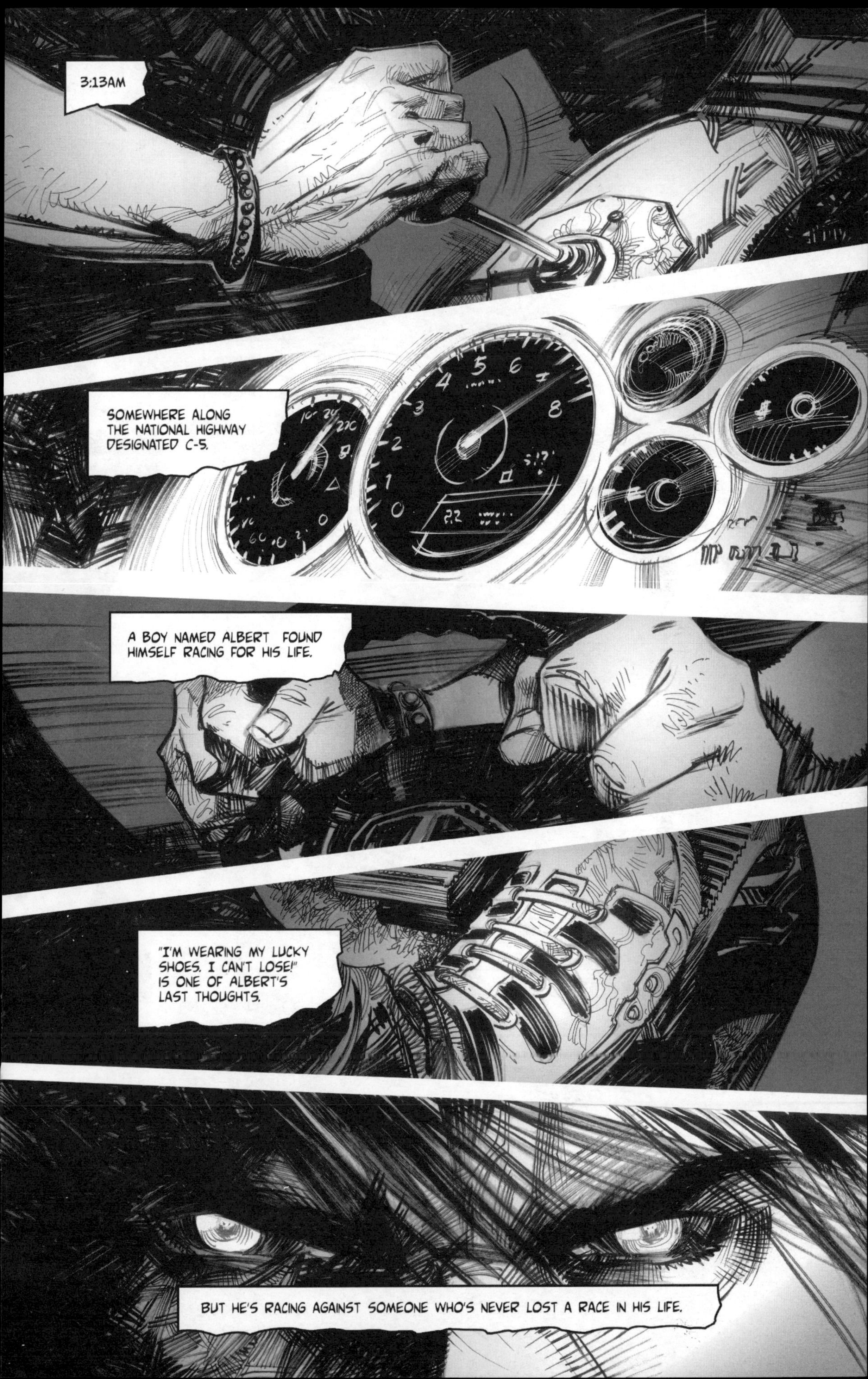
3:13AM
SOMEWHERE ALONG THE NATIONAL HIGHWAY DESIGNATED C-5.
A BOY NAMED ALBERT FOUND HIMSELF RACING FOR HIS LIFE.
"I'M WEARING MY LUCKY SHOES. I CAN'T LOSE!" IS ONE OF ALBERT'S LAST THOUGHTS.
BUT HE'S RACING AGAINST SOMEONE WHO'S NEVER LOST A RACE IN HIS LIFE.

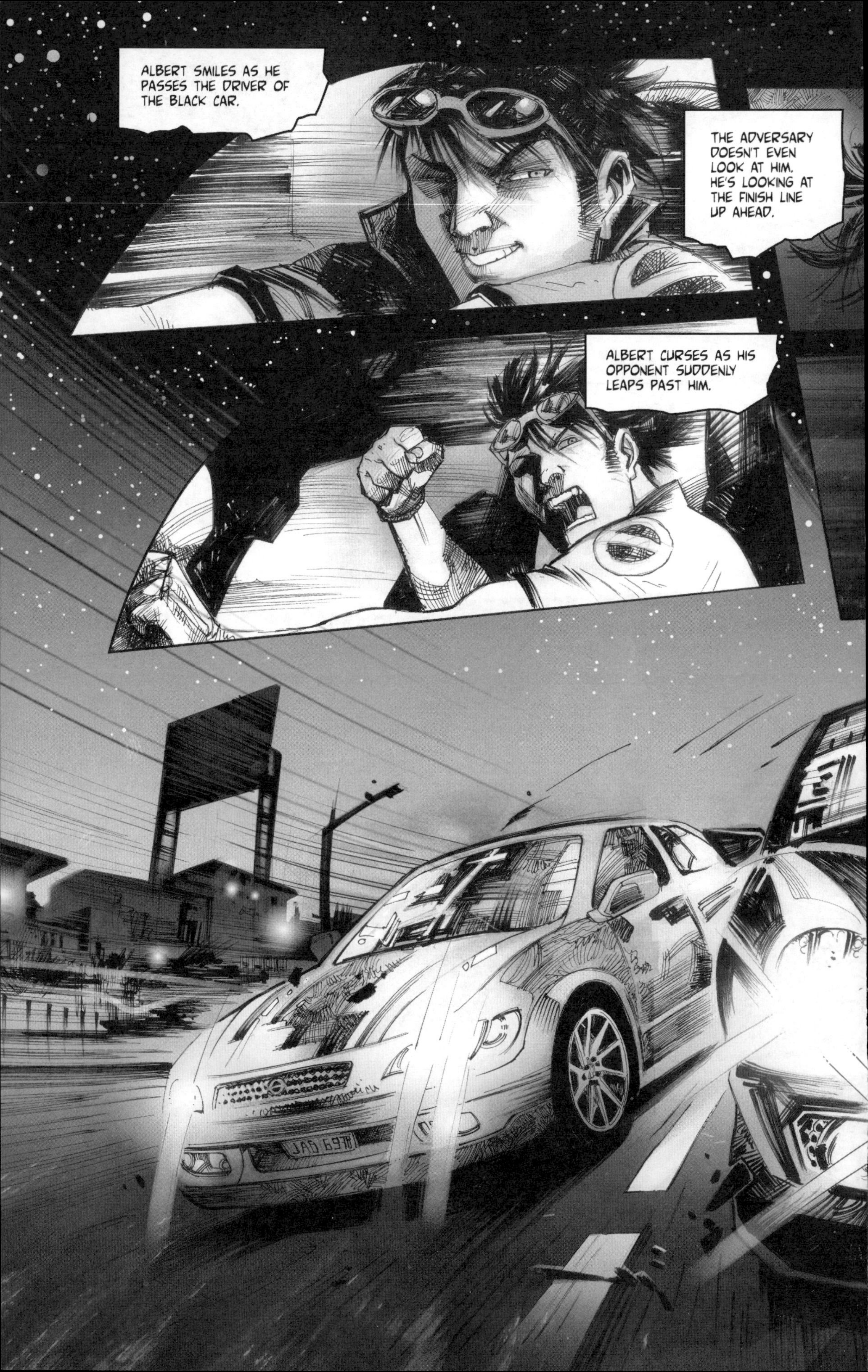
ALBERT SMILES AS HE PASSES THE DRIVER OF THE BLACK CAR.
THE ADVERSARY DOESN'T EVEN LOOK AT HIM. HE'S LOOKING AT THE FINISH LINE UP AHEAD.
ALBERT CURSES AS HIS OPPONENT SUDDENLY LEAPS PAST HIM.

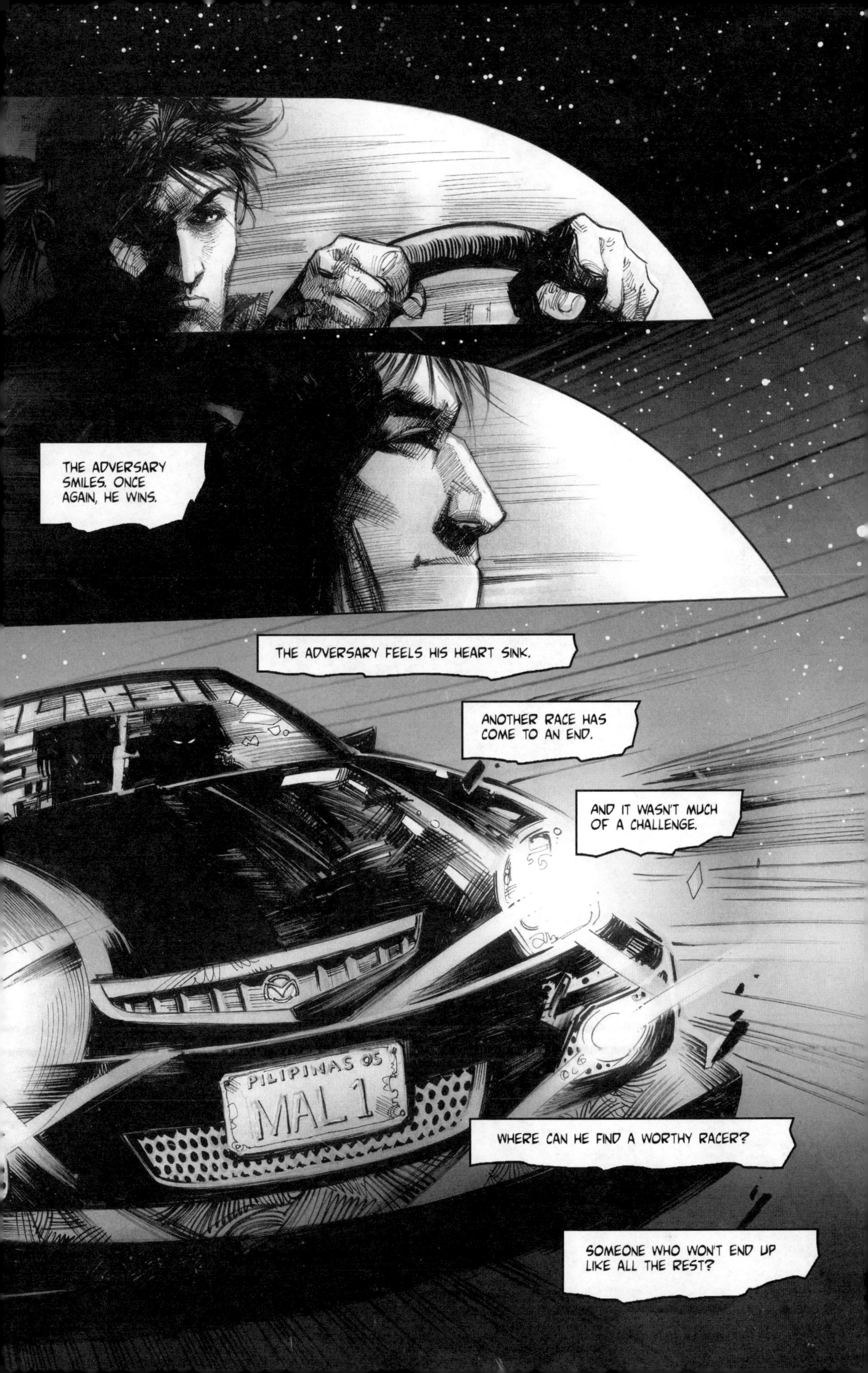
THE ADVERSARY SMILES. ONCE AGAIN, HE WINS.
THE ADVERSARY FEELS HIS HEART SINK.
ANOTHER RACE HAS COME TO AN END.
AND IT WASN'T MUCH OF A CHALLENGE.
PILIPINAS 05
MAL 1
WHERE CAN HE FIND A WORTHY RACER?
SOMEONE WHO WON'T END UP LIKE ALL THE REST?

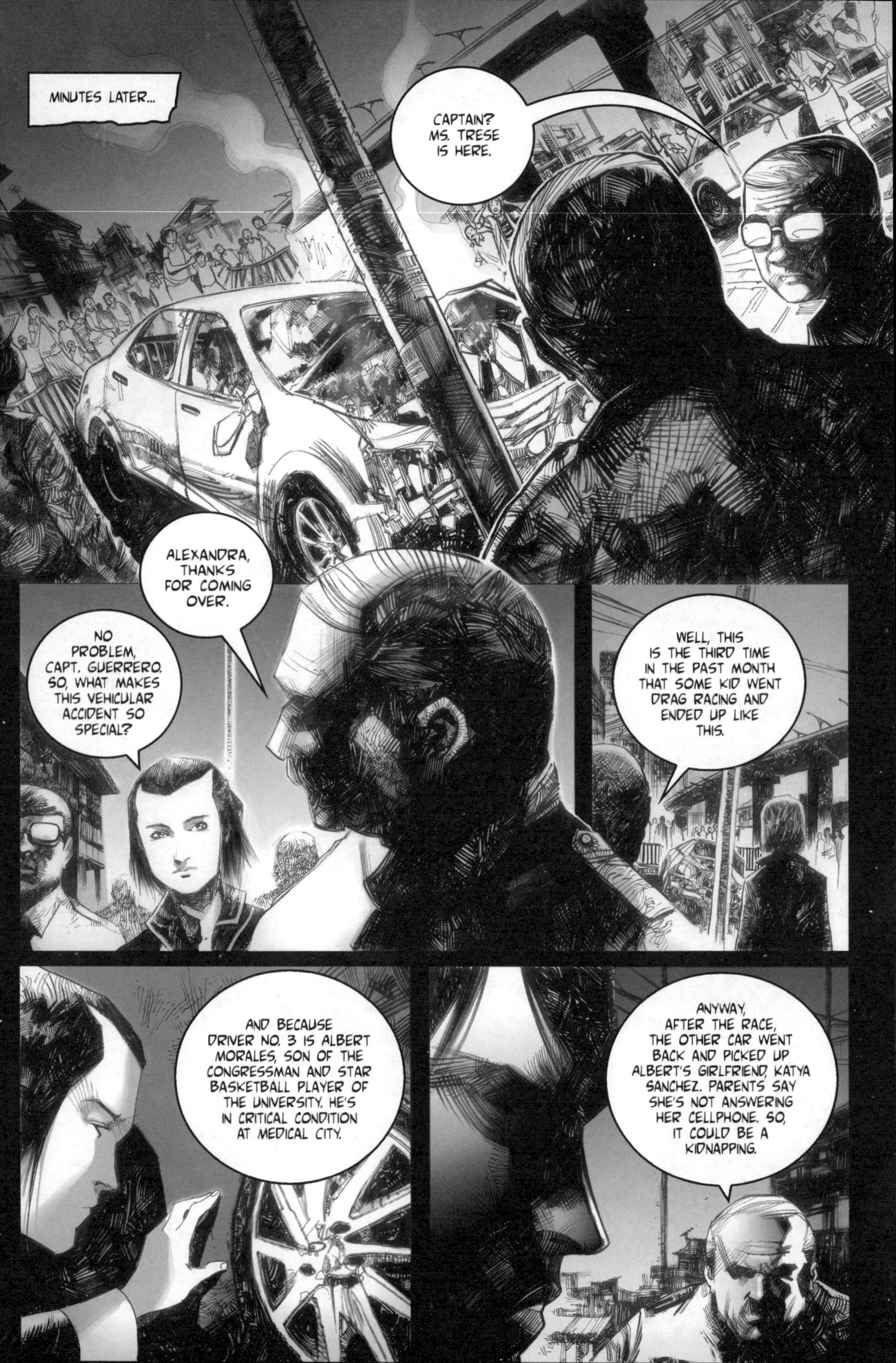
MINUTES LATER...
CAPTAIN? MS. TRESE IS HERE.
ALEXANDRA, THANKS FOR COMING OVER.
NO PROBLEM, CAPT. GUERRERO. SO, WHAT MAKES THIS VEHICULAR ACCIDENT SO SPECIAL?
WELL, THIS IS THE THIRD TIME IN THE PAST MONTH THAT SOME KID WENT DRAG RACING AND ENDED UP LIKE THIS.
AND BECAUSE DRIVER NO. 3 IS ALBERT MORALES, SON OF THE CONGRESSMAN AND STAR BASKETBALL PLAYER OF THE UNIVERSITY. HE'S IN CRITICAL CONDITION AT MEDICAL CITY.
ANYWAY, AFTER THE RACE, THE OTHER CAR WENT BACK AND PICKED UP ALBERT'S GIRLFRIEND, KATYA SANCHEZ. PARENTS SAY SHE'S NOT ANSWERING HER CELLPHONE. SO, IT COULD BE A KIDNAPPING.

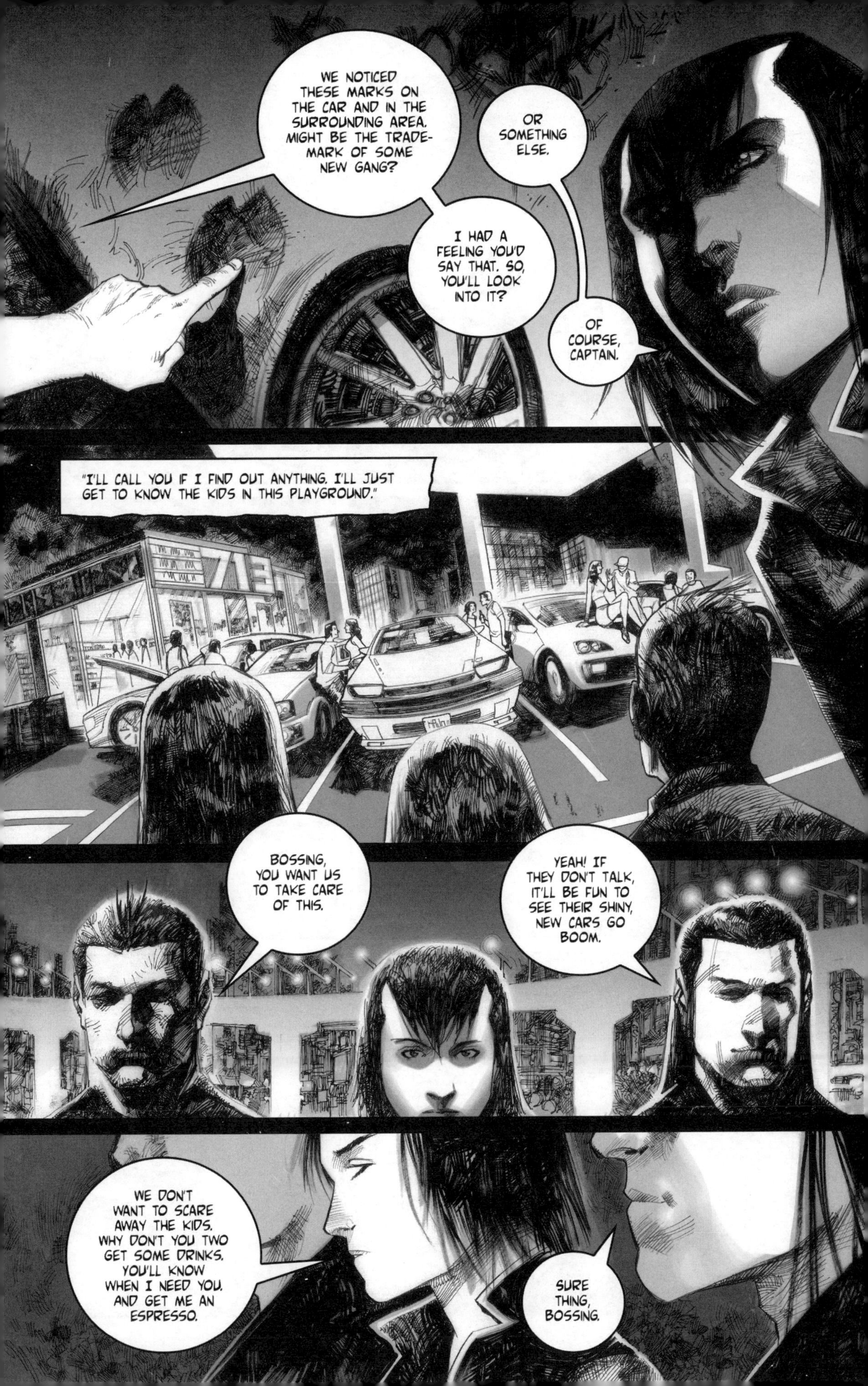
WE NOTICED THESE MARKS ON THE CAR AND IN THE SURROUNDING AREA. MIGHT BE THE TRADE-MARK OF SOME NEW GANG?
OR SOMETHING ELSE.
I HAD A FEELING YOU'D SAY THAT. SO, YOU'LL LOOK INTO IT?
OF COURSE, CAPTAIN.
"I'LL CALL YOU IF I FIND OUT ANYTHING. I'LL JUST GET TO KNOW THE KIDS IN THIS PLAYGROUND."
BOSSING, YOU WANT US TO TAKE CARE OF THIS.
YEAH! IF THEY DON'T TALK, IT'LL BE FUN TO SEE THEIR SHINY, NEW CARS GO BOOM.
WE DON'T WANT TO SCARE AWAY THE KIDS. WHY DON'T YOU TWO GET SOME DRINKS. YOU'LL KNOW WHEN I NEED YOU. AND GET ME AN ESPRESSO.
SURE THING, BOSSING.

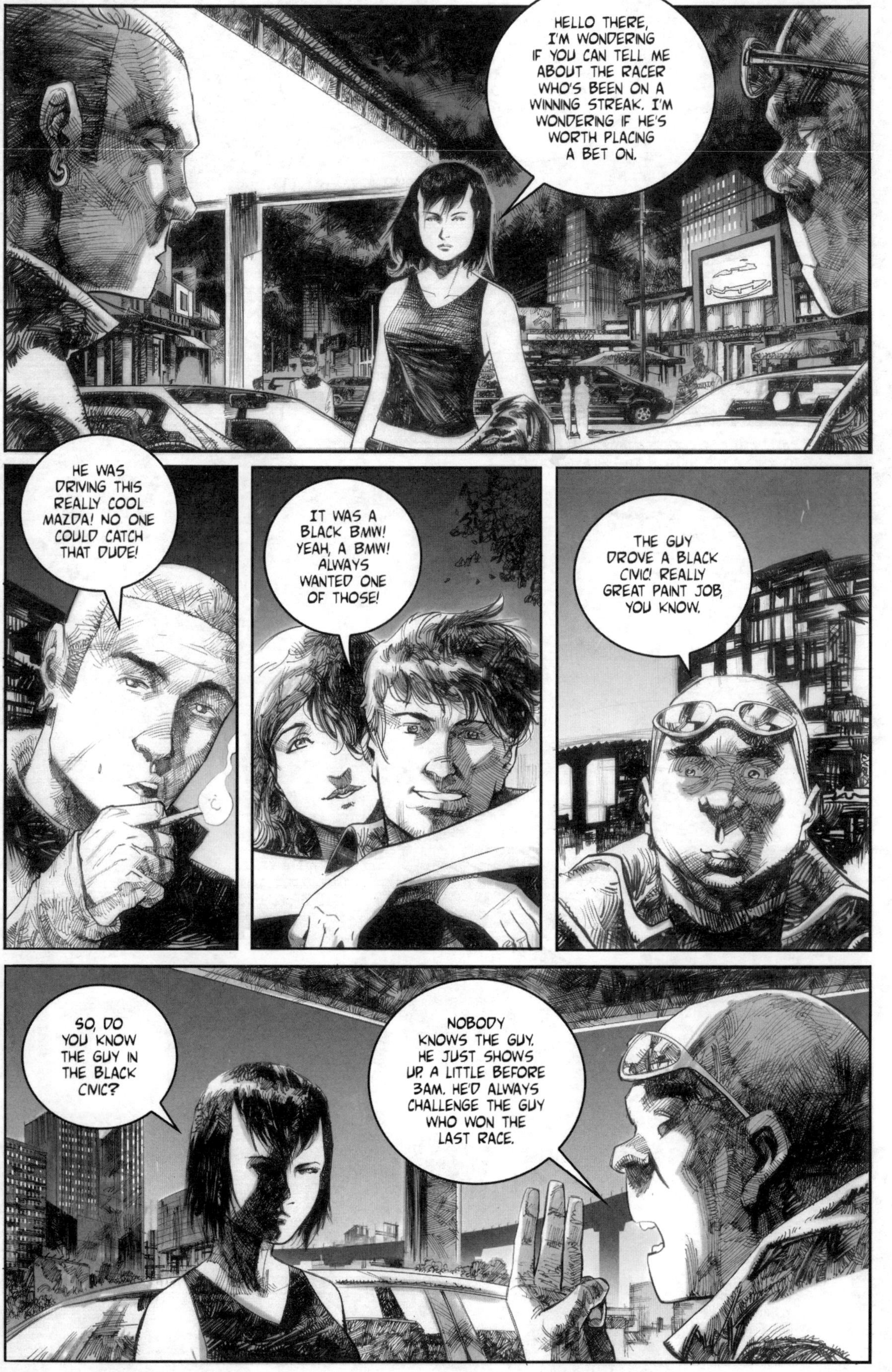
HELLO THERE, I'M WONDERING IF YOU CAN TELL ME ABOUT THE RACER WHO'S BEEN ON A WINNING STREAK. I'M WONDERING IF HE'S WORTH PLACING A BET ON.
HE WAS DRIVING THIS REALLY COOL MAZDA! NO ONE COULD CATCH THAT DUDE!
IT WAS A BLACK BMW! YEAH, A BMW! ALWAYS WANTED ONE OF THOSE!
THE GUY DROVE A BLACK CIVIC! REALLY GREAT PAINT JOB, YOU KNOW.
SO, DO YOU KNOW THE GUY IN THE BLACK CIVIC?
NOBODY KNOWS THE GUY. HE JUST SHOWS UP. A LITTLE BEFORE 3AM. HE'D ALWAYS CHALLENGE THE GUY WHO WON THE LAST RACE.

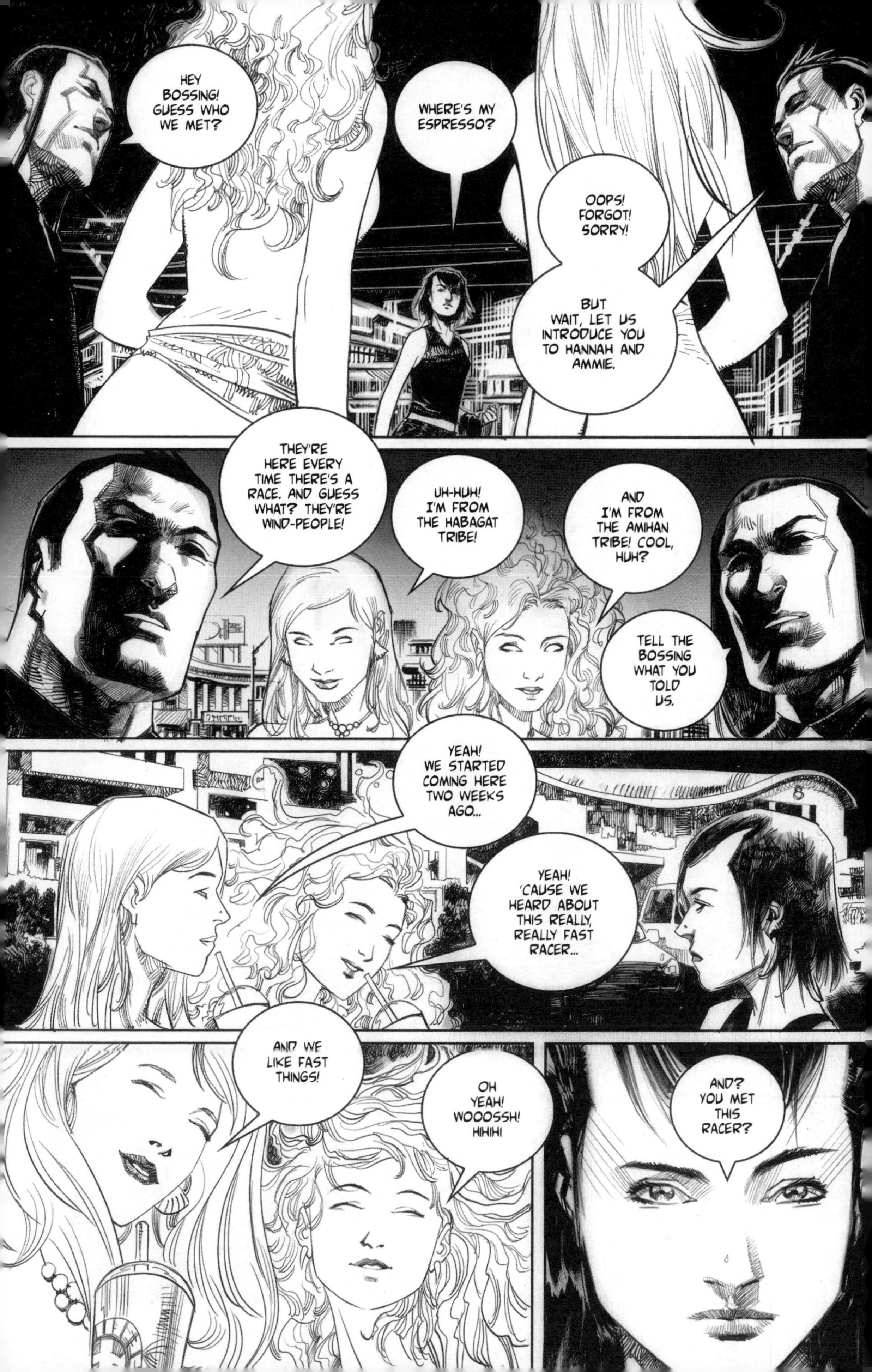
HEY BOSSING! GUESS WHO WE MET?
WHERE'S MY ESPRESSO?
OOPS! FORGOT! SORRY!
BUT WAIT, LET US INTRODUCE YOU TO HANNAH AND AMMIE.
THEY'RE HERE EVERY TIME THERE'S A RACE. AND GUESS WHAT? THEY'RE WIND-PEOPLE!
UH-HUH! I'M FROM THE HABAGAT TRIBE!
AND I'M FROM THE AMIHAN TRIBE! COOL, HUH?
TELL THE BOSSING WHAT YOU TOLD US.
YEAH! WE STARTED COMING HERE TWO WEEKS AGO...
YEAH! 'CAUSE WE HEARD ABOUT THIS REALLY, REALLY FAST RACER...
AND WE LIKE FAST THINGS!
OH YEAH! WOOOSSH! HIHIHI
AND? YOU MET THIS RACER?

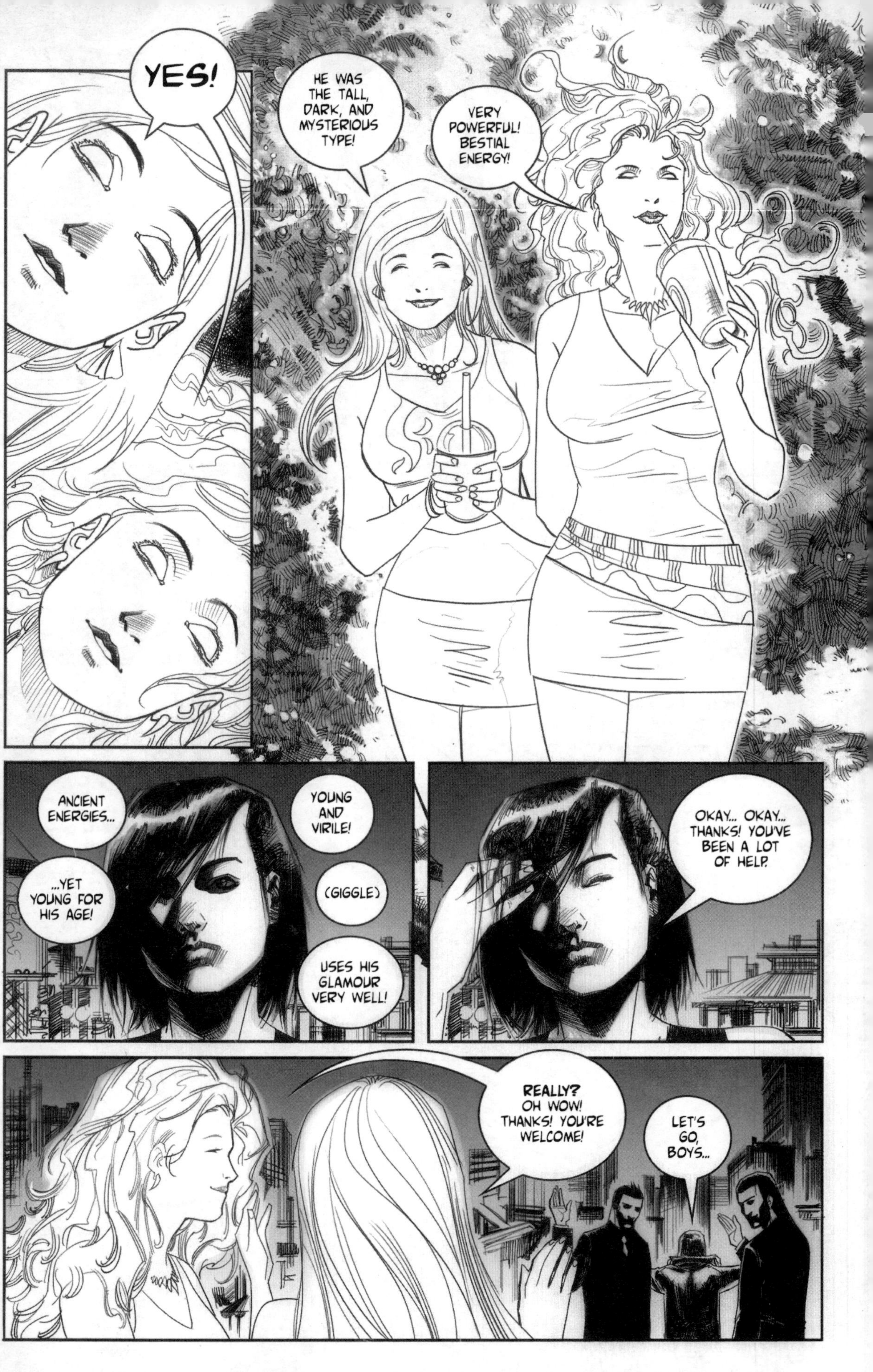
YES!
HE WAS THE TALL, DARK, AND MYSTERIOUS TYPE!
VERY POWERFUL! BESTIAL ENERGY!
ANCIENT ENERGIES...
...YET YOUNG FOR HIS AGE!
YOUNG AND VIRILE!
(GIGGLE)
USES HIS GLAMOUR VERY WELL!
OKAY... OKAY... THANKS! YOU'VE BEEN A LOT OF HELP.
REALLY? OH WOW! THANKS! YOU'RE WELCOME!
LET'S GO, BOYS...

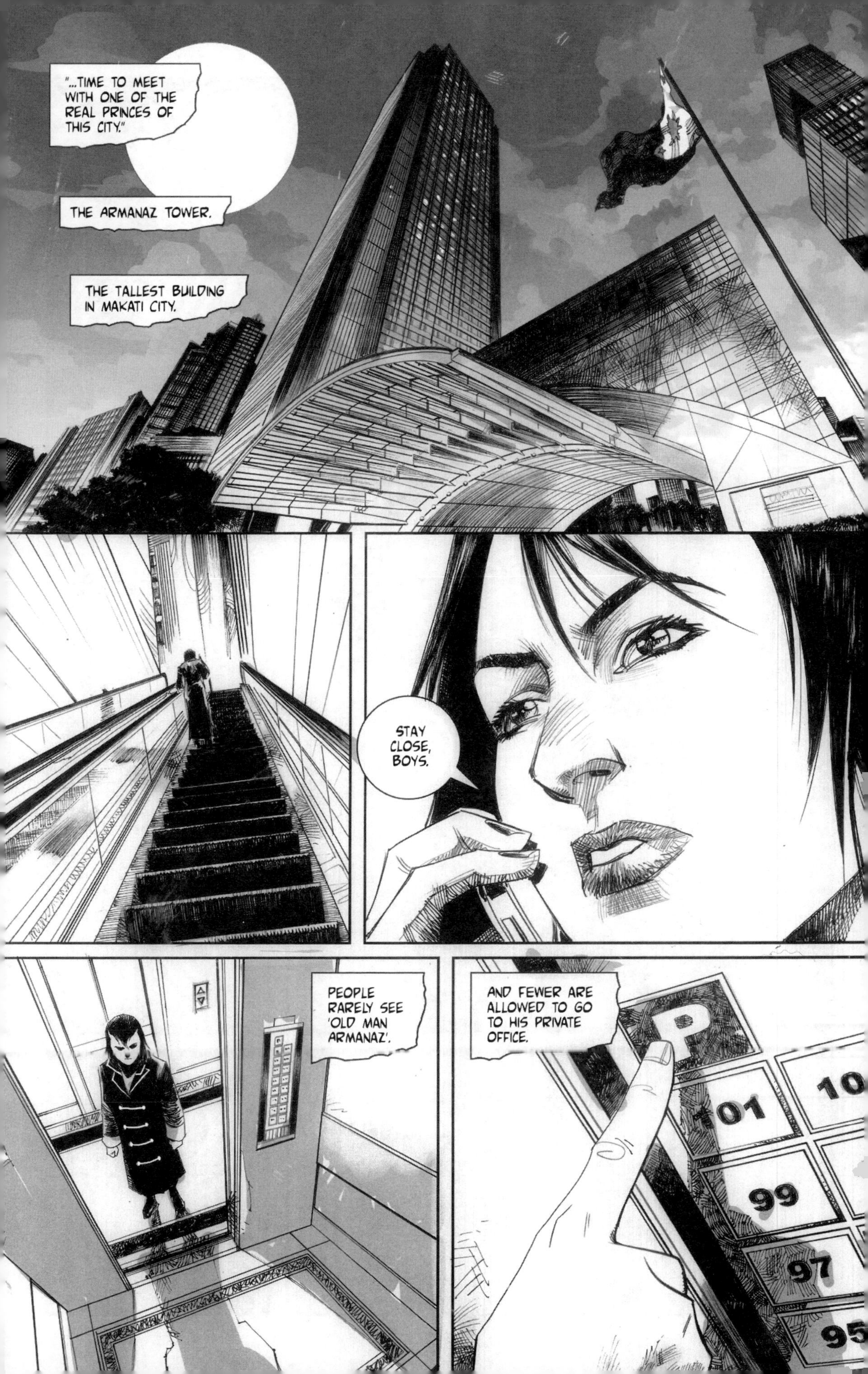
"...TIME TO MEET WITH ONE OF THE REAL PRINCES OF THIS CITY."
THE ARMANAZ TOWER.
THE TALLEST BUILDING IN MAKATI CITY.
STAY CLOSE, BOYS.
PEOPLE RARELY SEE 'OLD MAN ARMANAZ'.
AND FEWER ARE ALLOWED TO GO TO HIS PRIVATE OFFICE.
P
101
99
97
95

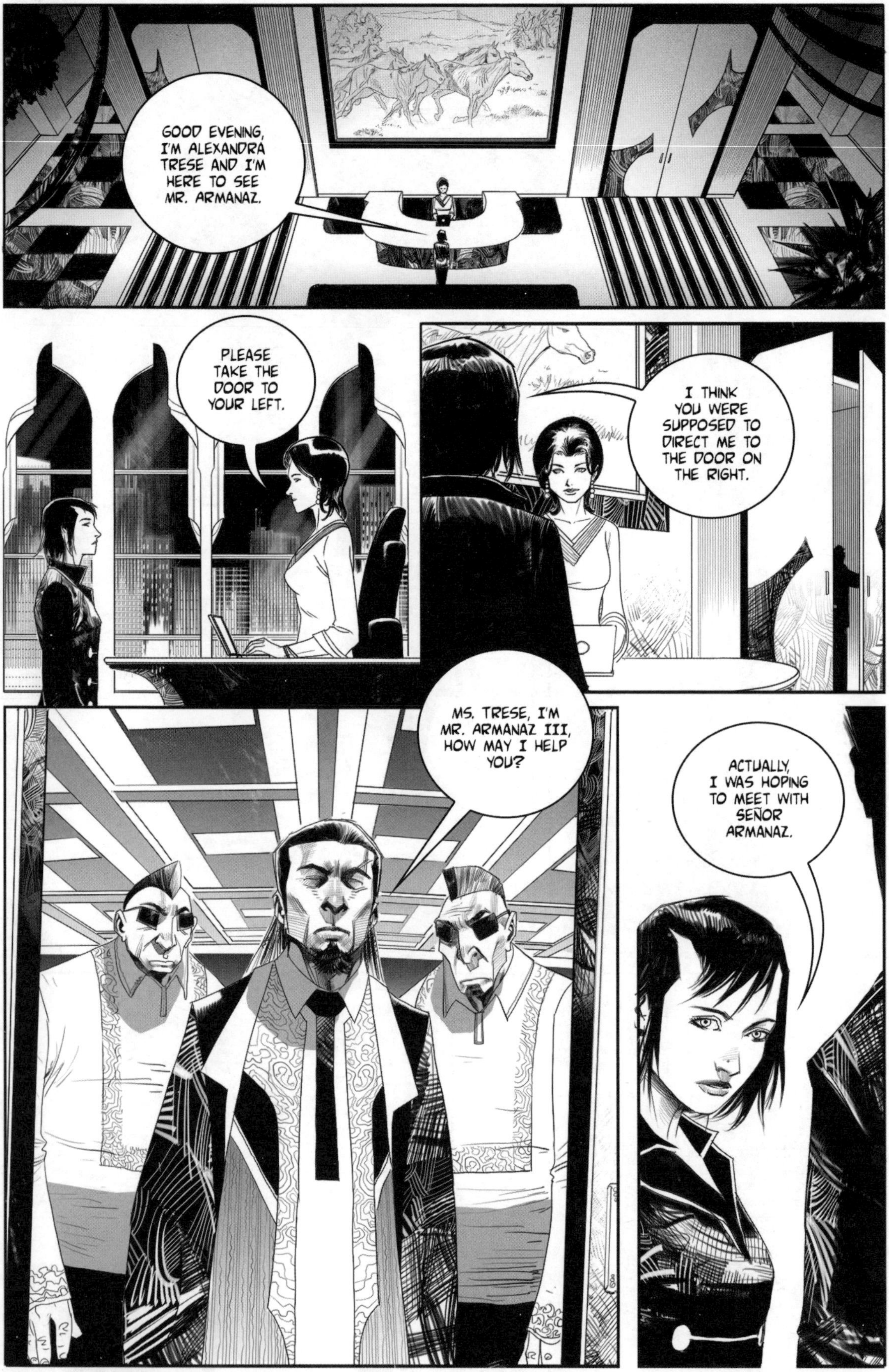
GOOD EVENING, I'M ALEXANDRA TRESE AND I'M HERE TO SEE MR. ARMANAZ.
PLEASE TAKE THE DOOR TO YOUR LEFT.
I THINK YOU WERE SUPPOSED TO DIRECT ME TO THE DOOR ON THE RIGHT.
MS. TRESE, I'M MR. ARMANAZ III, HOW MAY I HELP YOU?
ACTUALLY, I WAS HOPING TO MEET WITH SEÑOR ARMANAZ.

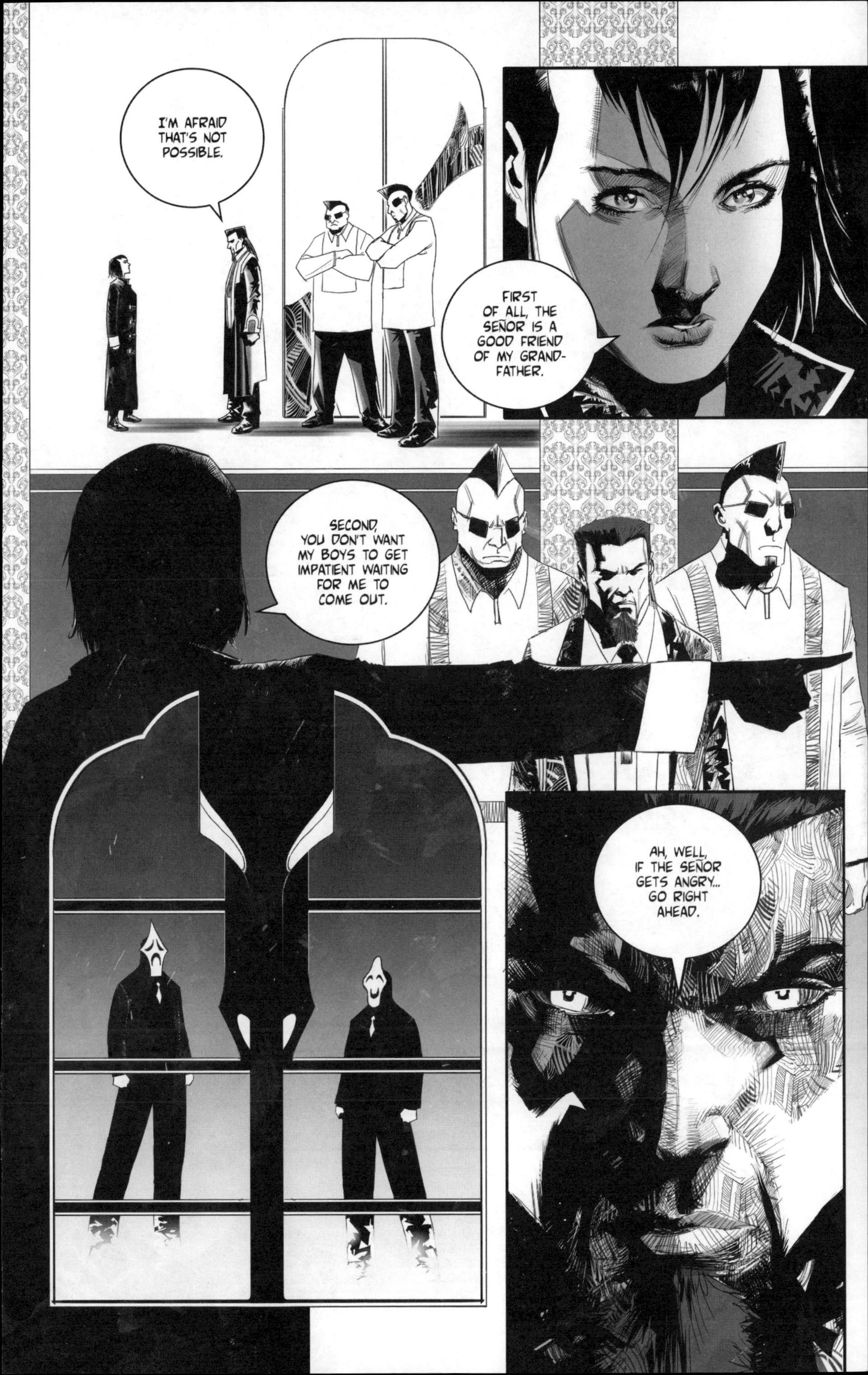
I'M AFRAID THAT'S NOT POSSIBLE.
FIRST OF ALL, THE SEÑOR IS A GOOD FRIEND OF MY GRAND-FATHER.
SECOND, YOU DON'T WANT MY BOYS TO GET IMPATIENT WAITING FOR ME TO COME OUT.
AH, WELL, IF THE SEÑOR GETS ANGRY... GO RIGHT AHEAD.

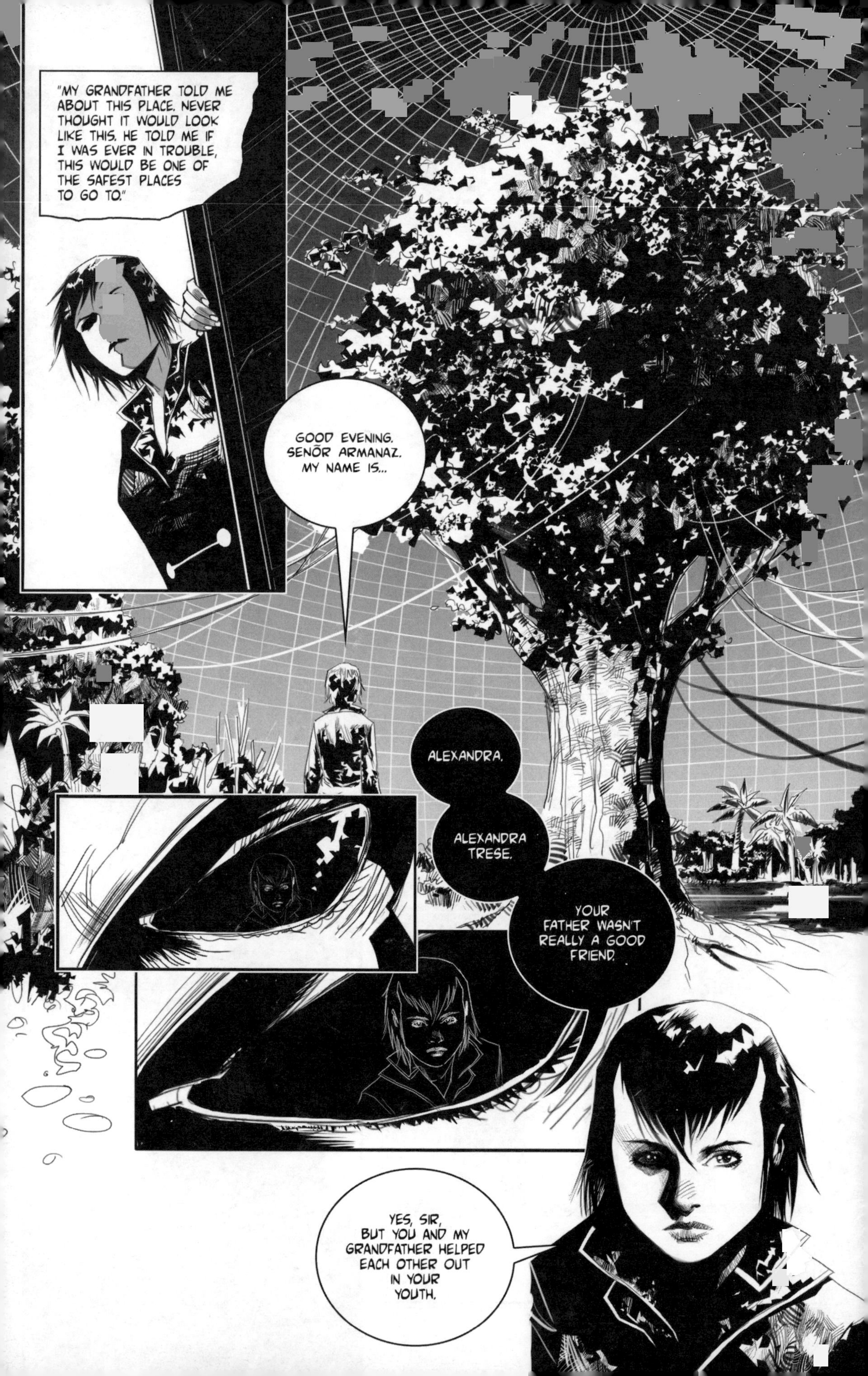
"MY GRANDFATHER TOLD ME ABOUT THIS PLACE. NEVER THOUGHT IT WOULD LOOK LIKE THIS. HE TOLD ME IF I WAS EVER IN TROUBLE, THIS WOULD BE ONE OF THE SAFEST PLACES TO GO TO."
GOOD EVENING. SEÑOR ARMANAZ. MY NAME IS...
ALEXANDRA.
ALEXANDRA TRESE.
YOUR FATHER WASN'T REALLY A GOOD FRIEND.
YES, SIR, BUT YOU AND MY GRANDFATHER HELPED EACH OTHER OUT IN YOUR YOUTH.

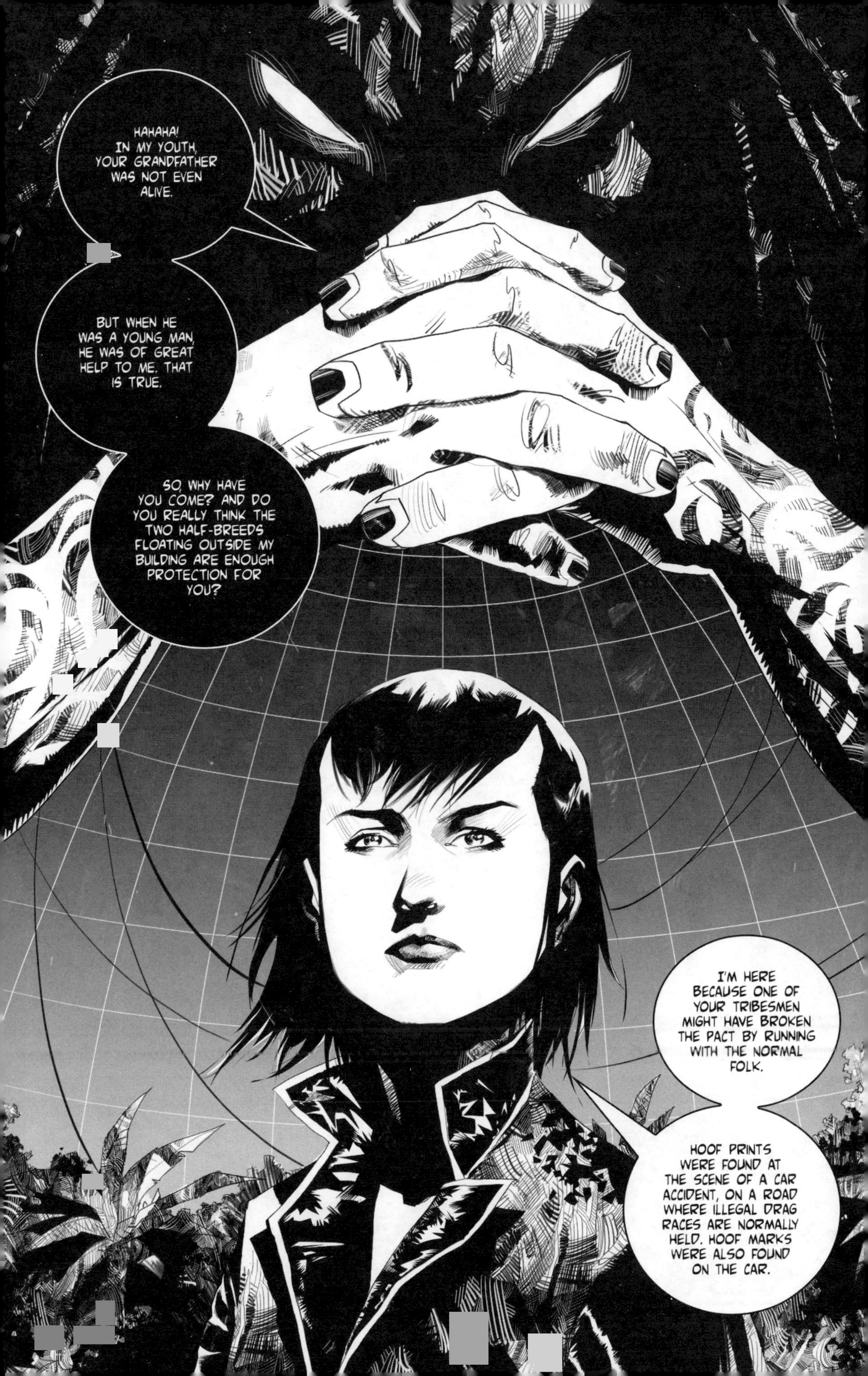
HAHAHA! IN MY YOUTH, YOUR GRANDFATHER WAS NOT EVEN ALIVE.
BUT WHEN HE WAS A YOUNG MAN, HE WAS OF GREAT HELP TO ME. THAT IS TRUE.
SO, WHY HAVE YOU COME? AND DO YOU REALLY THINK THE TWO HALF-BREEDS FLOATING OUTSIDE MY BUILDING ARE ENOUGH PROTECTION FOR YOU?
I'M HERE BECAUSE ONE OF YOUR TRIBESMEN MIGHT HAVE BROKEN THE PACT BY RUNNING WITH THE NORMAL FOLK.
HOOF PRINTS WERE FOUND AT THE SCENE OF A CAR ACCIDENT, ON A ROAD WHERE ILLEGAL DRAG RACES ARE NORMALLY HELD. HOOF MARKS WERE ALSO FOUND ON THE CAR.

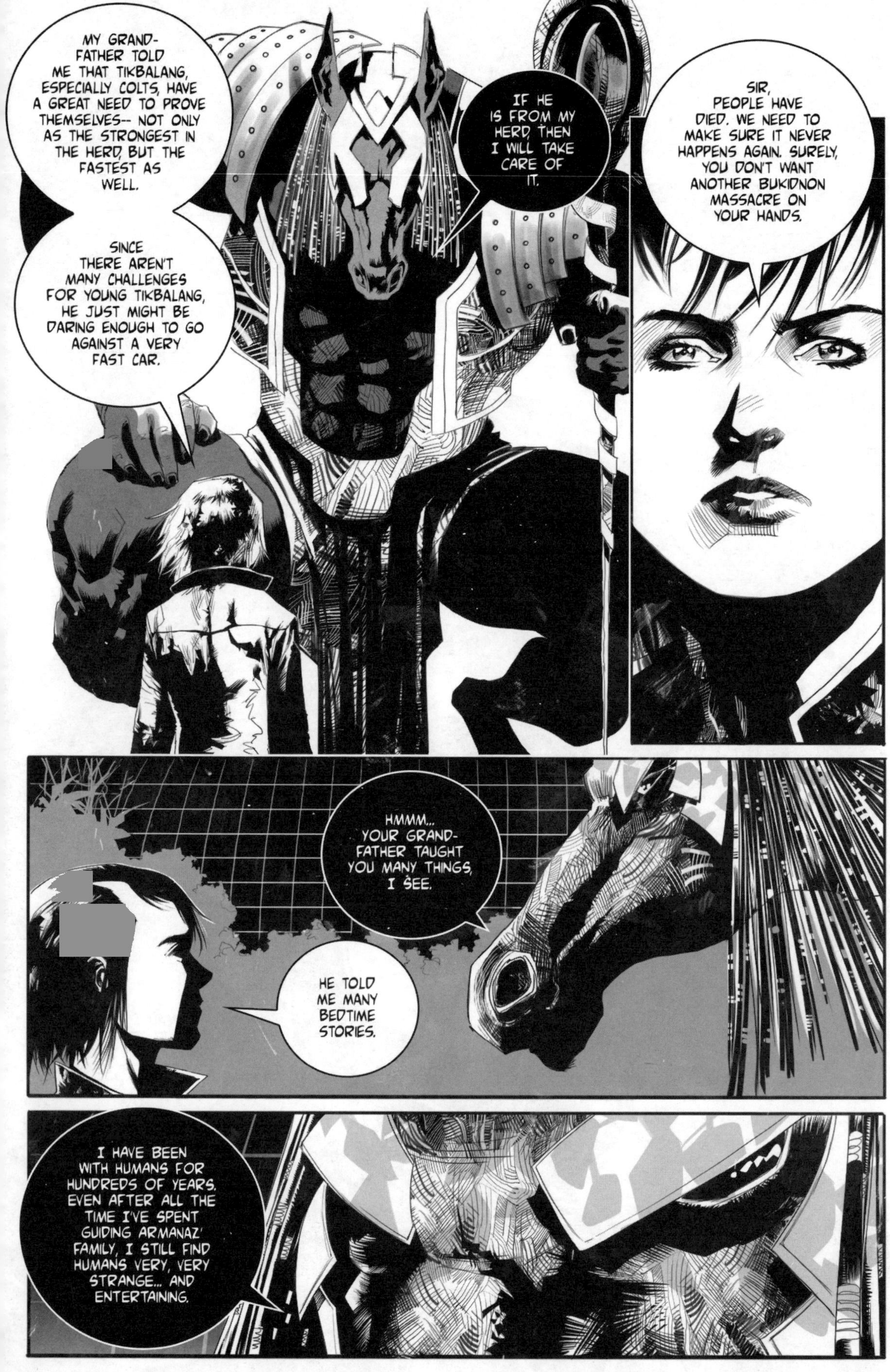
MY GRAND-FATHER TOLD ME THAT TIKBALANG, ESPECIALLY COLTS, HAVE A GREAT NEED TO PROVE THEMSELVES-- NOT ONLY AS THE STRONGEST IN THE HERD, BUT THE FASTEST AS WELL.
SINCE THERE AREN'T MANY CHALLENGES FOR YOUNG TIKBALANG, HE JUST MIGHT BE DARING ENOUGH TO GO AGAINST A VERY FAST CAR.
IF HE IS FROM MY HERD, THEN I WILL TAKE CARE OF IT.
SIR, PEOPLE HAVE DIED. WE NEED TO MAKE SURE IT NEVER HAPPENS AGAIN. SURELY, YOU DON'T WANT ANOTHER BUKIDNON MASSACRE ON YOUR HANDS.
HMMM... YOUR GRAND-FATHER TAUGHT YOU MANY THINGS, I SEE.
HE TOLD ME MANY BEDTIME STORIES.
I HAVE BEEN WITH HUMANS FOR HUNDREDS OF YEARS. EVEN AFTER ALL THE TIME I'VE SPENT GUIDING ARMANAZ' FAMILY, I STILL FIND HUMANS VERY, VERY STRANGE... AND ENTERTAINING.

HE ALSO TOLD ME THAT COLTS LIKE TO KEEP TROPHIES OF THEIR VICTORIES. A YOUNG GIRL WAS TAKEN BY THE DRIVER WHO WON THE RACE. SHE NEEDS TO BE FOUND, SIR.

I NEED A NAME.

LET ME FIND HIM. LET ME TAKE CARE OF IT.

NOT THAT I DOUBT YOUR POWERS, BUT I THINK I'LL FIND HIM FIRST, SIR. SO, I'LL NEED HIS NAME-- TO TAME HIM. SO, I CAN BRING HIM BACK TO YOU.

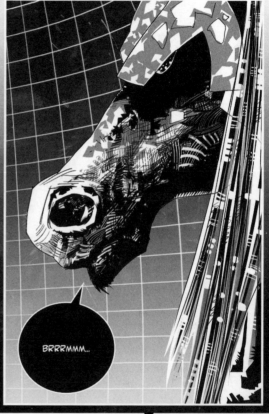

BRRRMMM...

TRUST ME, GREAT STALLION. I WILL BRING HIM BACK TO

MY PEOPLE HAVE TOLD ME THAT MALIKSI HAS NOT RETURNED FOR A MONTH. HE MIGHT BE THE MAVERICK YOU'RE LOOKING FOR.

THANK YOU, SIR. THANK YOU VERY MUCH.

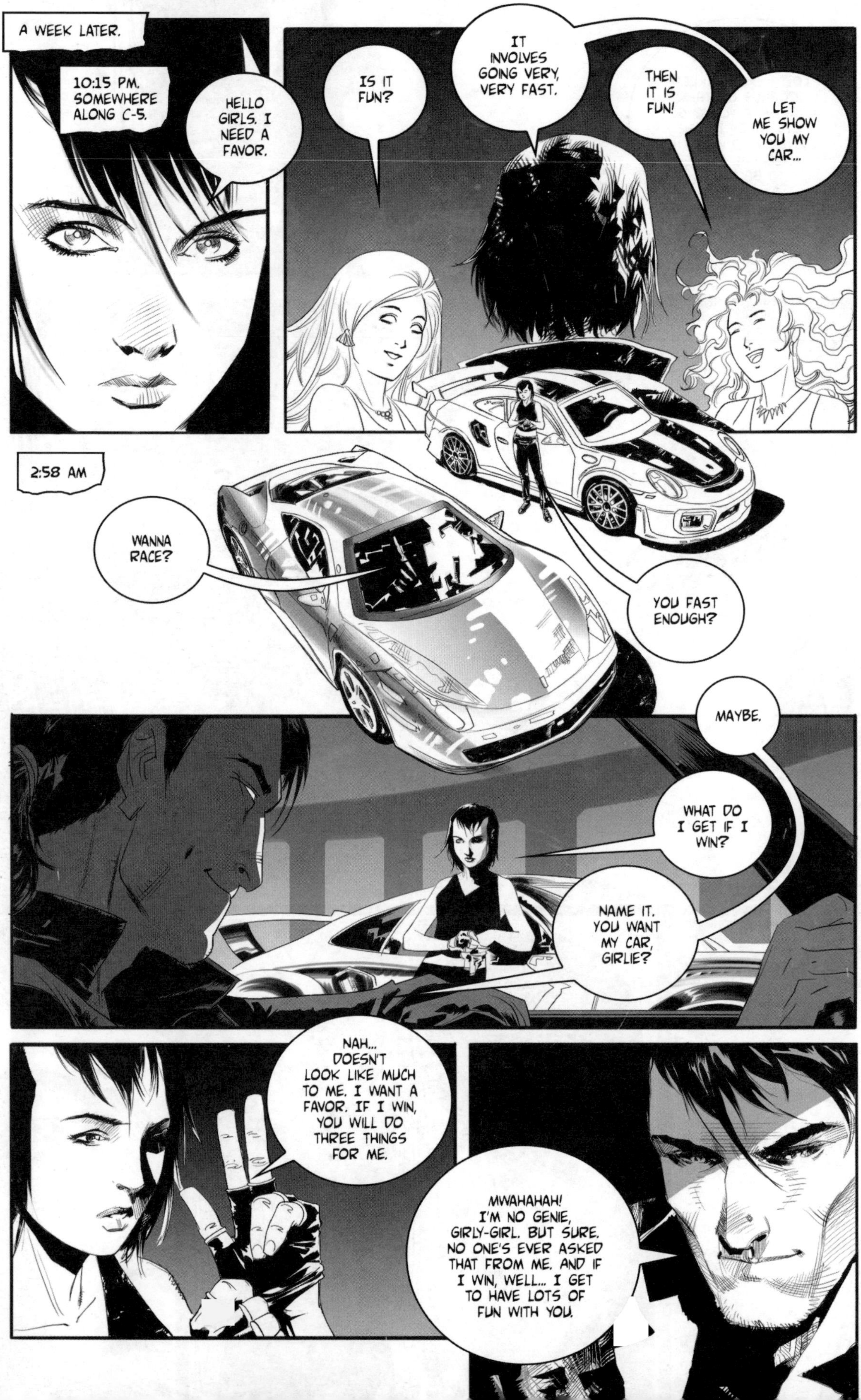

A WEEK LATER.
10:15 PM. SOMEWHERE ALONG C-5.
HELLO GIRLS. I NEED A FAVOR.
IS IT FUN?
IT INVOLVES GOING VERY, VERY FAST.
THEN IT IS FUN!
LET ME SHOW YOU MY CAR...
2:58 AM
WANNA RACE?
YOU FAST ENOUGH?
MAYBE.
WHAT DO I GET IF I WIN?
NAME IT. YOU WANT MY CAR, GIRLIE?
NAH... DOESN'T LOOK LIKE MUCH TO ME. I WANT A FAVOR. IF I WIN, YOU WILL DO THREE THINGS FOR ME.
MWAHAHAH! I'M NO GENIE, GIRLY-GIRL. BUT SURE. NO ONE'S EVER ASKED THAT FROM ME. AND IF I WIN, WELL... I GET TO HAVE LOTS OF FUN WITH YOU.

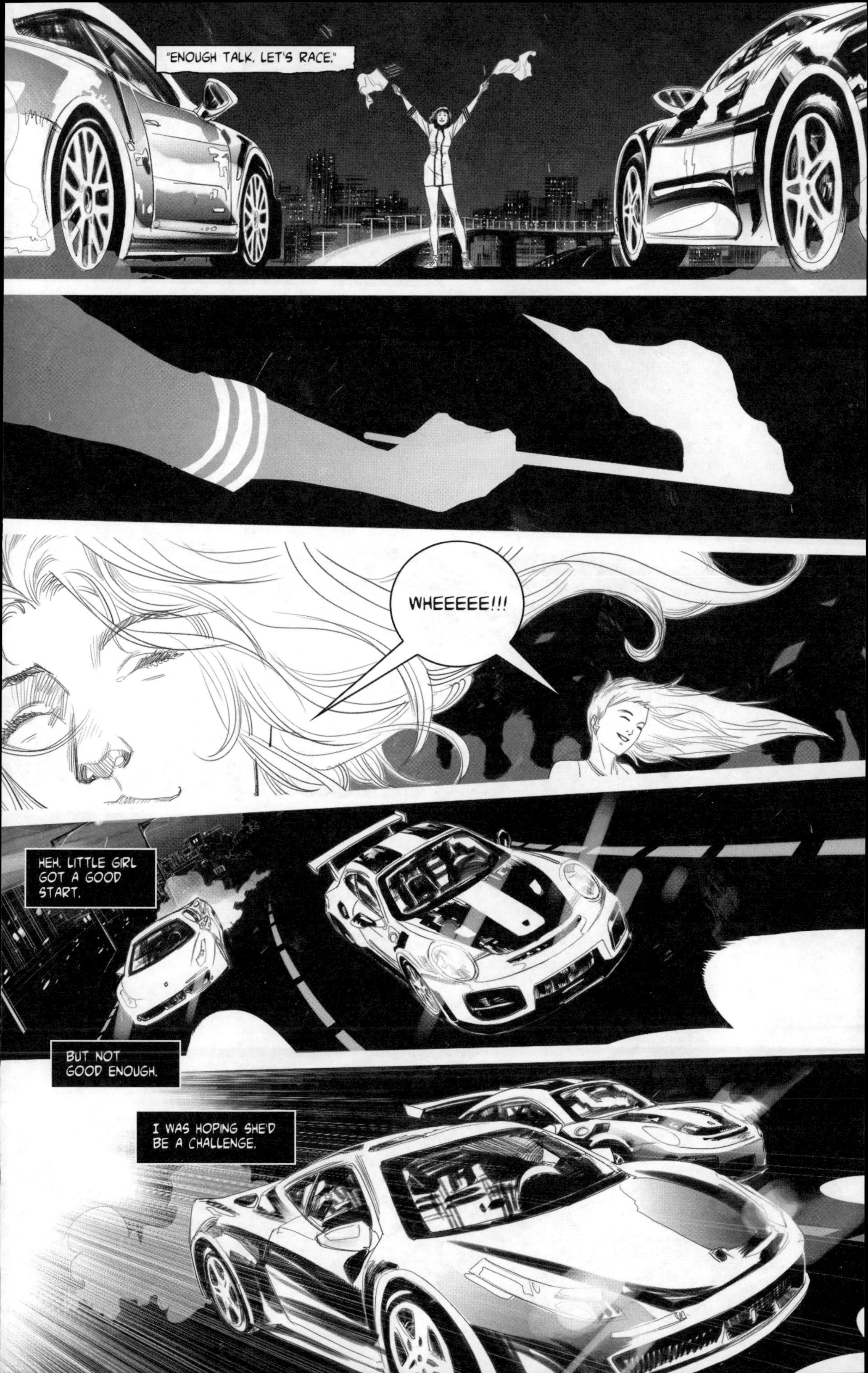
"ENOUGH TALK. LET'S RACE."
WHEEEEEE!!!
HEH. LITTLE GIRL GOT A GOOD START.
BUT NOT GOOD ENOUGH.
I WAS HOPING SHE'D BE A CHALLENGE.

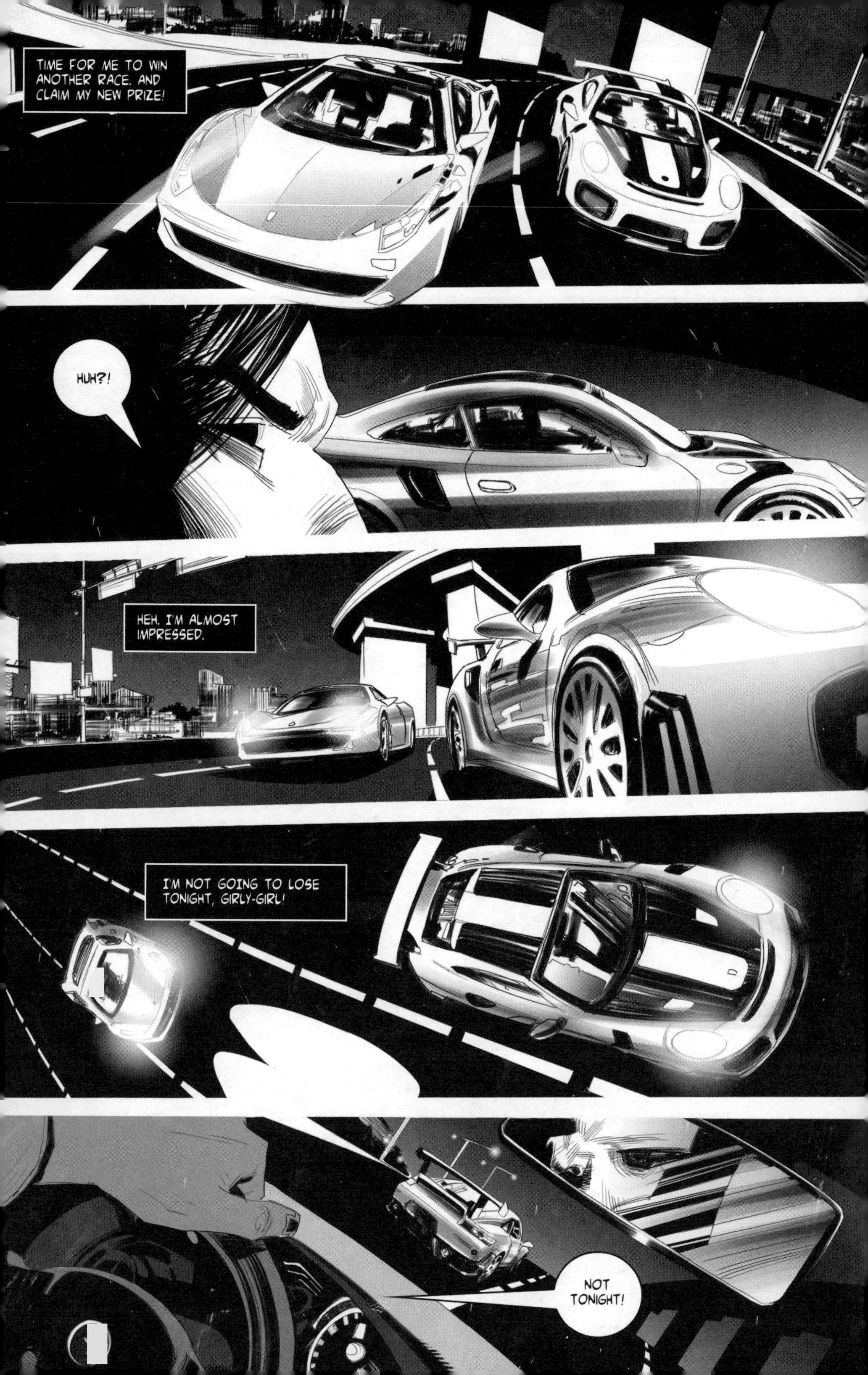
TIME FOR ME TO WIN ANOTHER RACE. AND CLAIM MY NEW PRIZE!
HUH?!
HEH. I'M ALMOST IMPRESSED.
I'M NOT GOING TO LOSE TONIGHT, GIRLY-GIRL!
NOT TONIGHT!

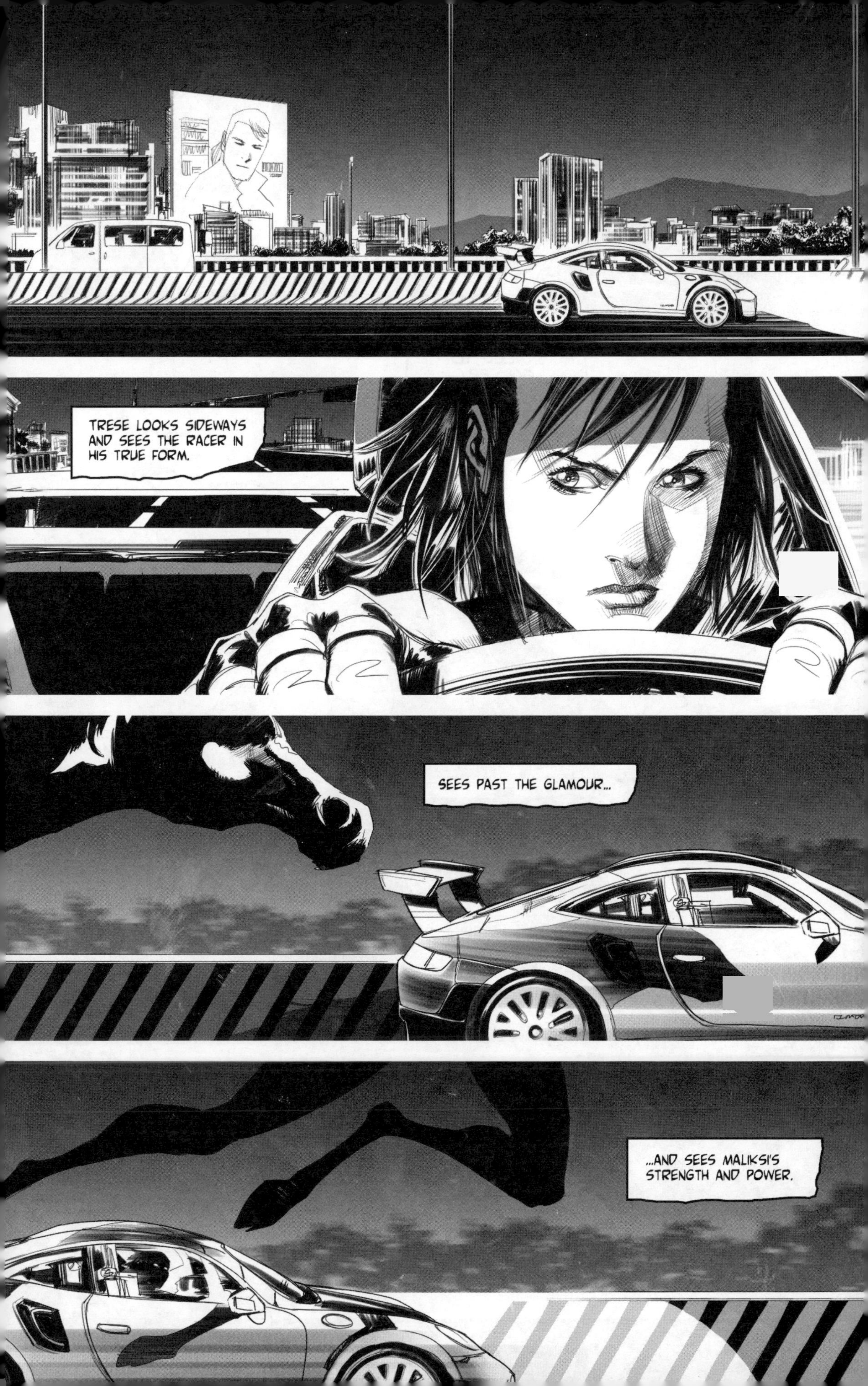
TRESE LOOKS SIDEWAYS AND SEES THE RACER IN HIS TRUE FORM.
SEES PAST THE GLAMOUR...
...AND SEES MALIKSI'S STRENGTH AND POWER.

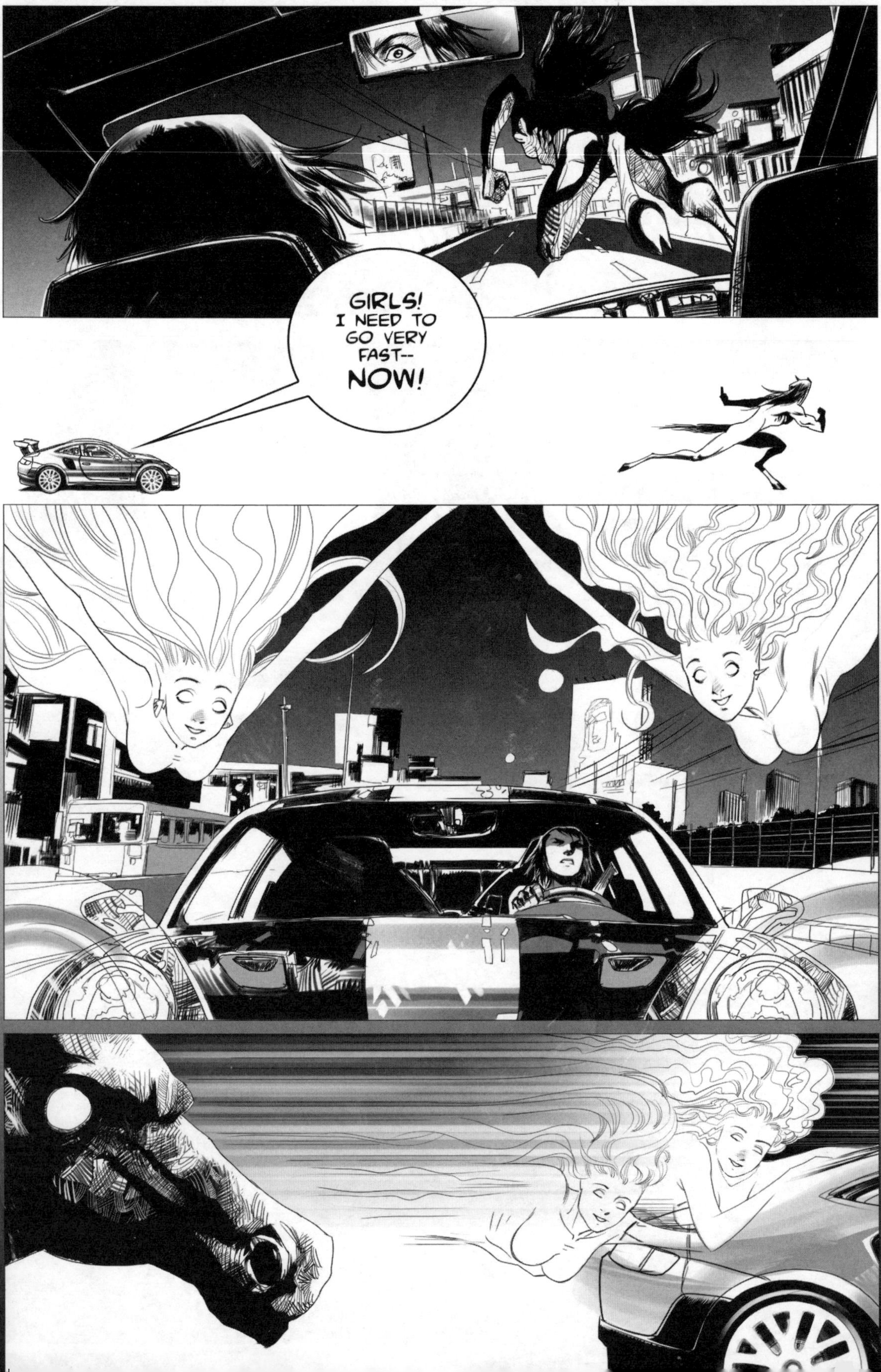
GIRLS! I NEED TO GO VERY FAST-- NOW!

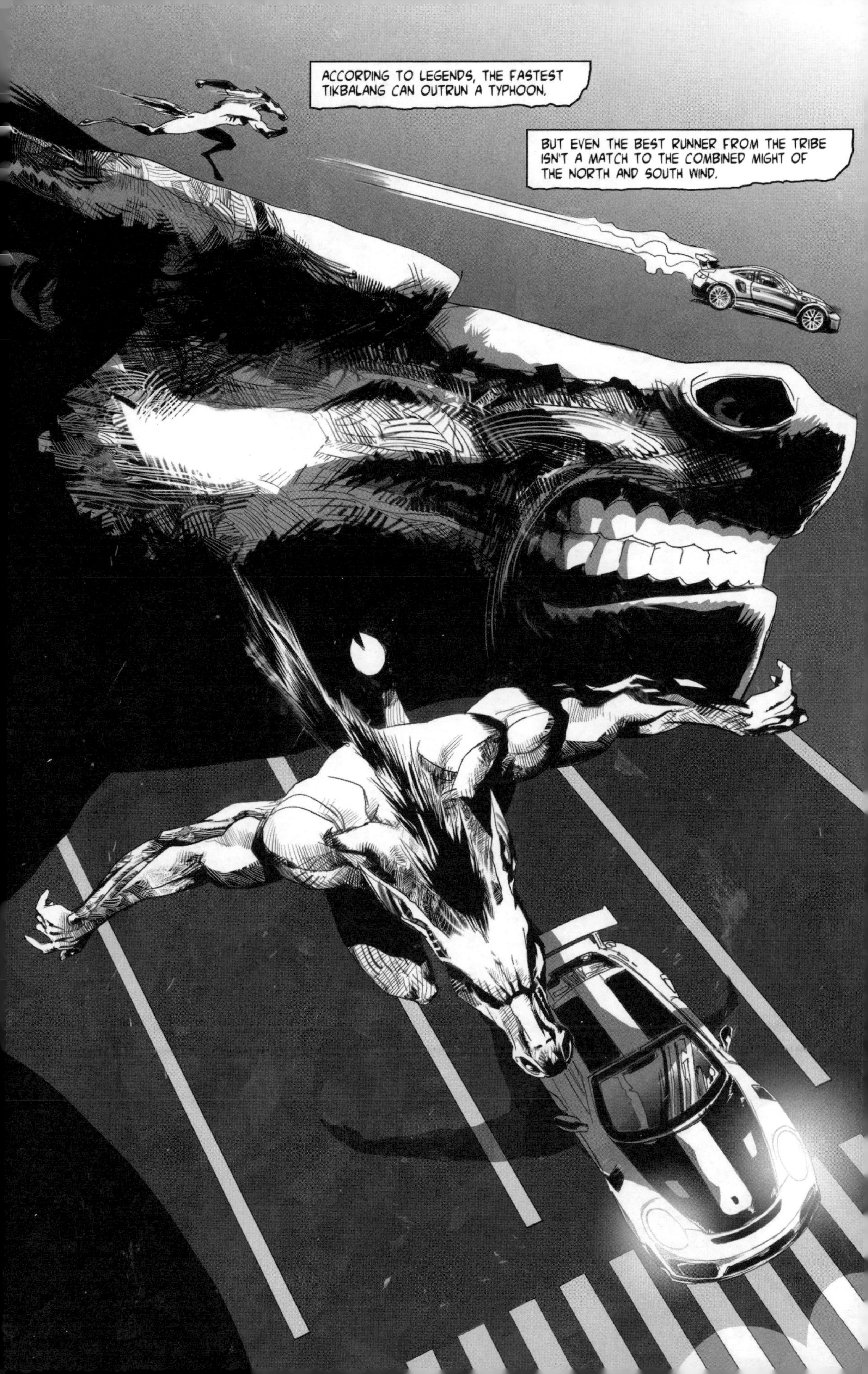
ACCORDING TO LEGENDS, THE FASTEST TIKBALANG CAN OUTRUN A TYPHOON.
BUT EVEN THE BEST RUNNER FROM THE TRIBE ISN'T A MATCH TO THE COMBINED MIGHT OF THE NORTH AND SOUTH WIND.

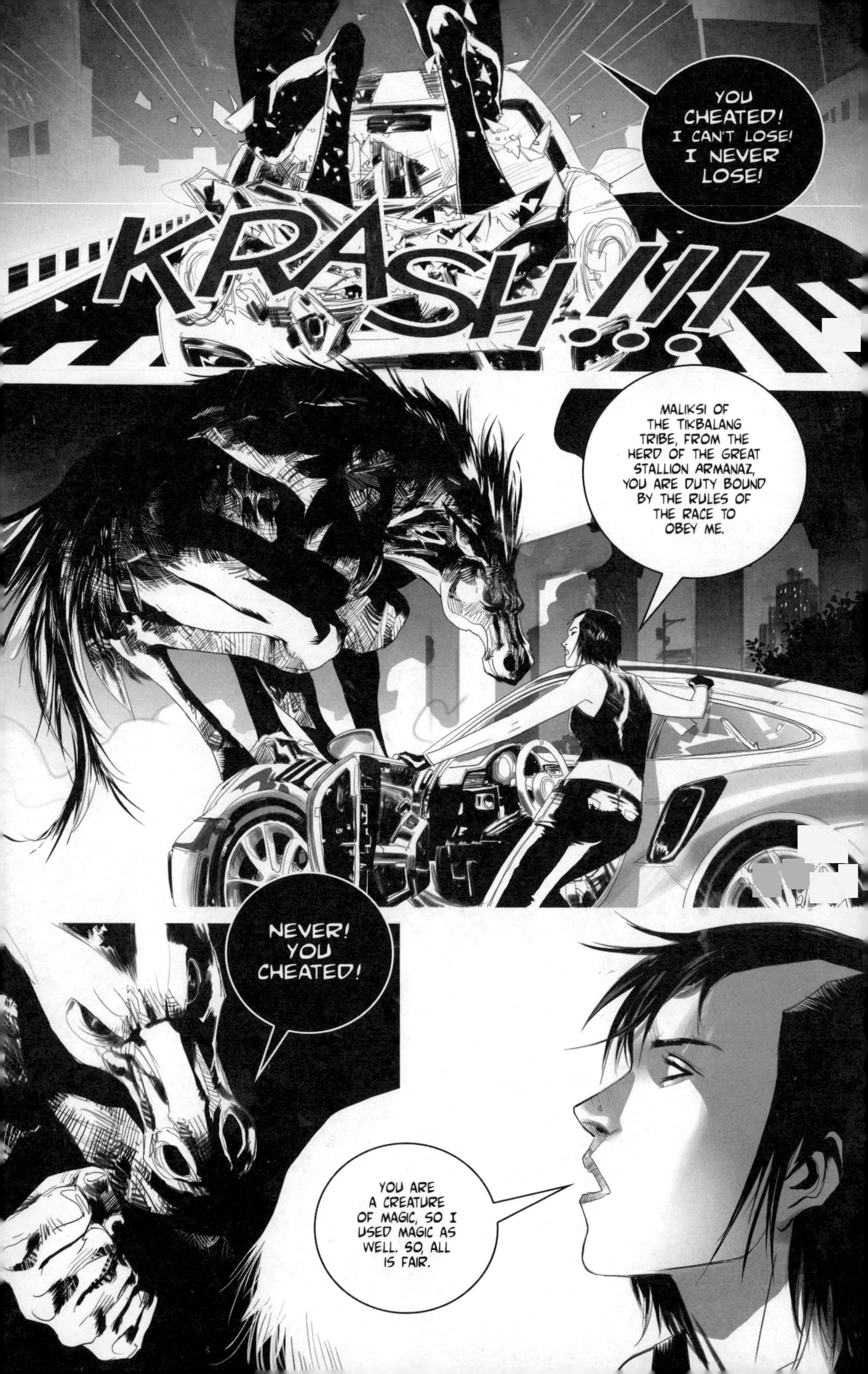
YOU CHEATED! I CAN'T LOSE! I NEVER LOSE!
KRASH!!!
MALIKSI OF THE TIKBALANG TRIBE, FROM THE HERD OF THE GREAT STALLION ARMANAZ, YOU ARE DUTY BOUND BY THE RULES OF THE RACE TO OBEY ME.
NEVER! YOU CHEATED!
YOU ARE A CREATURE OF MAGIC, SO I USED MAGIC AS WELL. SO, ALL IS FAIR.

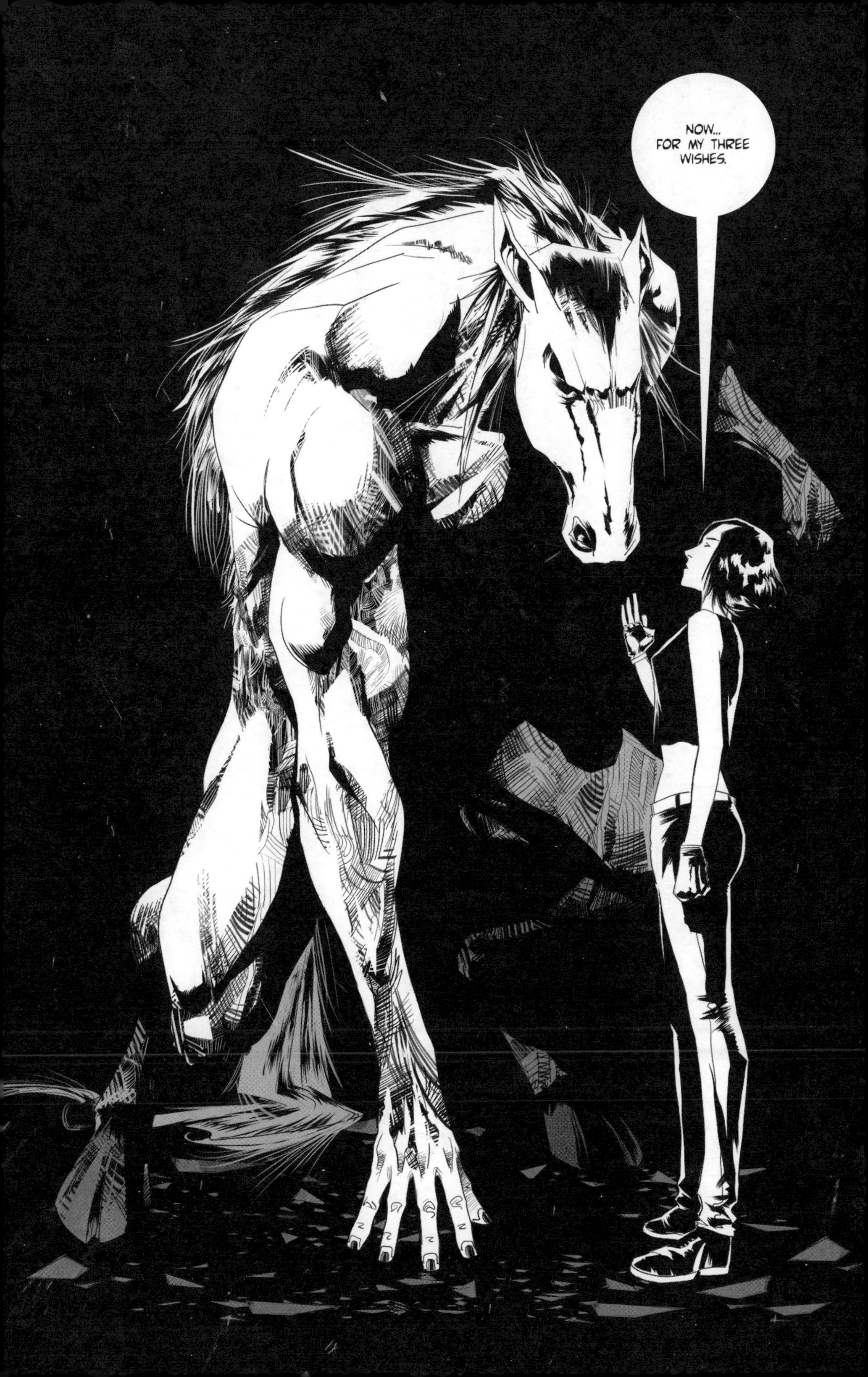
NOW... FOR MY THREE WISHES.

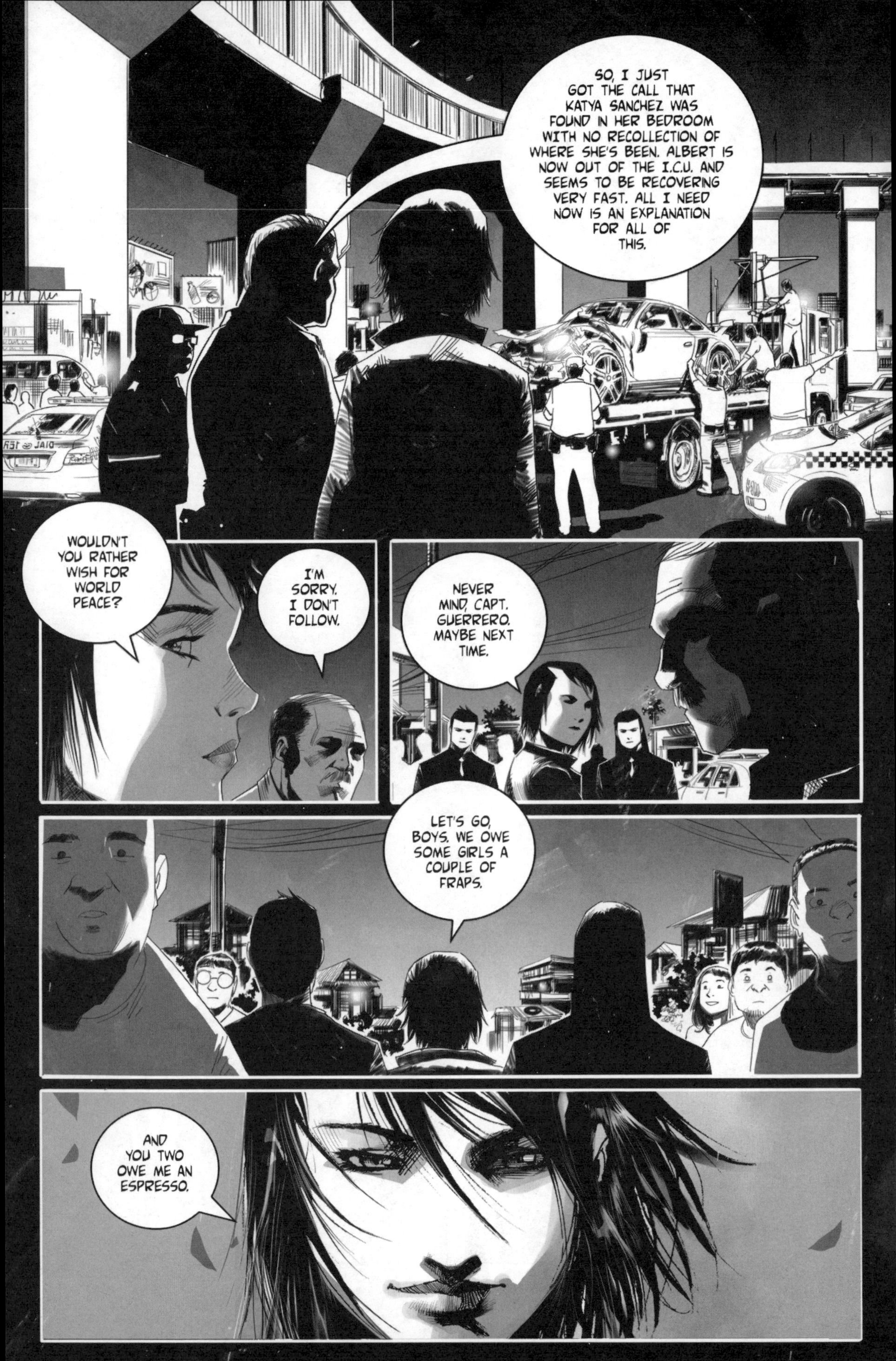
SO, I JUST GOT THE CALL THAT KATYA SANCHEZ WAS FOUND IN HER BEDROOM WITH NO RECOLLECTION OF WHERE SHE'S BEEN. ALBERT IS NOW OUT OF THE I.C.U. AND SEEMS TO BE RECOVERING VERY FAST. ALL I NEED NOW IS AN EXPLANATION FOR ALL OF THIS.
WOULDN'T YOU RATHER WISH FOR WORLD PEACE?
I'M SORRY. I DON'T FOLLOW.
NEVER MIND, CAPT. GUERRERO. MAYBE NEXT TIME.
LET'S GO, BOYS. WE OWE SOME GIRLS A COUPLE OF FRAPS.
AND YOU TWO OWE ME AN ESPRESSO.

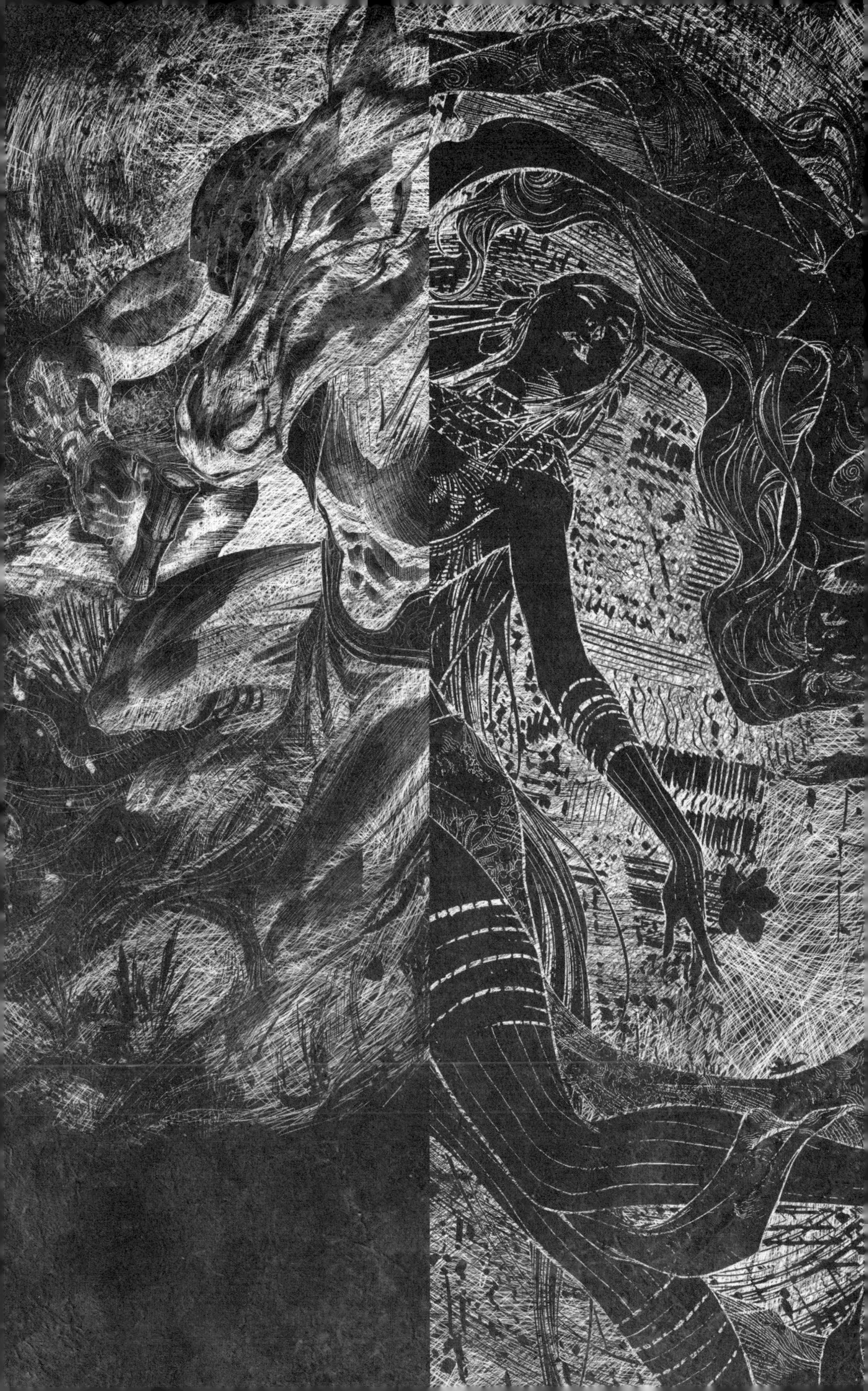

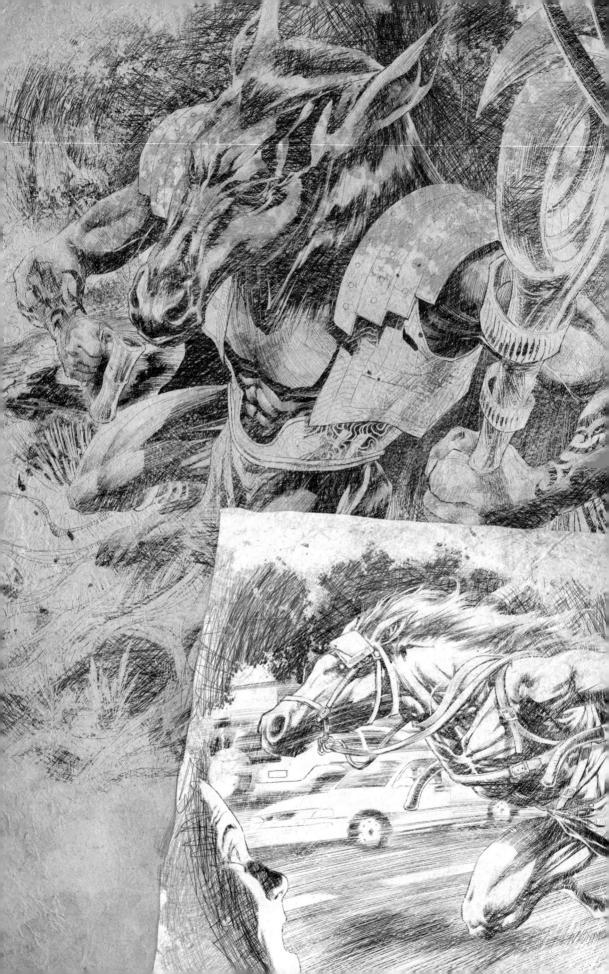

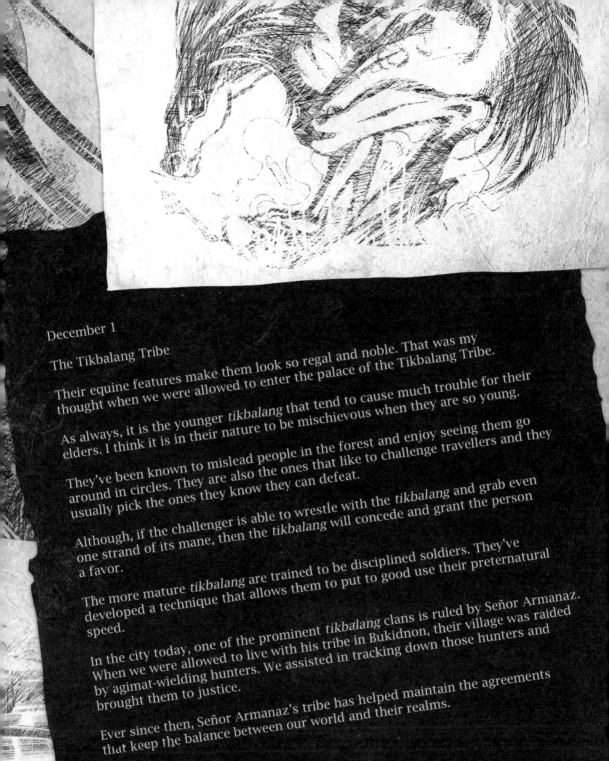

December 1

The Tikbalang Tribe

Their equine features make them look so regal and noble. That was my thought when we were allowed to enter the palace of the Tikbalang Tribe.

As always, it is the younger *tikbalang* that tend to cause much trouble for their elders. I think it is in their nature to be mischievous when they are so young.

They've been known to mislead people in the forest and enjoy seeing them go around in circles. They are also the ones that like to challenge travellers and they usually pick the ones they know they can defeat.

Although, if the challenger is able to wrestle with the *tikbalang* and grab even one strand of its mane, then the *tikbalang* will concede and grant the person a favor.

The more mature *tikbalang* are trained to be disciplined soldiers. They've developed a technique that allows them to put to good use their preternatural speed.

In the city today, one of the prominent *tikbalang* clans is ruled by Señor Armanaz. When we were allowed to live with his tribe in Bukidnon, their village was raided by agimat-wielding hunters. We assisted in tracking down those hunters and brought them to justice.

Ever since then, Señor Armanaz's tribe has helped maintain the agreements that keep the balance between our world and their realms.

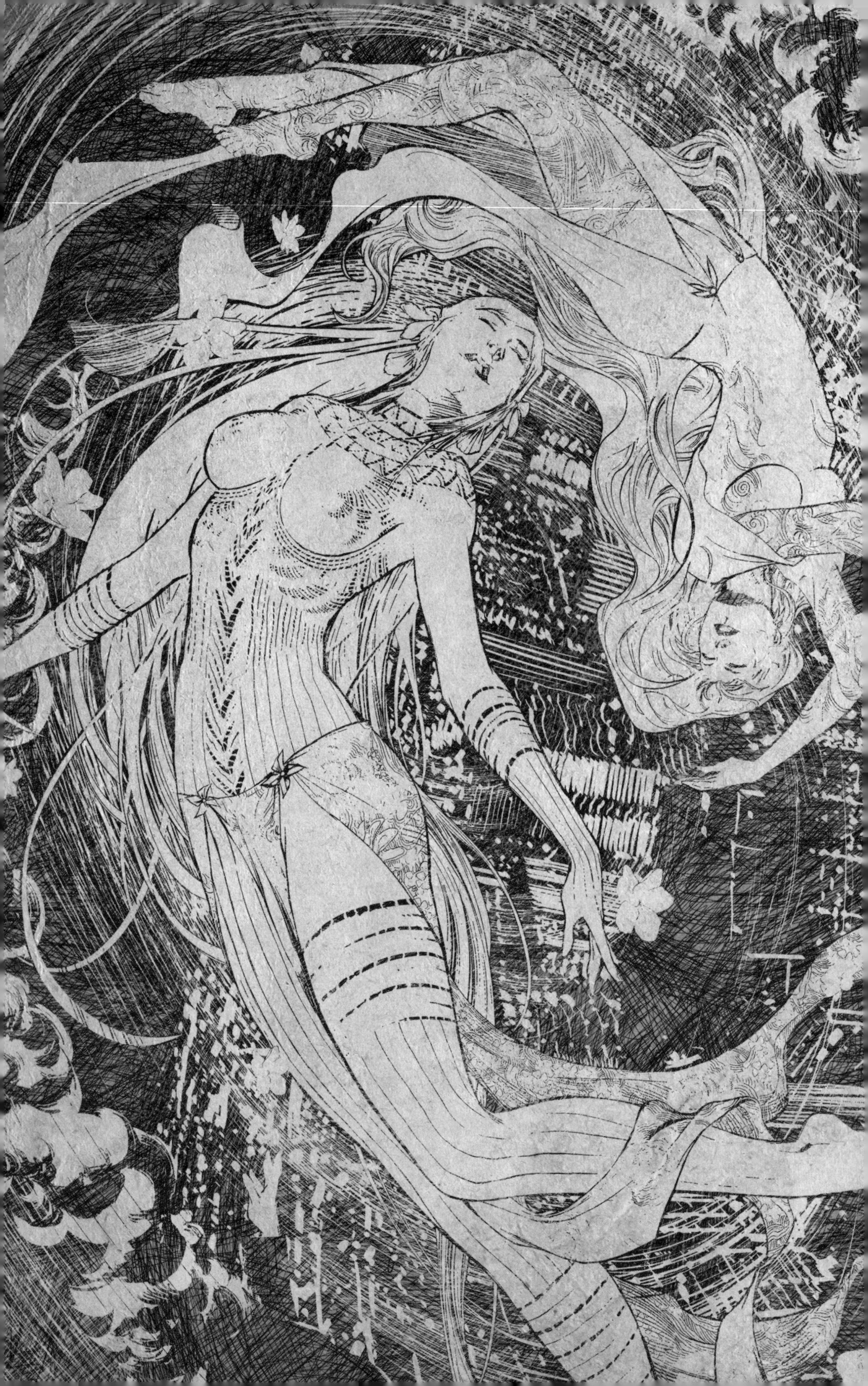

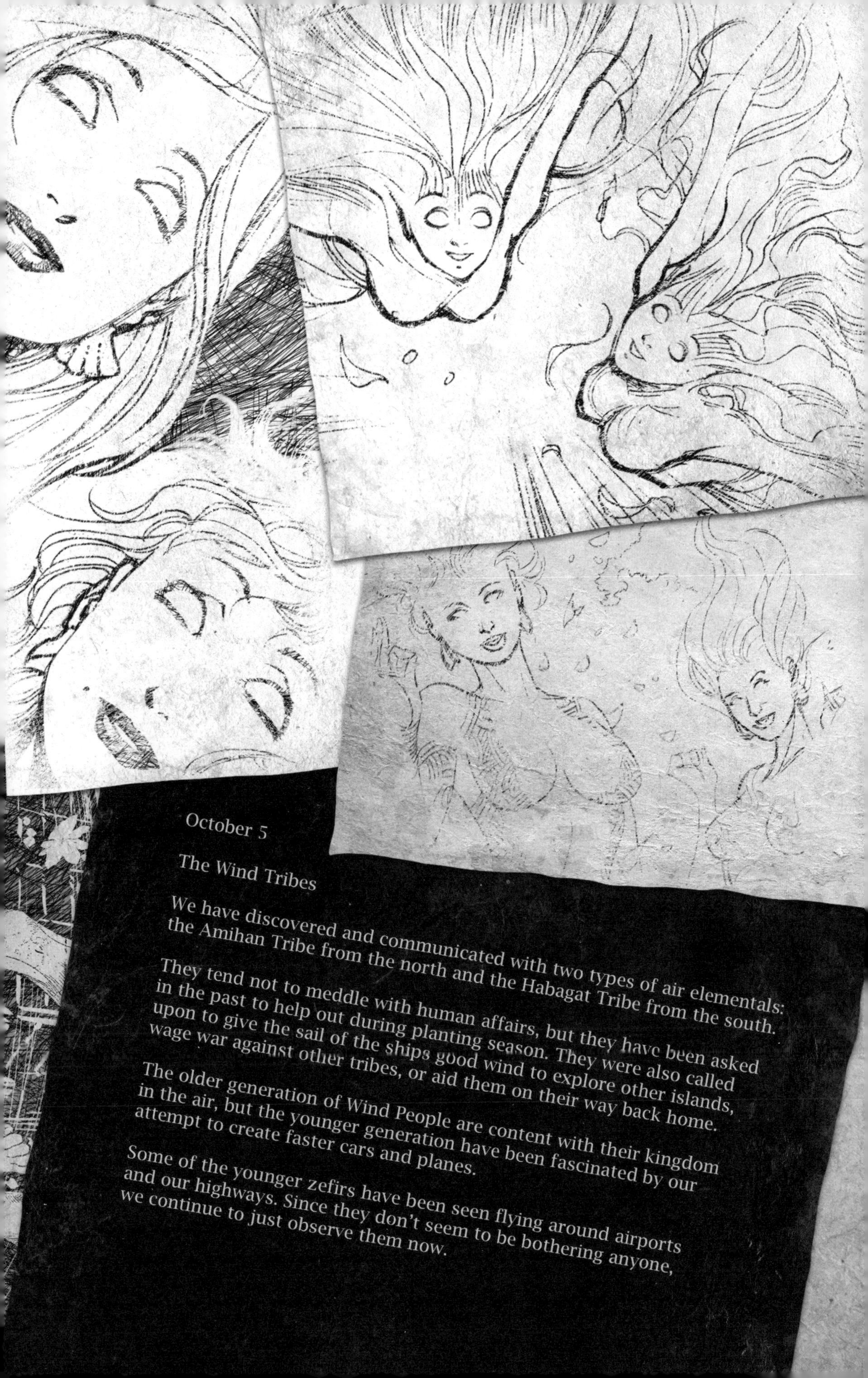

October 5

The Wind Tribes

We have discovered and communicated with two types of air elementals: the Amihan Tribe from the north and the Habagat Tribe from the south.

They tend not to meddle with human affairs, but they have been asked in the past to help out during planting season. They were also called upon to give the sail of the ships good wind to explore other islands, wage war against other tribes, or aid them on their way back home.

The older generation of Wind People are content with their kingdom in the air, but the younger generation have been fascinated by our attempt to create faster cars and planes.

Some of the younger zefirs have been seen flying around airports and our highways. Since they don't seem to be bothering anyone, we continue to just observe them now.

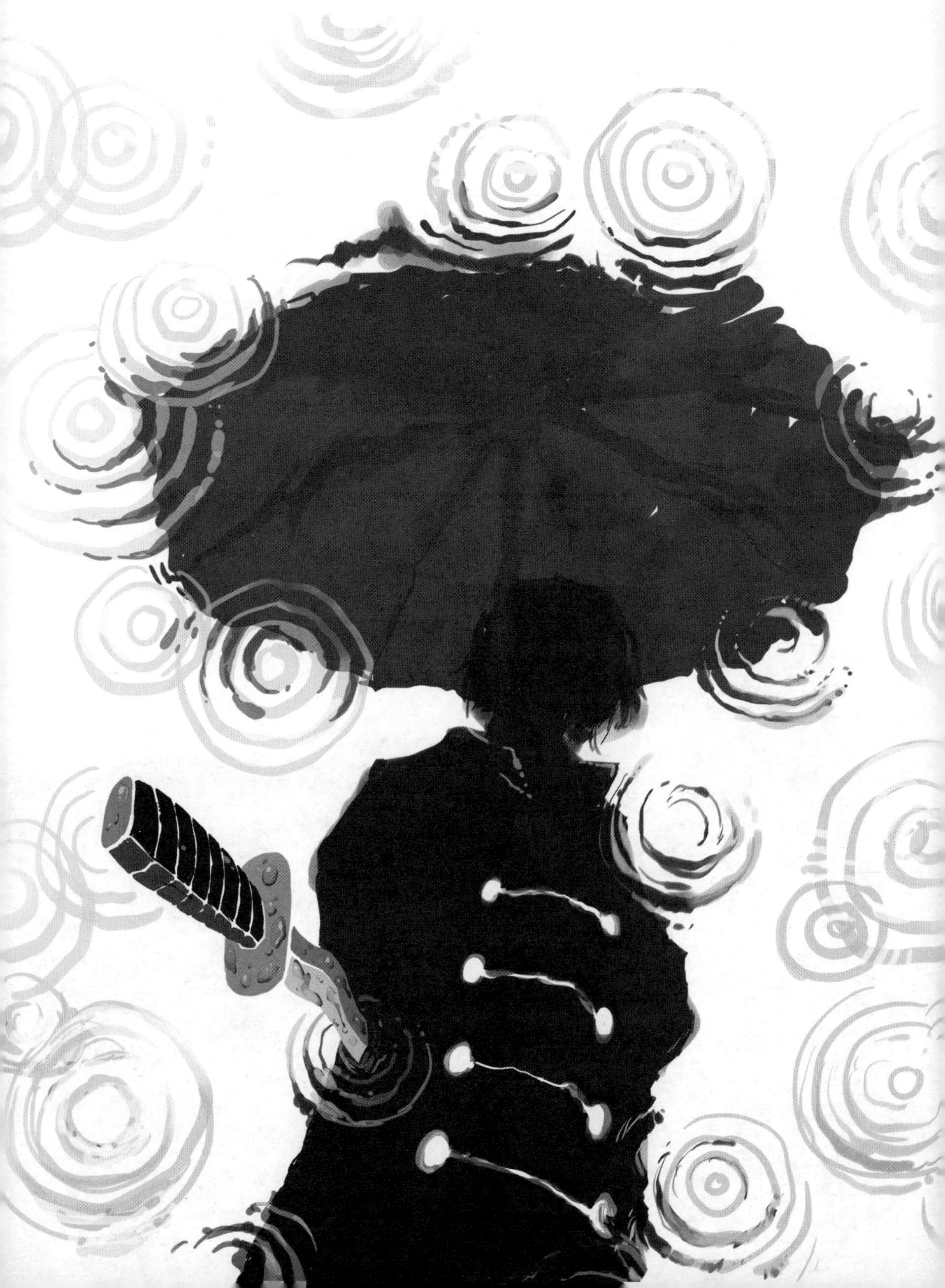

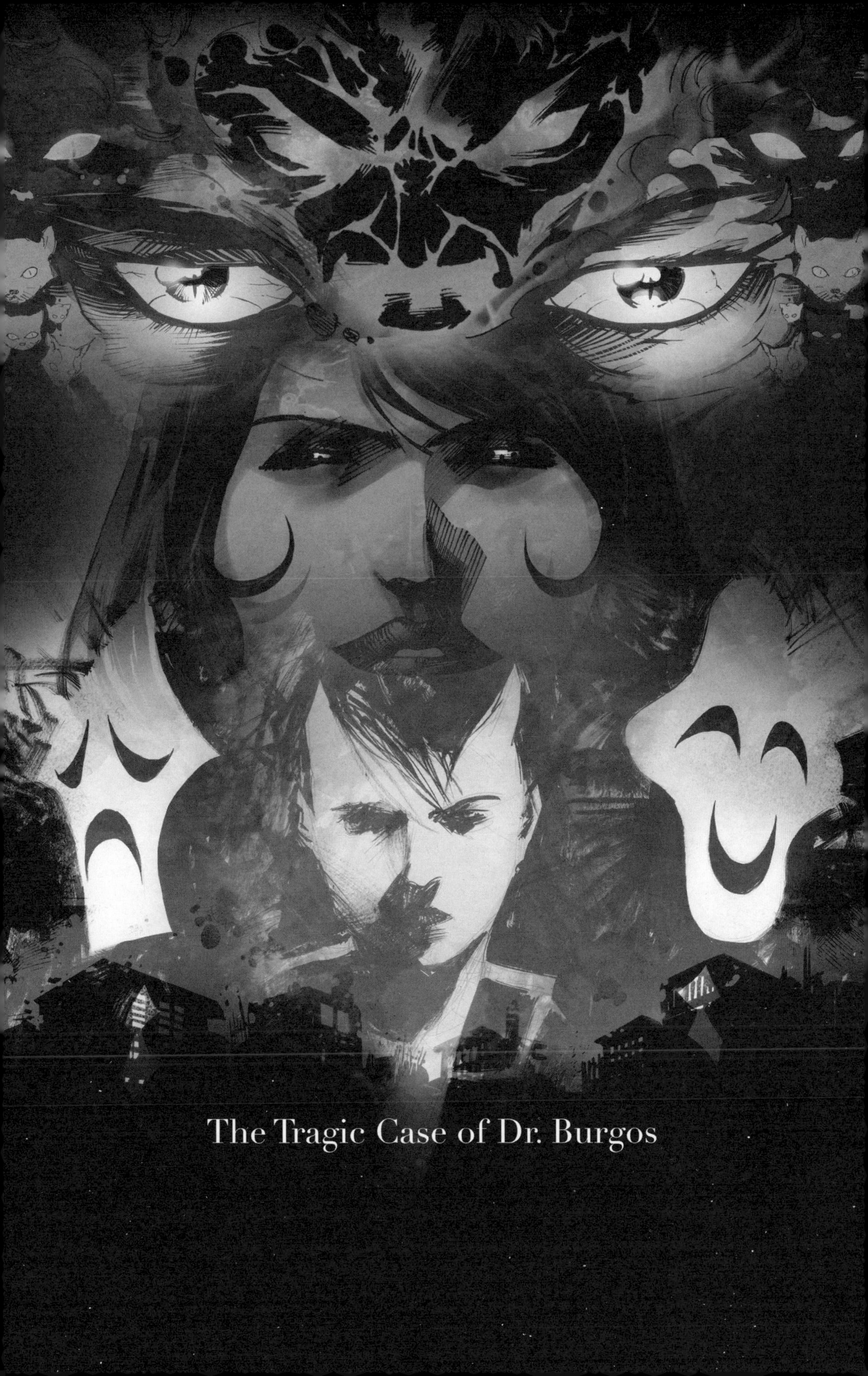

The Tragic Case of Dr. Burgos

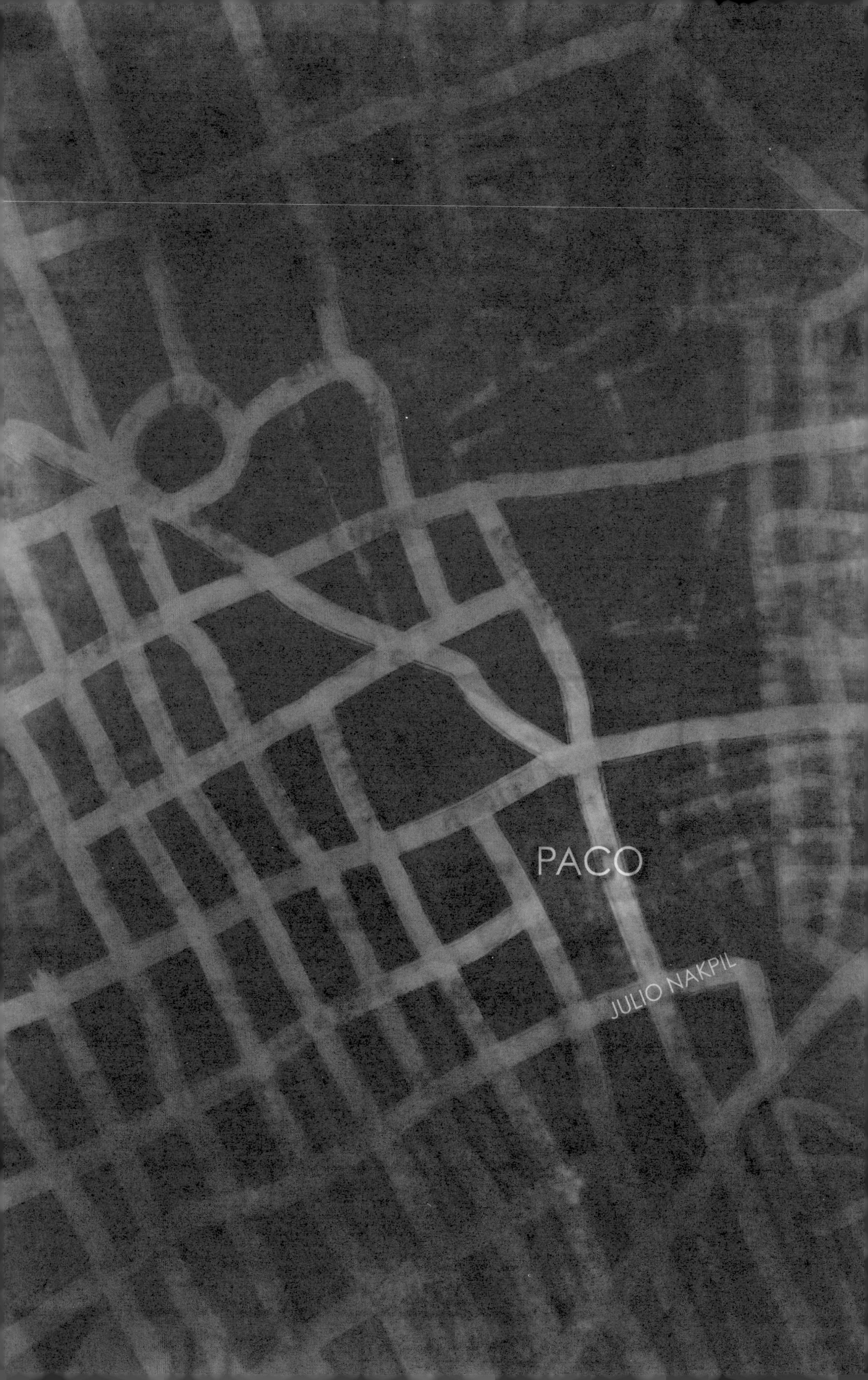
PACO
JULIO NAKPIL

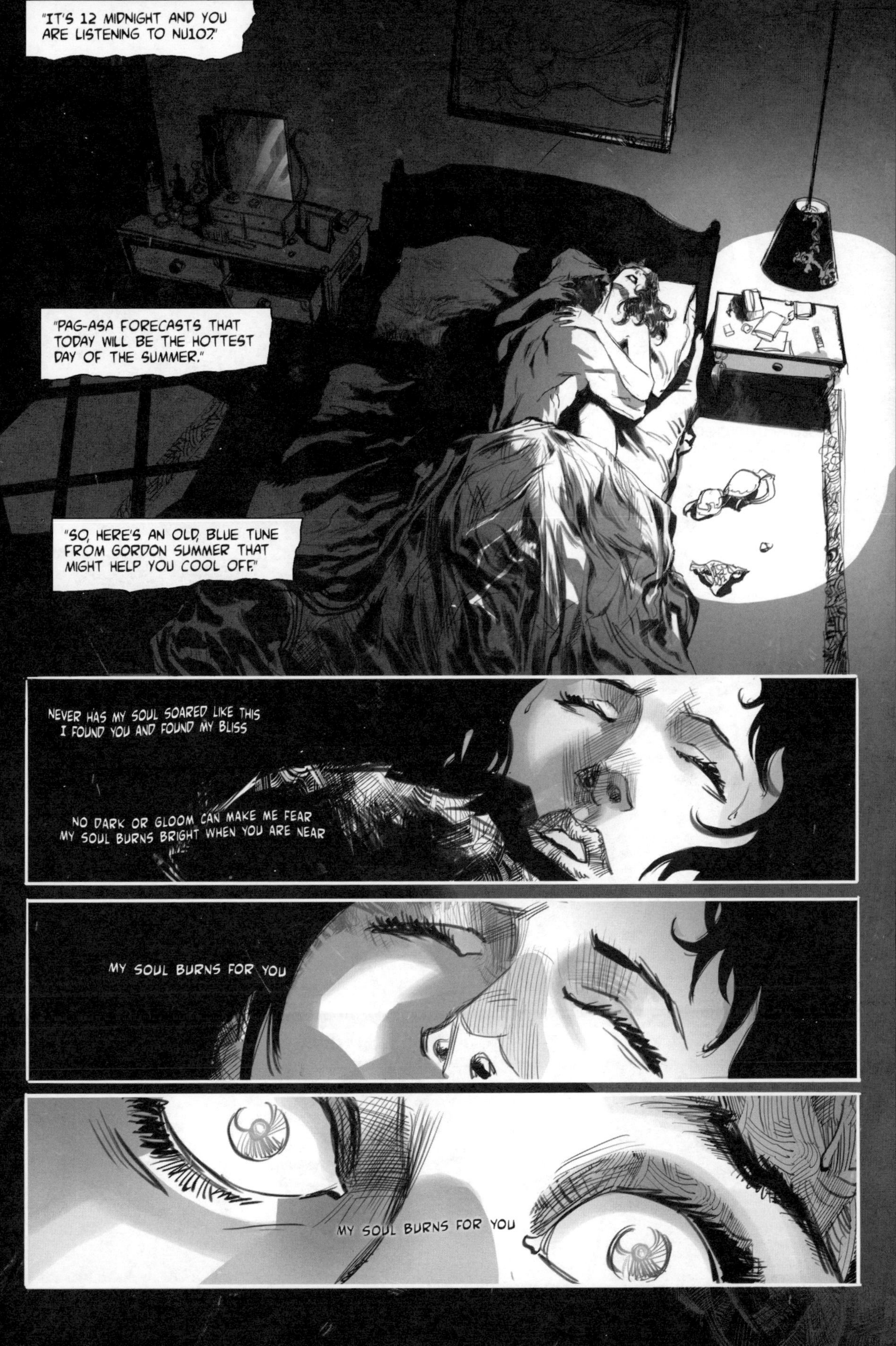
"IT'S 12 MIDNIGHT AND YOU ARE LISTENING TO NU107."
"PAG-ASA FORECASTS THAT TODAY WILL BE THE HOTTEST DAY OF THE SUMMER."
"SO, HERE'S AN OLD, BLUE TUNE FROM GORDON SUMMER THAT MIGHT HELP YOU COOL OFF."
NEVER HAS MY SOUL SOARED LIKE THIS
I FOUND YOU AND FOUND MY BLISS
NO DARK OR GLOOM CAN MAKE ME FEAR
MY SOUL BURNS BRIGHT WHEN YOU ARE NEAR
MY SOUL BURNS FOR YOU
MY SOUL BURNS FOR YOU

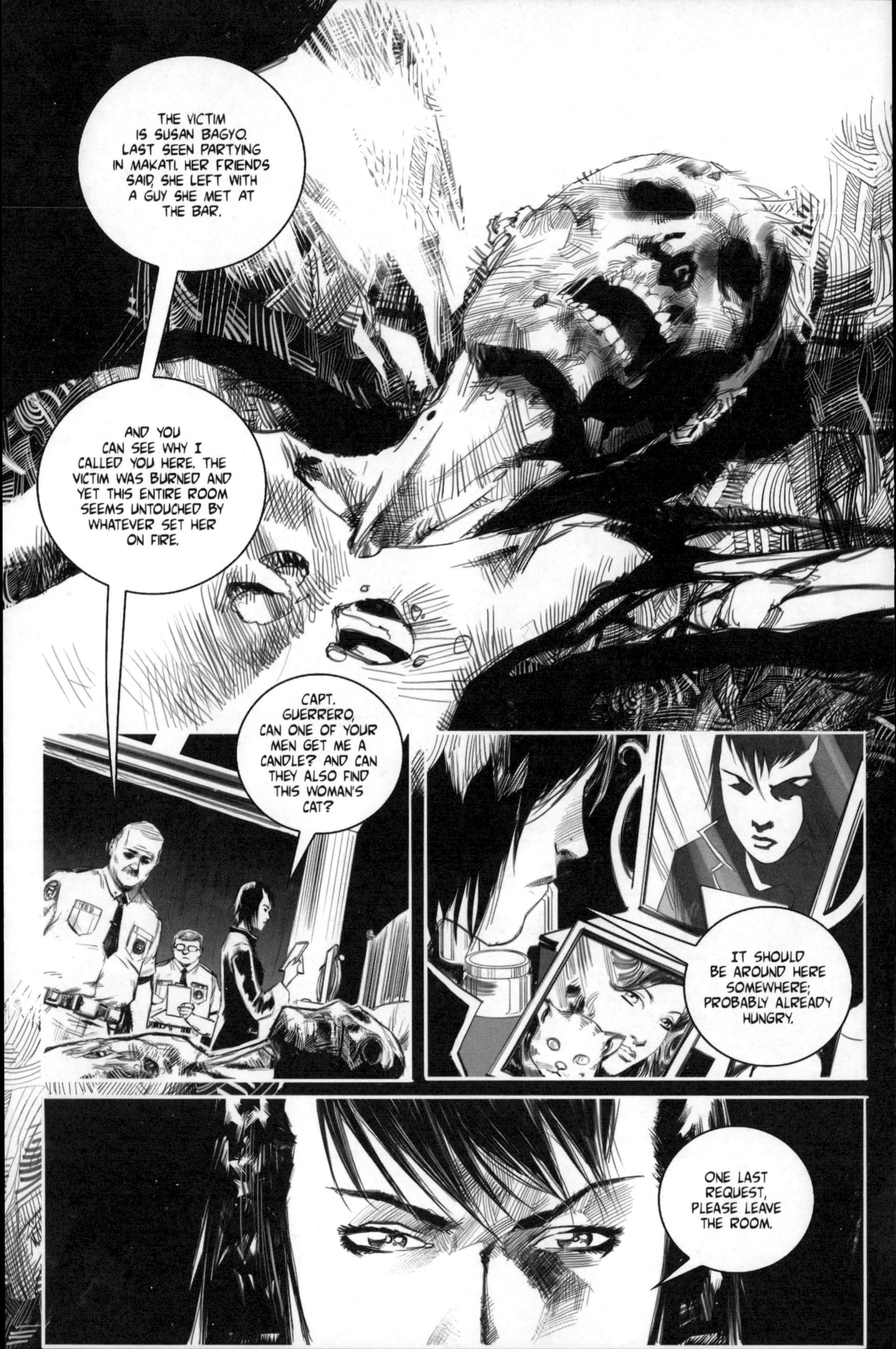
THE VICTIM IS SUSAN BAGYO. LAST SEEN PARTYING IN MAKATI. HER FRIENDS SAID, SHE LEFT WITH A GUY SHE MET AT THE BAR.
AND YOU CAN SEE WHY I CALLED YOU HERE. THE VICTIM WAS BURNED AND YET THIS ENTIRE ROOM SEEMS UNTOUCHED BY WHATEVER SET HER ON FIRE.
CAPT. GUERRERO, CAN ONE OF YOUR MEN GET ME A CANDLE? AND CAN THEY ALSO FIND THIS WOMAN'S CAT?
IT SHOULD BE AROUND HERE SOMEWHERE; PROBABLY ALREADY HUNGRY.
ONE LAST REQUEST, PLEASE LEAVE THE ROOM.

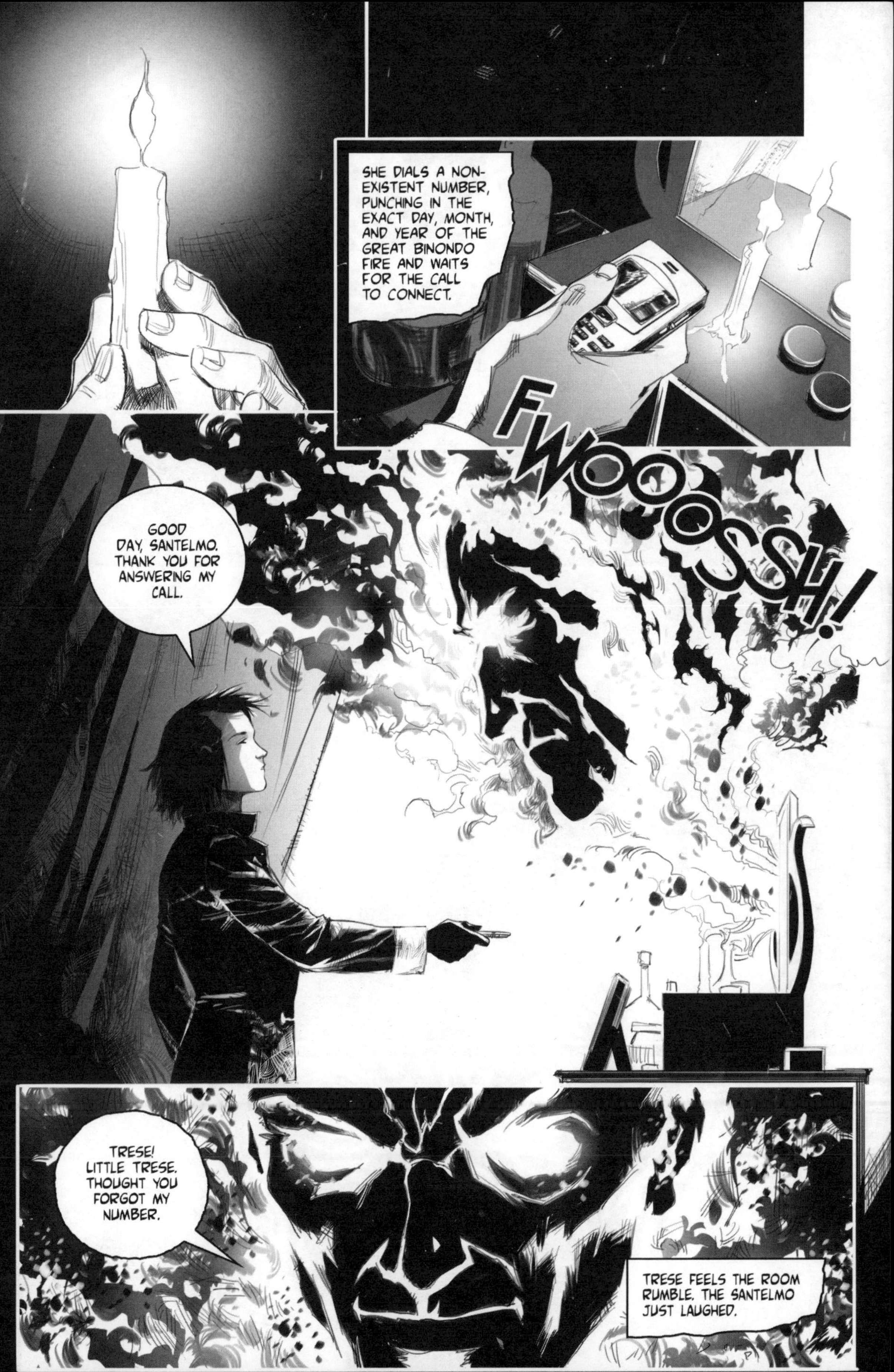
SHE DIALS A NON-EXISTENT NUMBER, PUNCHING IN THE EXACT DAY, MONTH, AND YEAR OF THE GREAT BINONDO FIRE AND WAITS FOR THE CALL TO CONNECT.
FWOOOOSSH!
GOOD DAY, SANTELMO. THANK YOU FOR ANSWERING MY CALL.
TRESE! LITTLE TRESE. THOUGHT YOU FORGOT MY NUMBER.
TRESE FEELS THE ROOM RUMBLE. THE SANTELMO JUST LAUGHED.

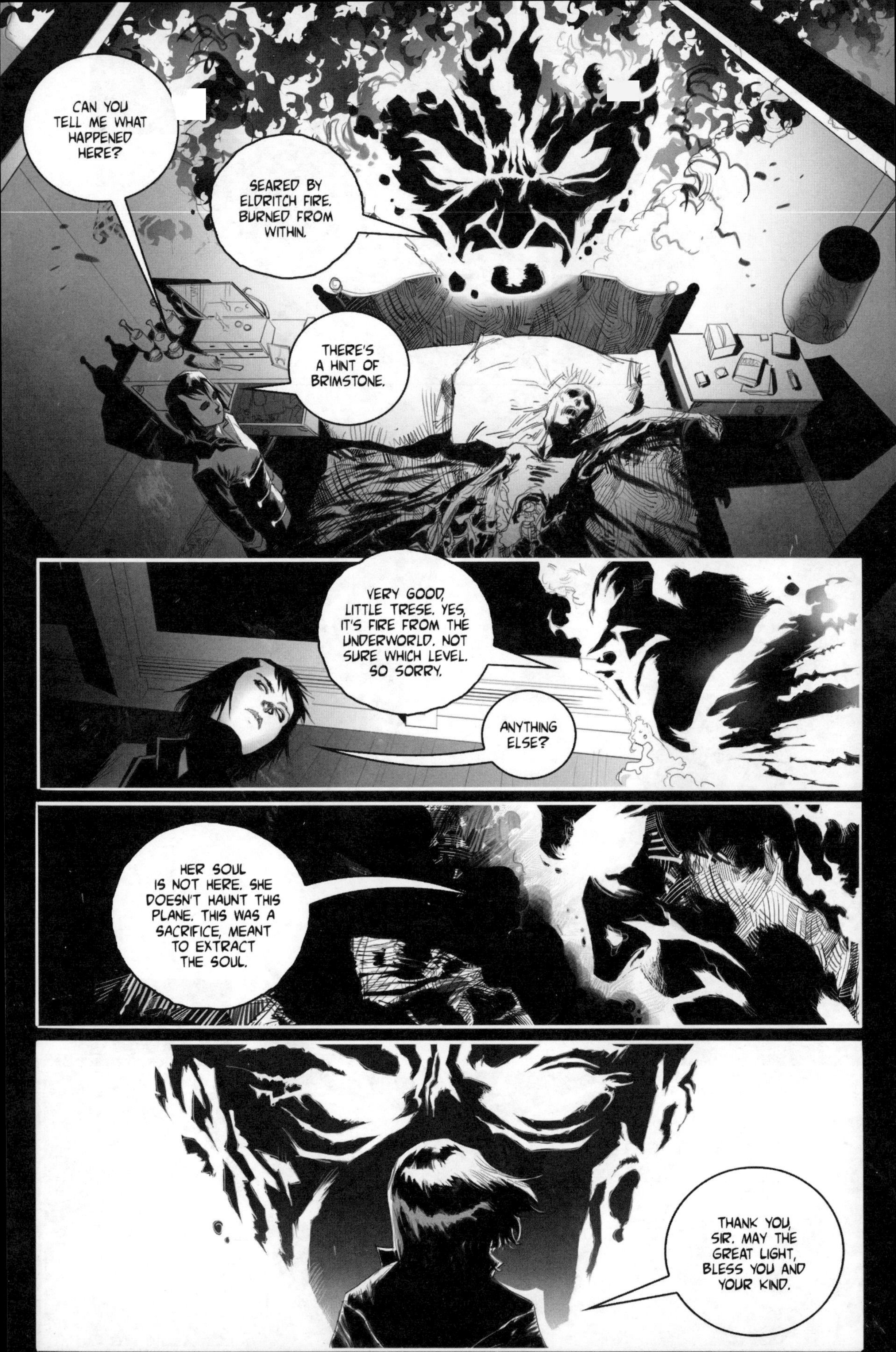
CAN YOU TELL ME WHAT HAPPENED HERE?
SEARED BY ELDRITCH FIRE. BURNED FROM WITHIN.
THERE'S A HINT OF BRIMSTONE.
VERY GOOD, LITTLE TRESE. YES, IT'S FIRE FROM THE UNDERWORLD. NOT SURE WHICH LEVEL. SO SORRY.
ANYTHING ELSE?
HER SOUL IS NOT HERE. SHE DOESN'T HAUNT THIS PLANE. THIS WAS A SACRIFICE, MEANT TO EXTRACT THE SOUL.
THANK YOU, SIR. MAY THE GREAT LIGHT, BLESS YOU AND YOUR KIND.

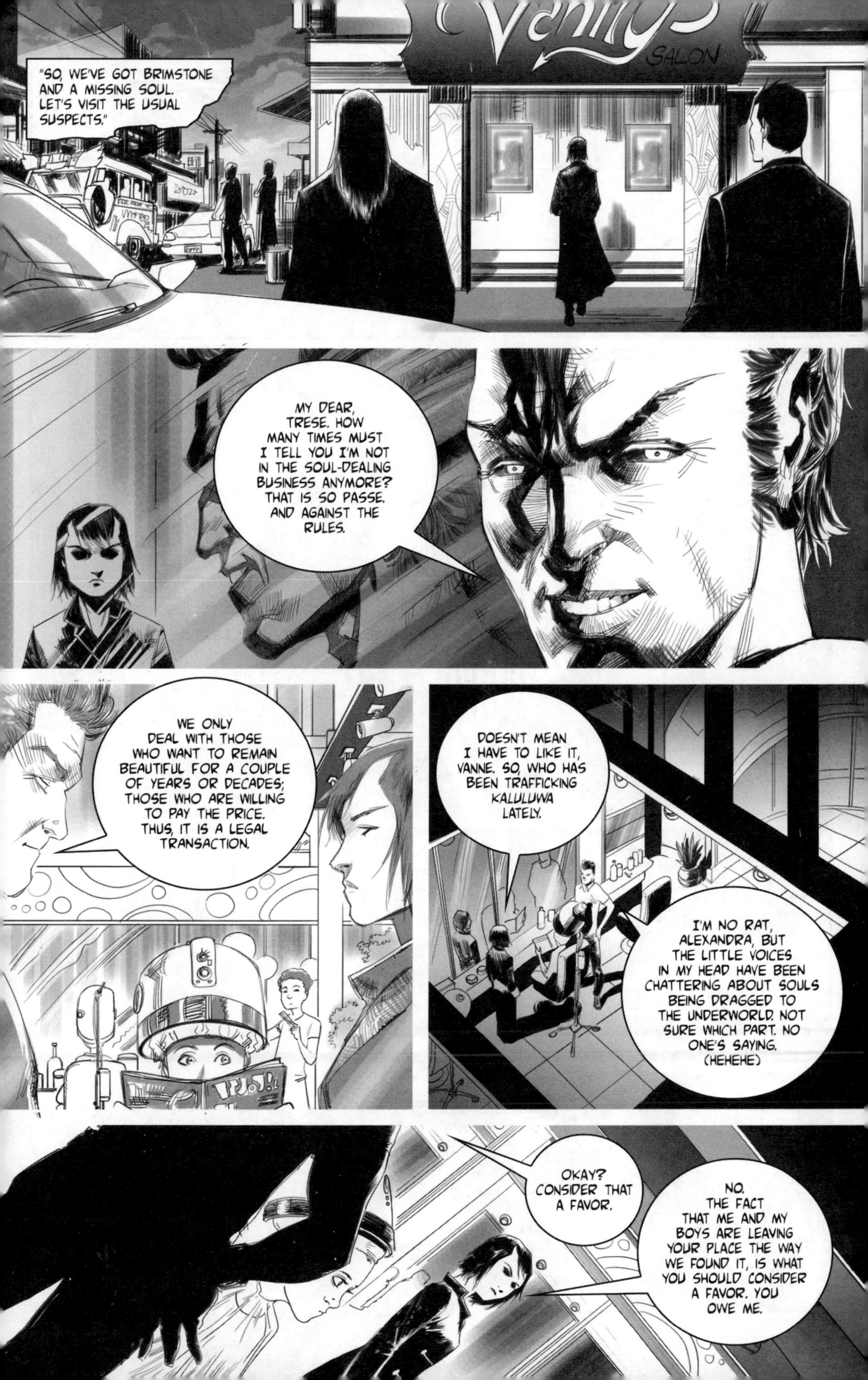
SALON
"SO, WE'VE GOT BRIMSTONE AND A MISSING SOUL. LET'S VISIT THE USUAL SUSPECTS."
MY DEAR, TRESE. HOW MANY TIMES MUST I TELL YOU I'M NOT IN THE SOUL-DEALING BUSINESS ANYMORE? THAT IS SO PASSE. AND AGAINST THE RULES.
WE ONLY DEAL WITH THOSE WHO WANT TO REMAIN BEAUTIFUL FOR A COUPLE OF YEARS OR DECADES; THOSE WHO ARE WILLING TO PAY THE PRICE. THUS, IT IS A LEGAL TRANSACTION.
DOESN'T MEAN I HAVE TO LIKE IT, VANNE. SO, WHO HAS BEEN TRAFFICKING KALULUWA LATELY.
I'M NO RAT, ALEXANDRA, BUT THE LITTLE VOICES IN MY HEAD HAVE BEEN CHATTERING ABOUT SOULS BEING DRAGGED TO THE UNDERWORLD. NOT SURE WHICH PART. NO ONE'S SAYING. (HEHEHE)
OKAY? CONSIDER THAT A FAVOR.
NO. THE FACT THAT ME AND MY BOYS ARE LEAVING YOUR PLACE THE WAY WE FOUND IT, IS WHAT YOU SHOULD CONSIDER A FAVOR. YOU OWE ME.

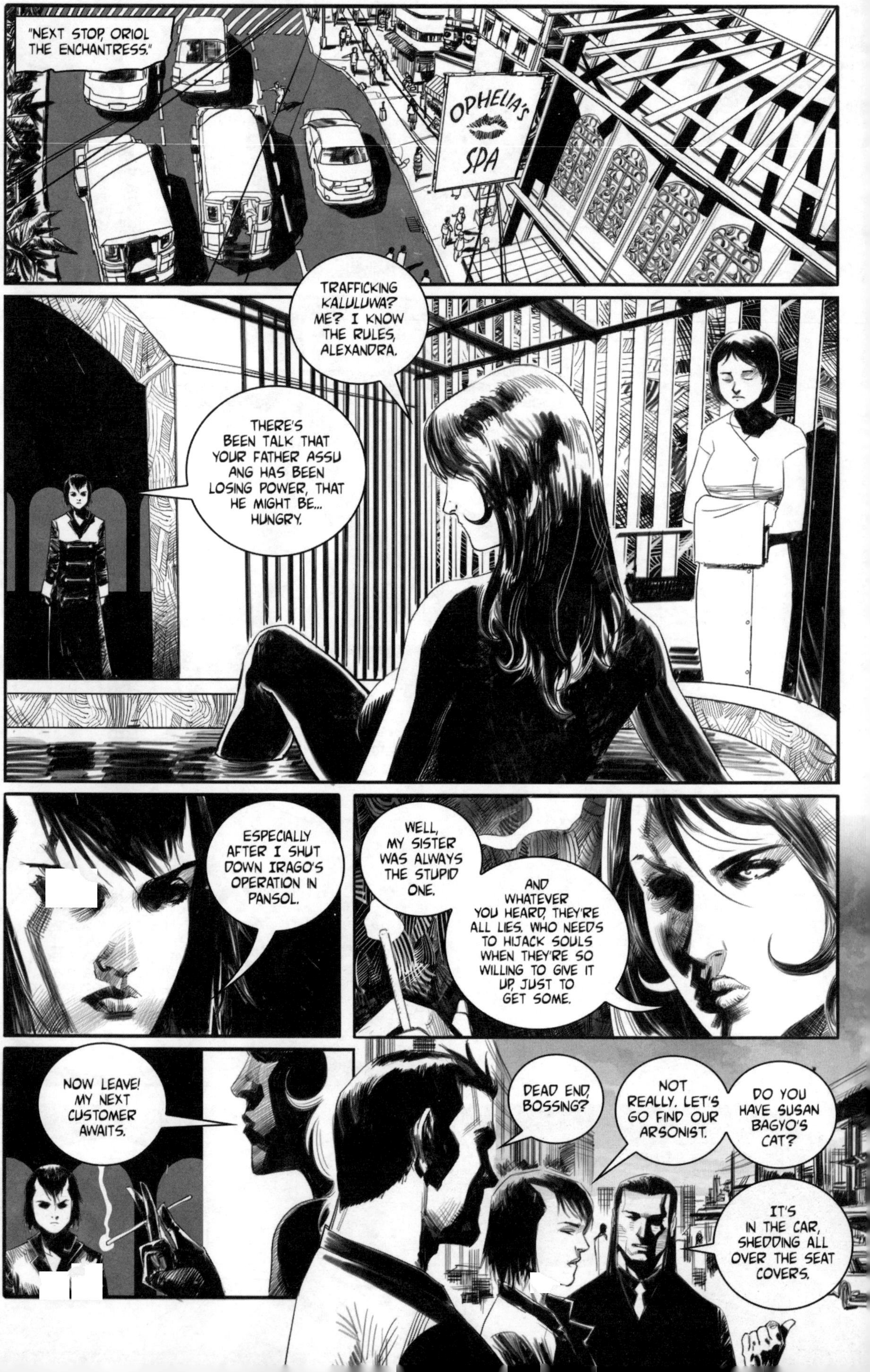
"NEXT STOP, ORIOL THE ENCHANTRESS."
OPHELIA'S SPA
TRAFFICKING KALULUWA? ME? I KNOW THE RULES, ALEXANDRA.
THERE'S BEEN TALK THAT YOUR FATHER ASSU ANG HAS BEEN LOSING POWER, THAT HE MIGHT BE... HUNGRY.
ESPECIALLY AFTER I SHUT DOWN IRAGO'S OPERATION IN PANSOL.
WELL, MY SISTER WAS ALWAYS THE STUPID ONE.
AND WHATEVER YOU HEARD, THEY'RE ALL LIES. WHO NEEDS TO HIJACK SOULS WHEN THEY'RE SO WILLING TO GIVE IT UP, JUST TO GET SOME.
NOW LEAVE! MY NEXT CUSTOMER AWAITS.
DEAD END, BOSSING?
NOT REALLY. LET'S GO FIND OUR ARSONIST.
DO YOU HAVE SUSAN BAGYO'S CAT?
IT'S IN THE CAR, SHEDDING ALL OVER THE SEAT COVERS.

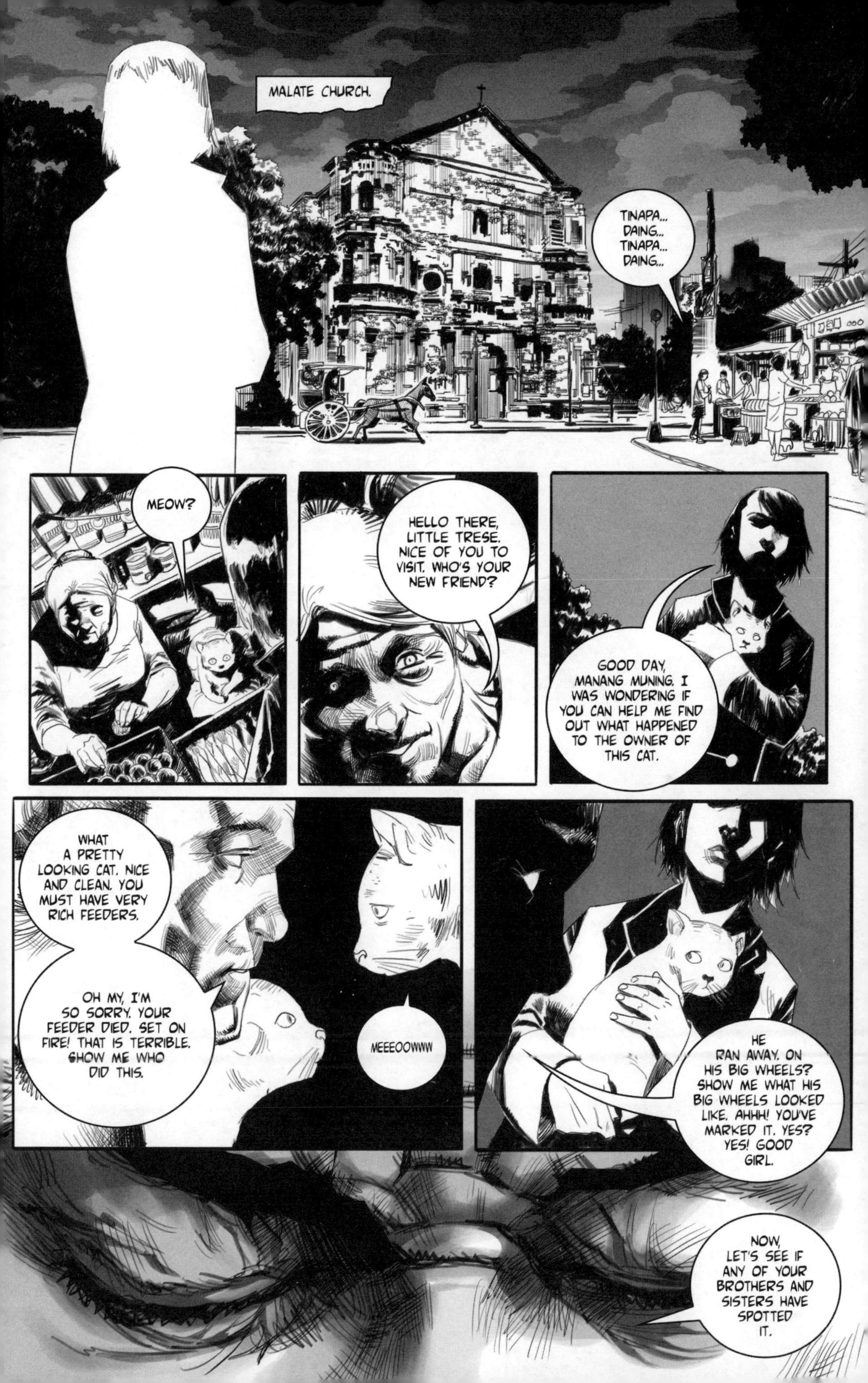
MALATE CHURCH.
TINAPA... DAING... TINAPA... DAING...
MEOW?
HELLO THERE, LITTLE TRESE. NICE OF YOU TO VISIT. WHO'S YOUR NEW FRIEND?
GOOD DAY, MANANG MUNING. I WAS WONDERING IF YOU CAN HELP ME FIND OUT WHAT HAPPENED TO THE OWNER OF THIS CAT.
WHAT A PRETTY LOOKING CAT. NICE AND CLEAN. YOU MUST HAVE VERY RICH FEEDERS.
OH MY, I'M SO SORRY. YOUR FEEDER DIED. SET ON FIRE! THAT IS TERRIBLE. SHOW ME WHO DID THIS.
MEEEOOWWW
HE RAN AWAY. ON HIS BIG WHEELS? SHOW ME WHAT HIS BIG WHEELS LOOKED LIKE. AHHH! YOU'VE MARKED IT. YES? YES! GOOD GIRL.
NOW, LET'S SEE IF ANY OF YOUR BROTHERS AND SISTERS HAVE SPOTTED IT.

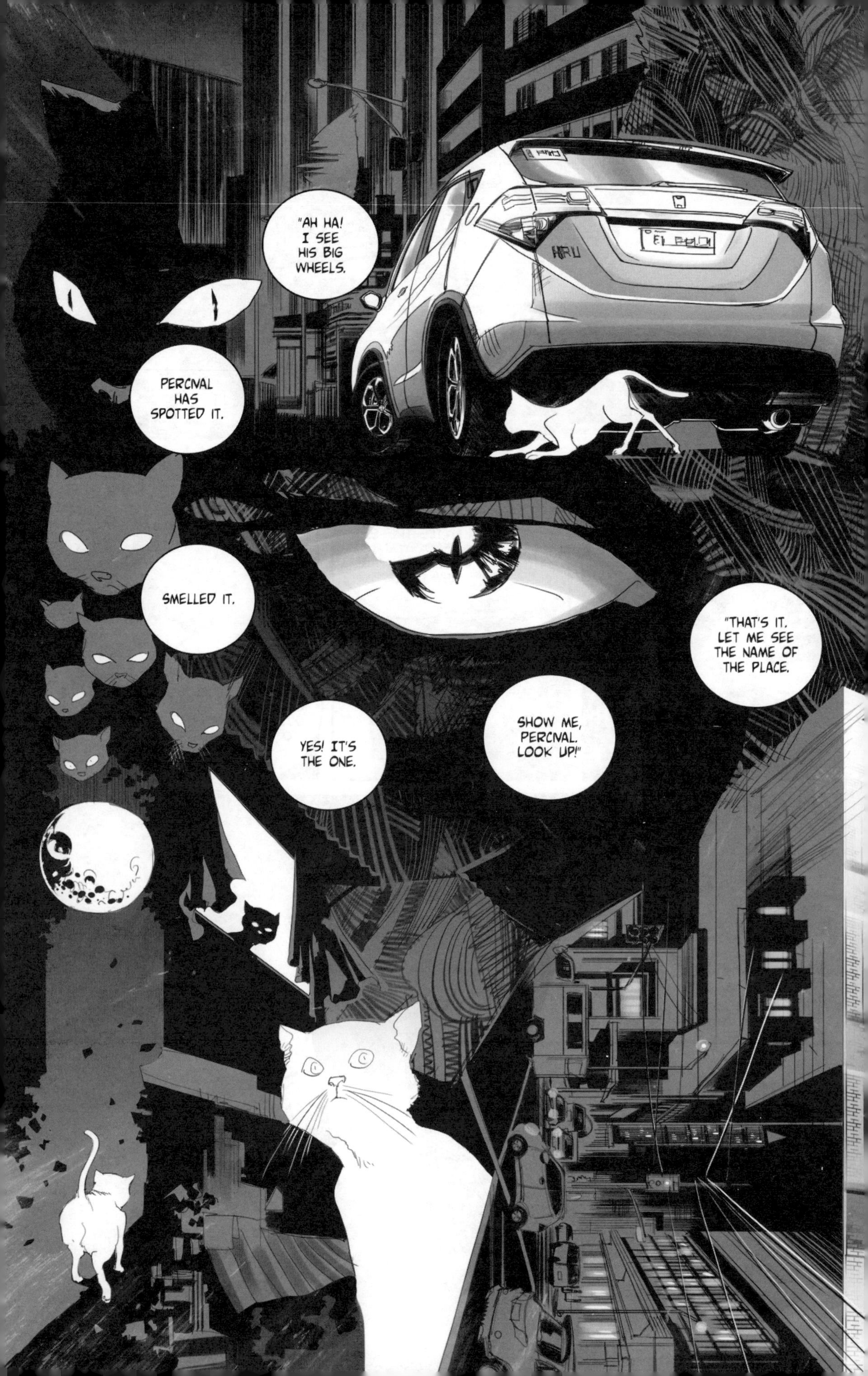
"AH HA! I SEE HIS BIG WHEELS.
PERCIVAL HAS SPOTTED IT.
SMELLED IT.
YES! IT'S THE ONE.
SHOW ME, PERCIVAL. LOOK UP!"
"THAT'S IT. LET ME SEE THE NAME OF THE PLACE.

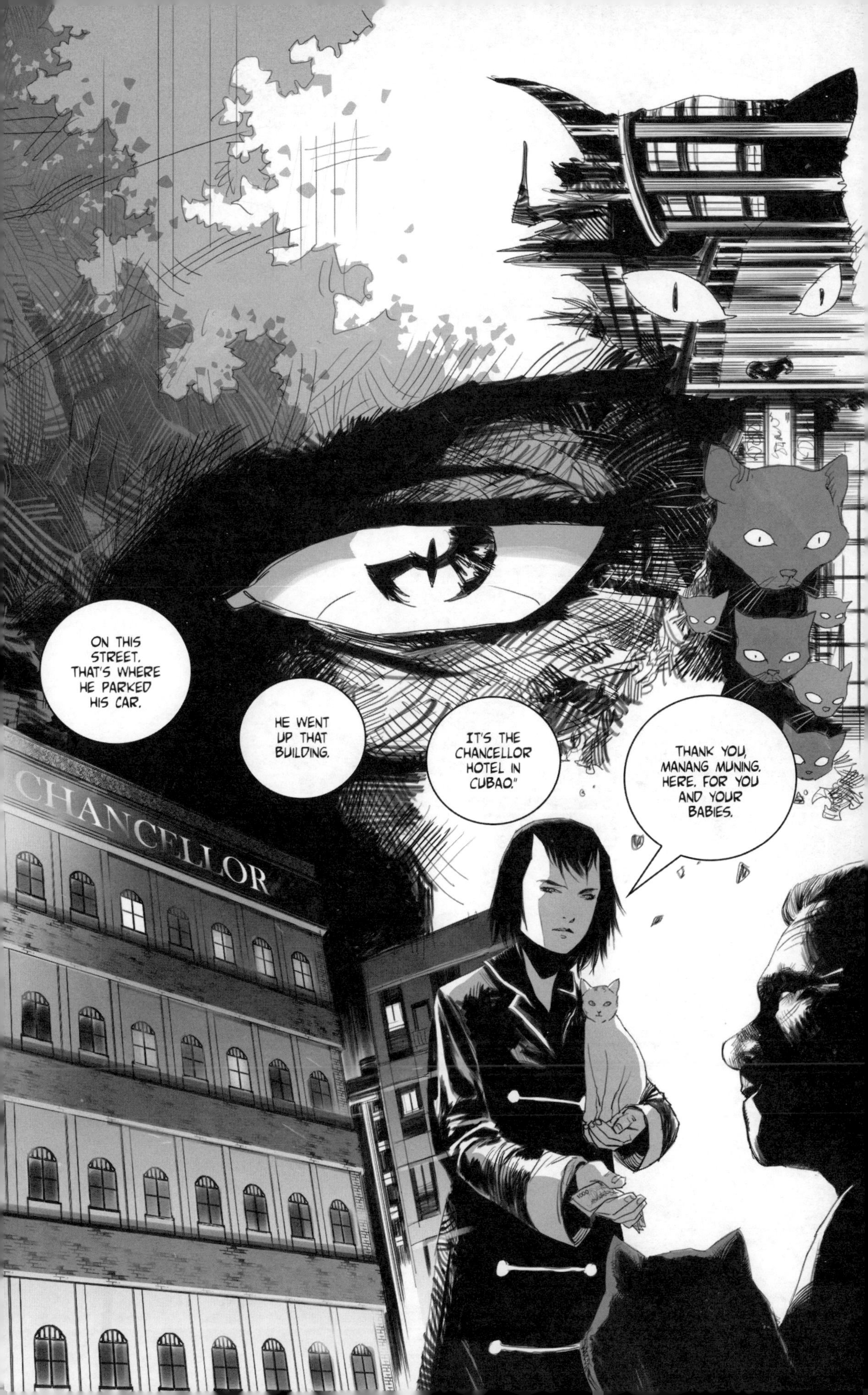
ON THIS STREET. THAT'S WHERE HE PARKED HIS CAR.
HE WENT UP THAT BUILDING.
IT'S THE CHANCELLOR HOTEL IN CUBAO."
THANK YOU, MANANG MUNING. HERE. FOR YOU AND YOUR BABIES.
CHANCELLOR

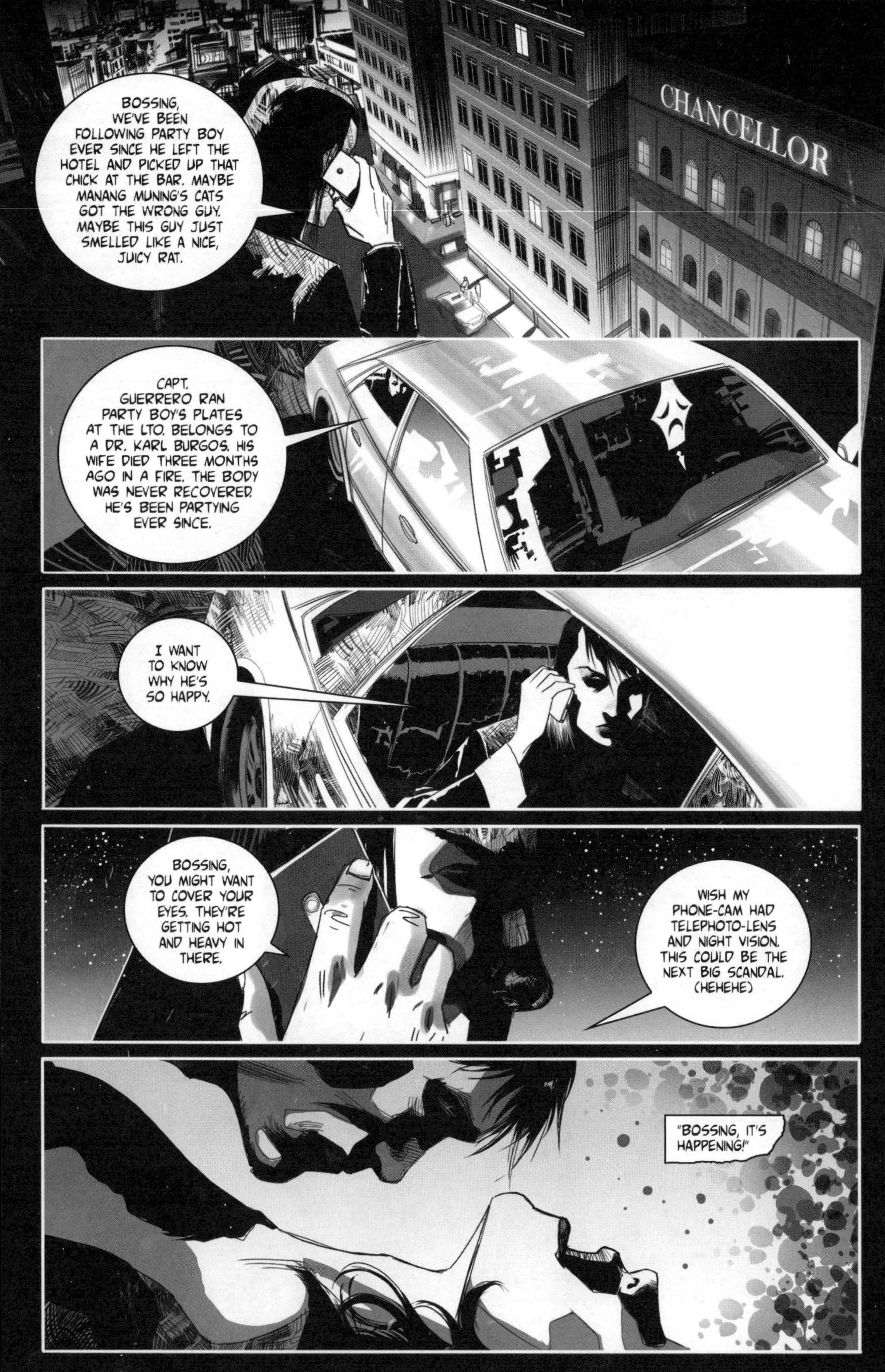
CHANCELLOR
BOSSING, WE'VE BEEN FOLLOWING PARTY BOY EVER SINCE HE LEFT THE HOTEL AND PICKED UP THAT CHICK AT THE BAR. MAYBE MANANG MUNING'S CATS GOT THE WRONG GUY. MAYBE THIS GUY JUST SMELLED LIKE A NICE, JUICY RAT.
CAPT. GUERRERO RAN PARTY BOY'S PLATES AT THE LTO. BELONGS TO A DR. KARL BURGOS. HIS WIFE DIED THREE MONTHS AGO IN A FIRE. THE BODY WAS NEVER RECOVERED. HE'S BEEN PARTYING EVER SINCE.
I WANT TO KNOW WHY HE'S SO HAPPY.
BOSSING, YOU MIGHT WANT TO COVER YOUR EYES. THEY'RE GETTING HOT AND HEAVY IN THERE.
WISH MY PHONE-CAM HAD TELEPHOTO-LENS AND NIGHT VISION. THIS COULD BE THE NEXT BIG SCANDAL. (HEHEHE)
"BOSSING, IT'S HAPPENING!"

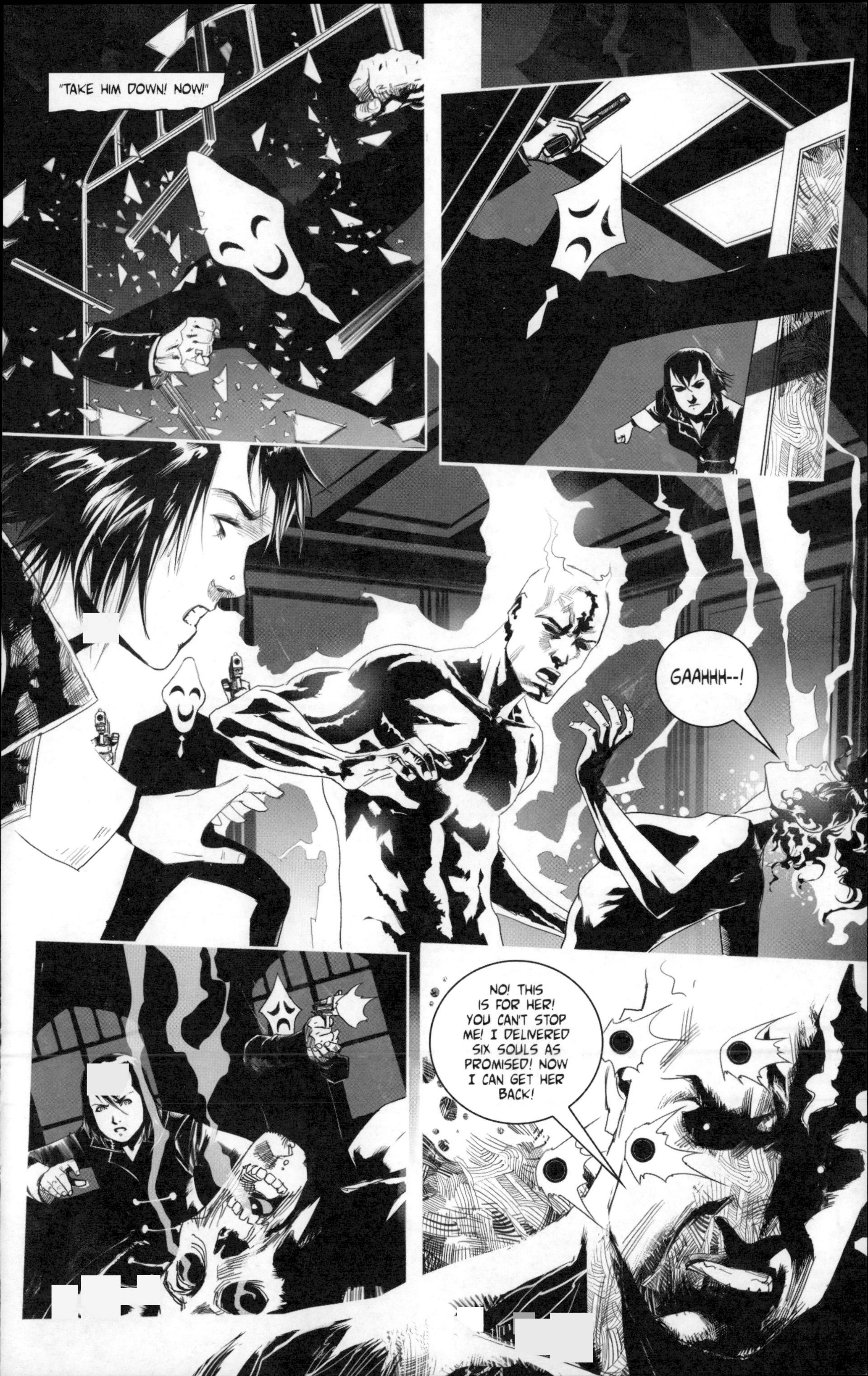
"TAKE HIM DOWN! NOW!"
GAAHHH--!
NO! THIS IS FOR HER! YOU CAN'T STOP ME! I DELIVERED SIX SOULS AS PROMISED! NOW I CAN GET HER BACK!

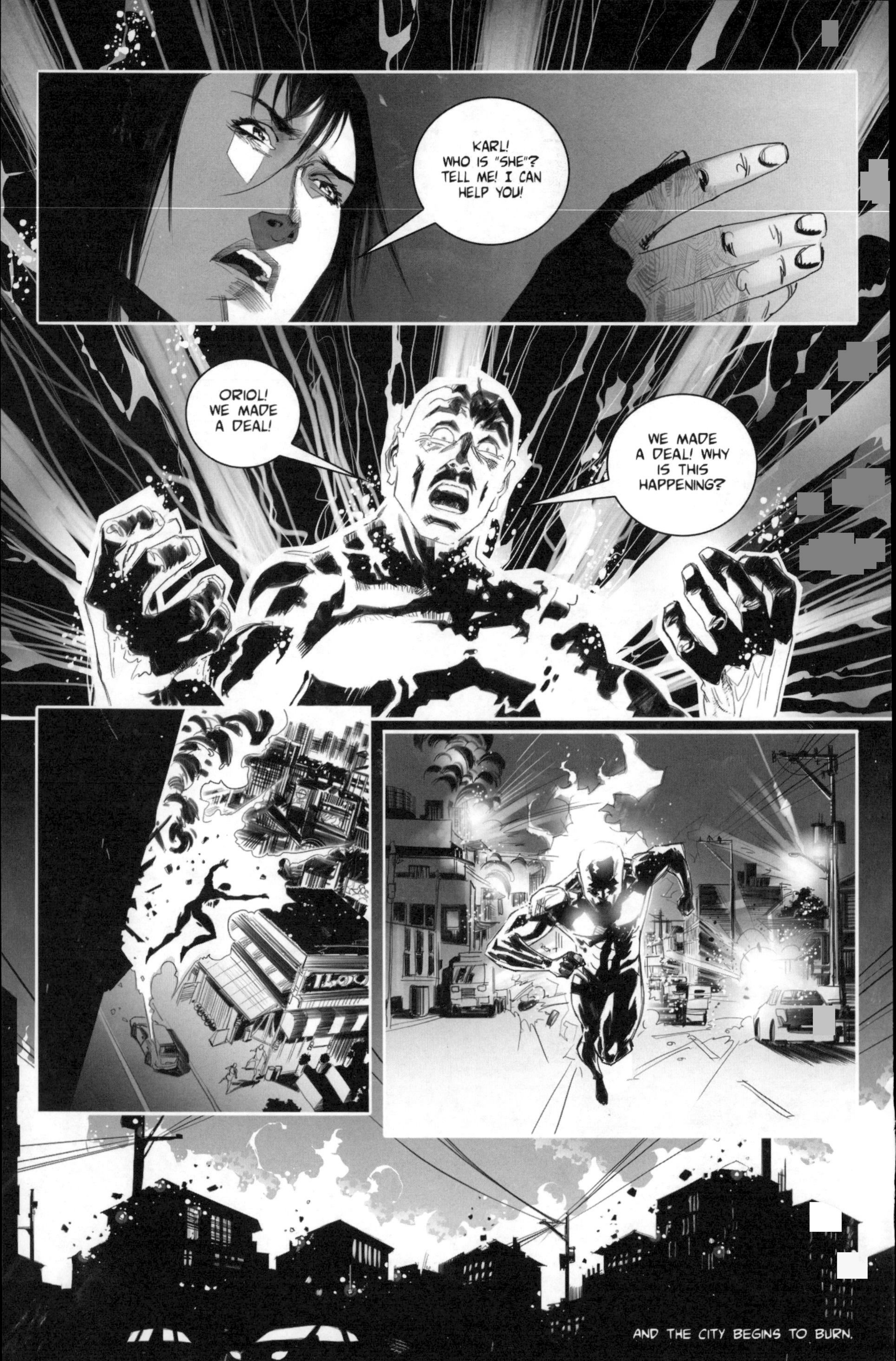
KARL! WHO IS "SHE"? TELL ME! I CAN HELP YOU!
ORIOL! WE MADE A DEAL!
WE MADE A DEAL! WHY IS THIS HAPPENING?
AND THE CITY BEGINS TO BURN.

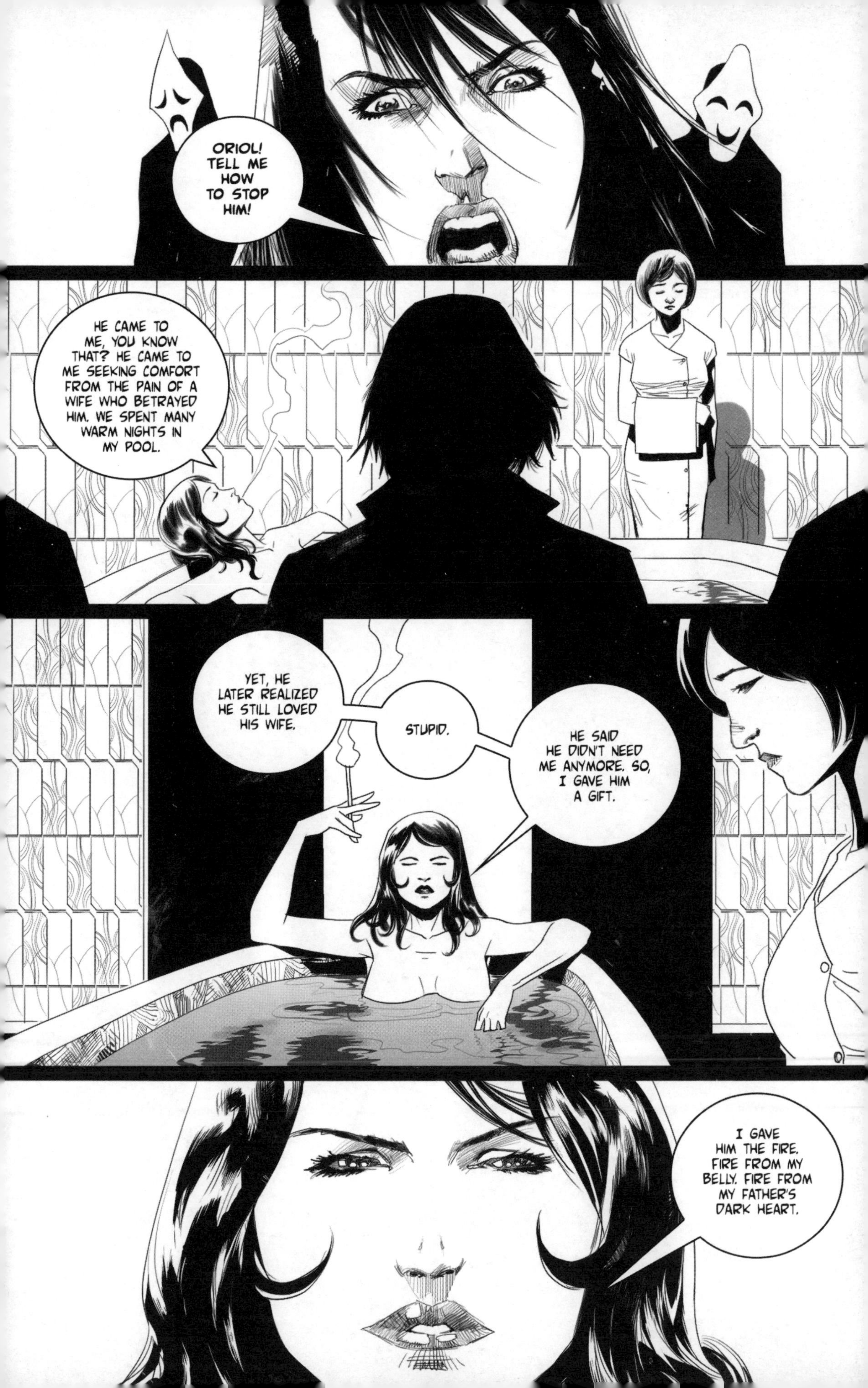
ORIOL! TELL ME HOW TO STOP HIM!
HE CAME TO ME, YOU KNOW THAT? HE CAME TO ME SEEKING COMFORT FROM THE PAIN OF A WIFE WHO BETRAYED HIM. WE SPENT MANY WARM NIGHTS IN MY POOL.
YET, HE LATER REALIZED HE STILL LOVED HIS WIFE.
STUPID.
HE SAID HE DIDN'T NEED ME ANYMORE. SO, I GAVE HIM A GIFT.
I GAVE HIM THE FIRE. FIRE FROM MY BELLY. FIRE FROM MY FATHER'S DARK HEART.

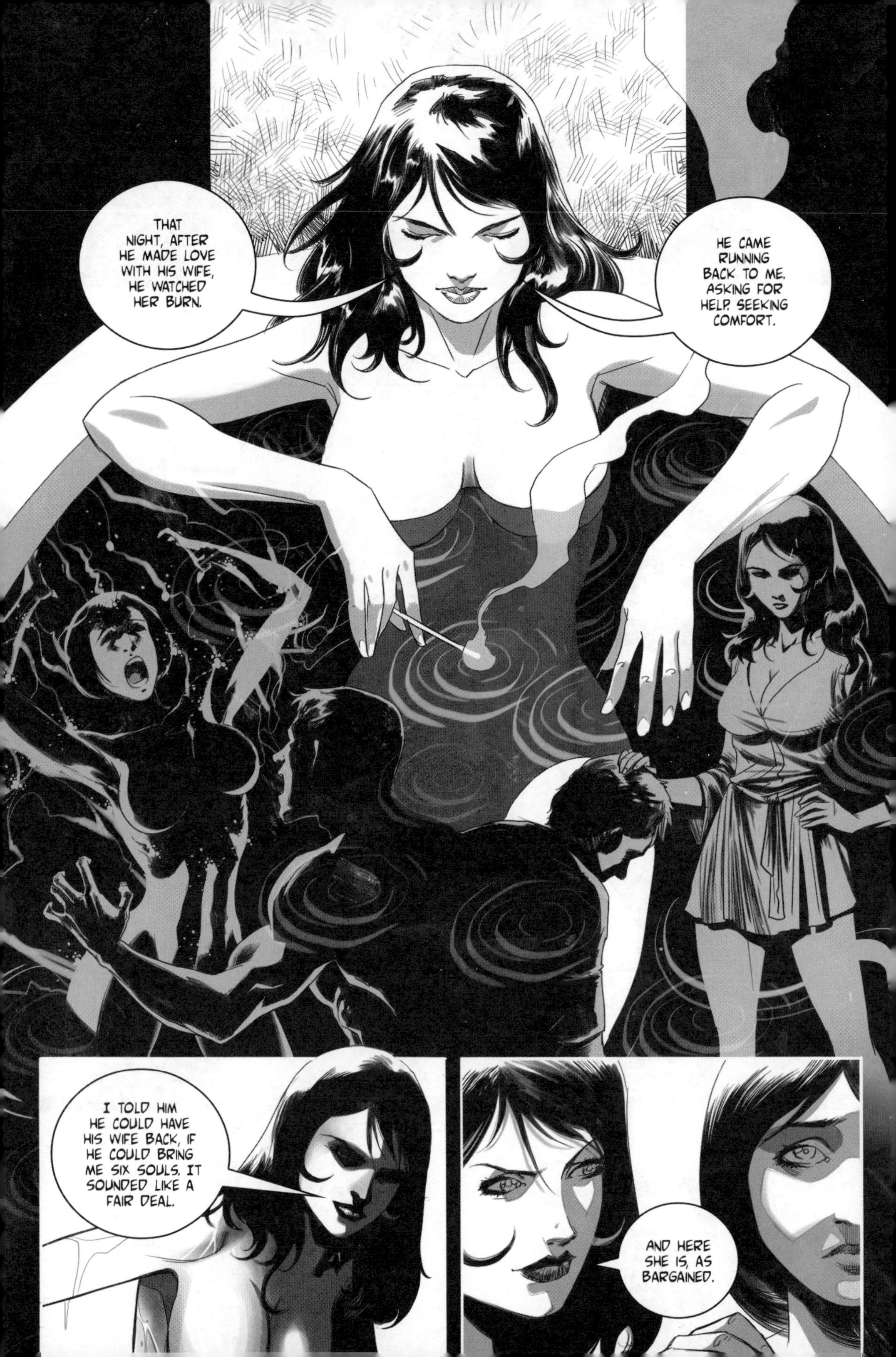

THAT NIGHT, AFTER HE MADE LOVE WITH HIS WIFE, HE WATCHED HER BURN.
HE CAME RUNNING BACK TO ME. ASKING FOR HELP. SEEKING COMFORT.
I TOLD HIM HE COULD HAVE HIS WIFE BACK, IF HE COULD BRING ME SIX SOULS. IT SOUNDED LIKE A FAIR DEAL.
AND HERE SHE IS, AS BARGAINED.

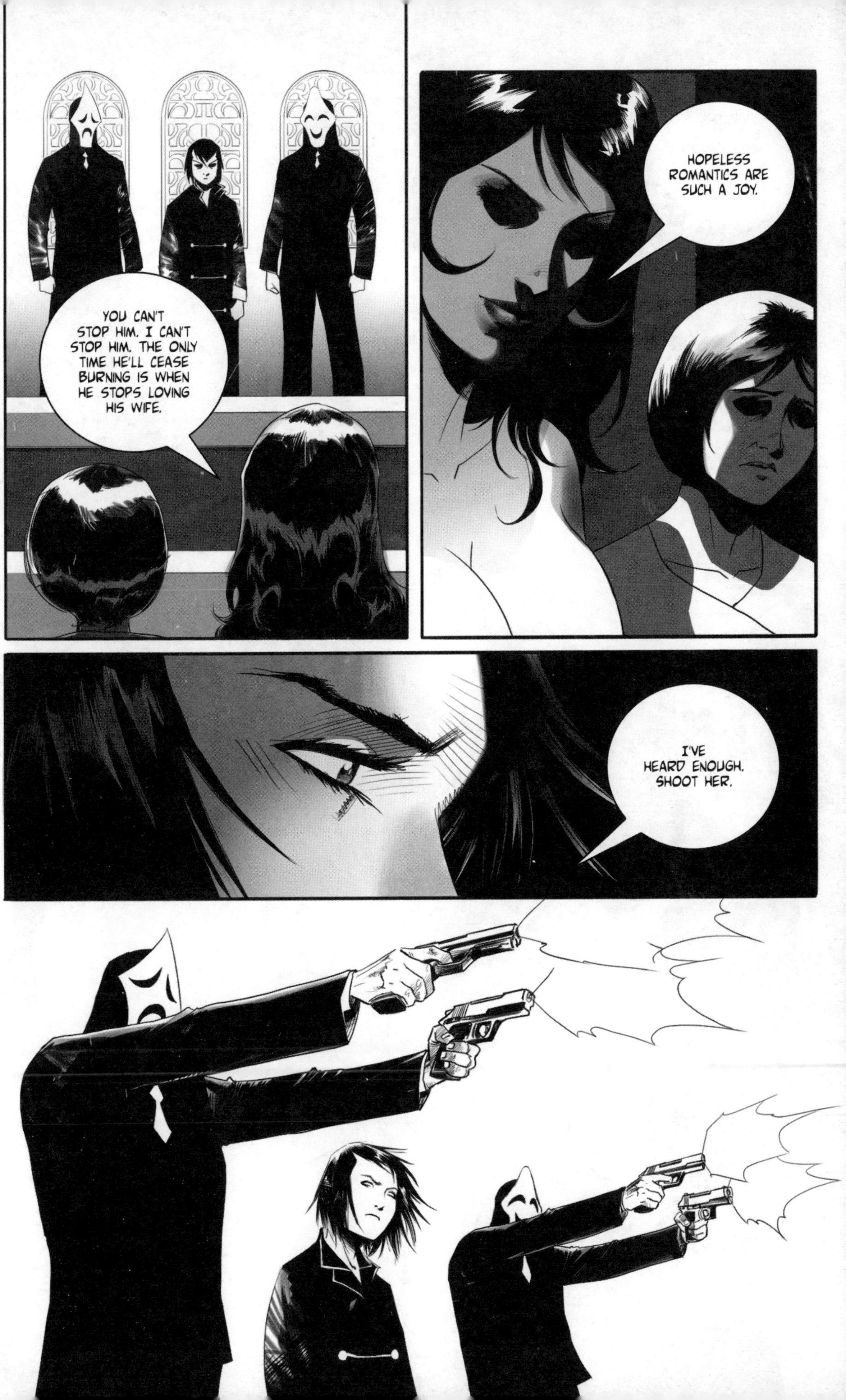
YOU CAN'T STOP HIM. I CAN'T STOP HIM. THE ONLY TIME HE'LL CEASE BURNING IS WHEN HE STOPS LOVING HIS WIFE.
HOPELESS ROMANTICS ARE SUCH A JOY.
I'VE HEARD ENOUGH. SHOOT HER.

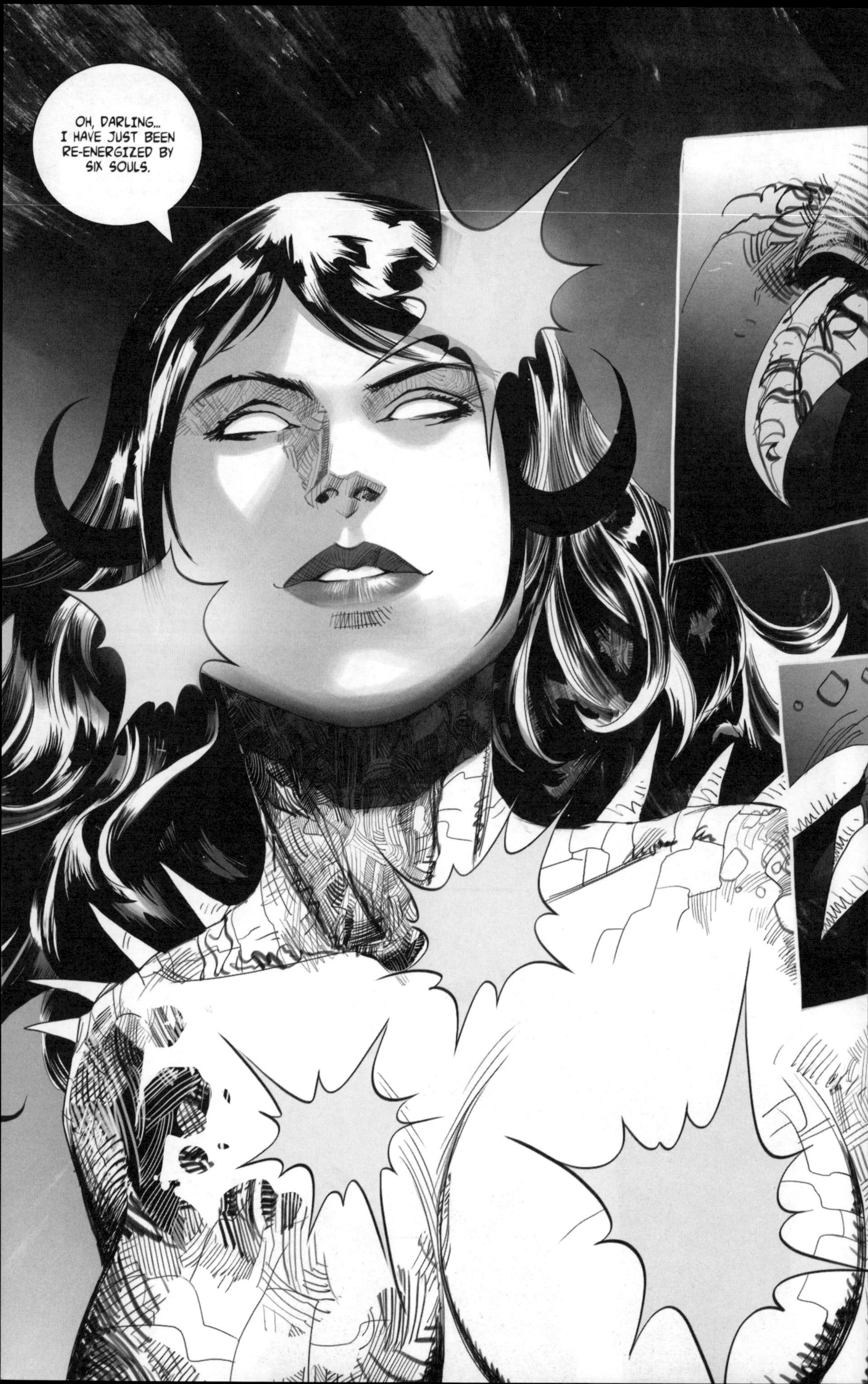
OH, DARLING... I HAVE JUST BEEN RE-ENERGIZED BY SIX SOULS.

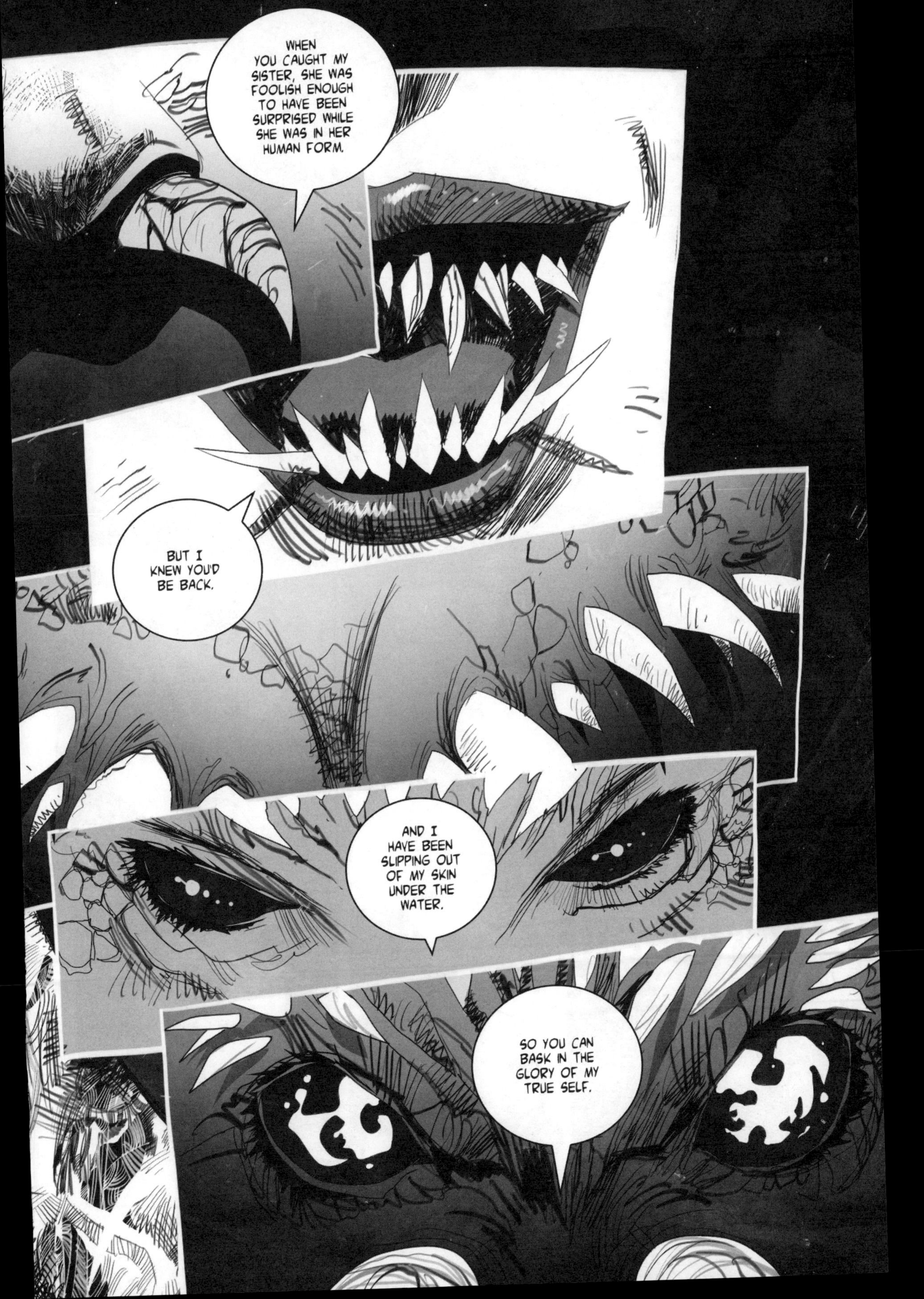
WHEN YOU CAUGHT MY SISTER, SHE WAS FOOLISH ENOUGH TO HAVE BEEN SURPRISED WHILE SHE WAS IN HER HUMAN FORM.
BUT I KNEW YOU'D BE BACK.
AND I HAVE BEEN SLIPPING OUT OF MY SKIN UNDER THE WATER.
SO YOU CAN BASK IN THE GLORY OF MY TRUE SELF.

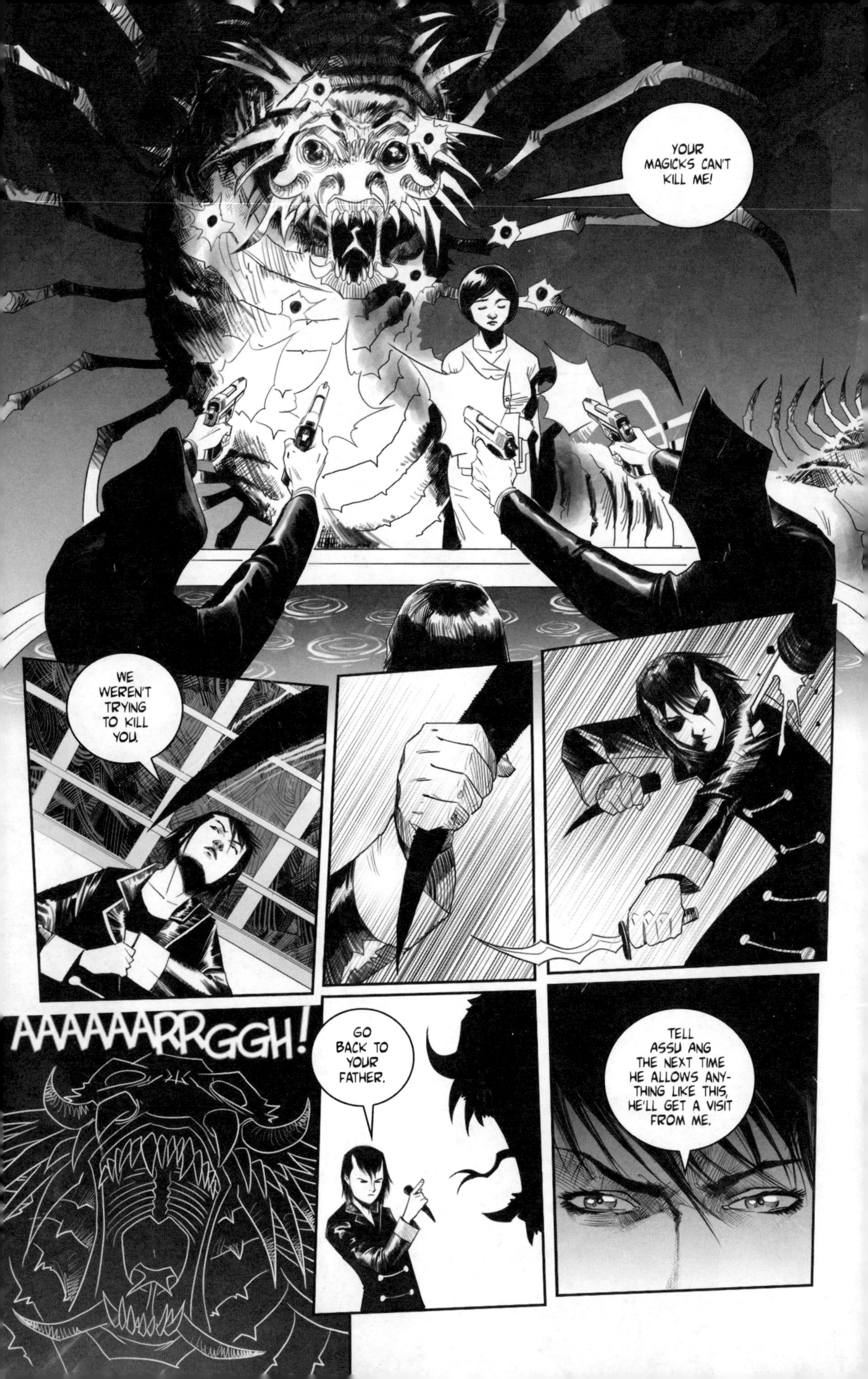
YOUR MAGICKS CAN'T KILL ME!
WE WEREN'T TRYING TO KILL YOU.
AAAAAARRGGH!
GO BACK TO YOUR FATHER.
TELL ASSU ANG THE NEXT TIME HE ALLOWS ANY-THING LIKE THIS, HE'LL GET A VISIT FROM ME.

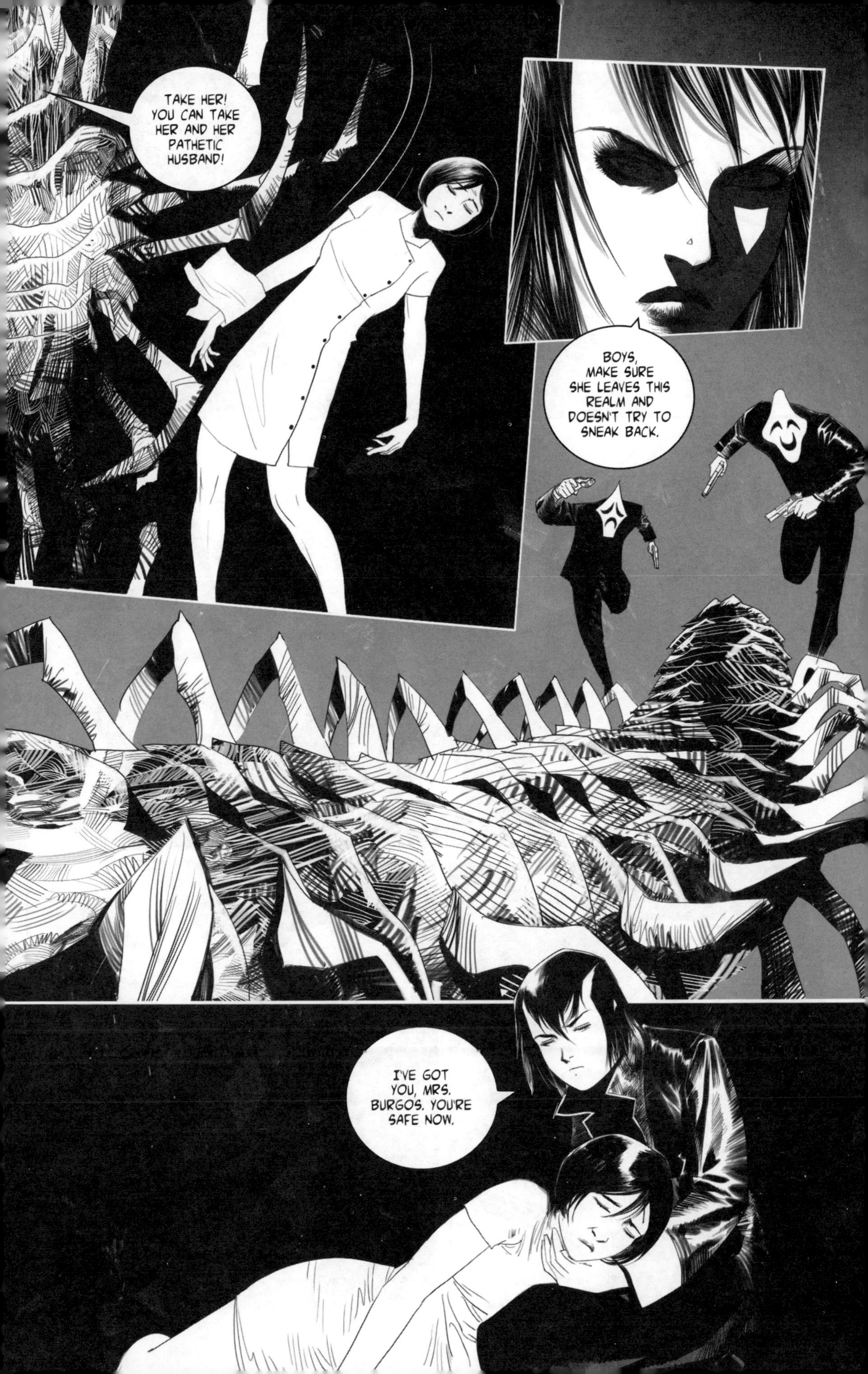
TAKE HER! YOU CAN TAKE HER AND HER PATHETIC HUSBAND!
BOYS, MAKE SURE SHE LEAVES THIS REALM AND DOESN'T TRY TO SNEAK BACK.
I'VE GOT YOU, MRS. BURGOS. YOU'RE SAFE NOW.

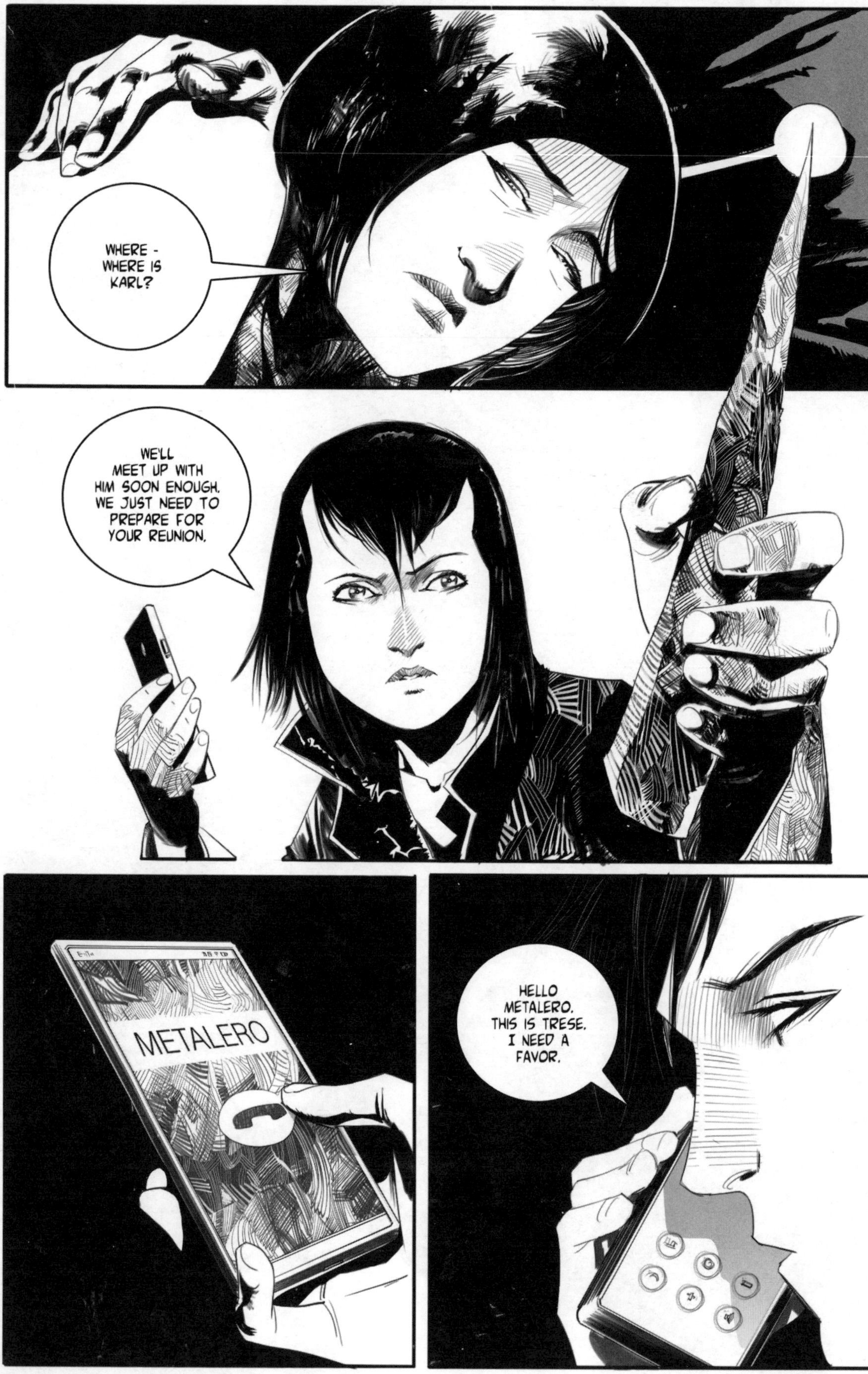
WHERE - WHERE IS KARL?
WE'LL MEET UP WITH HIM SOON ENOUGH. WE JUST NEED TO PREPARE FOR YOUR REUNION.
METALERO
HELLO METALERO. THIS IS TRESE. I NEED A FAVOR.

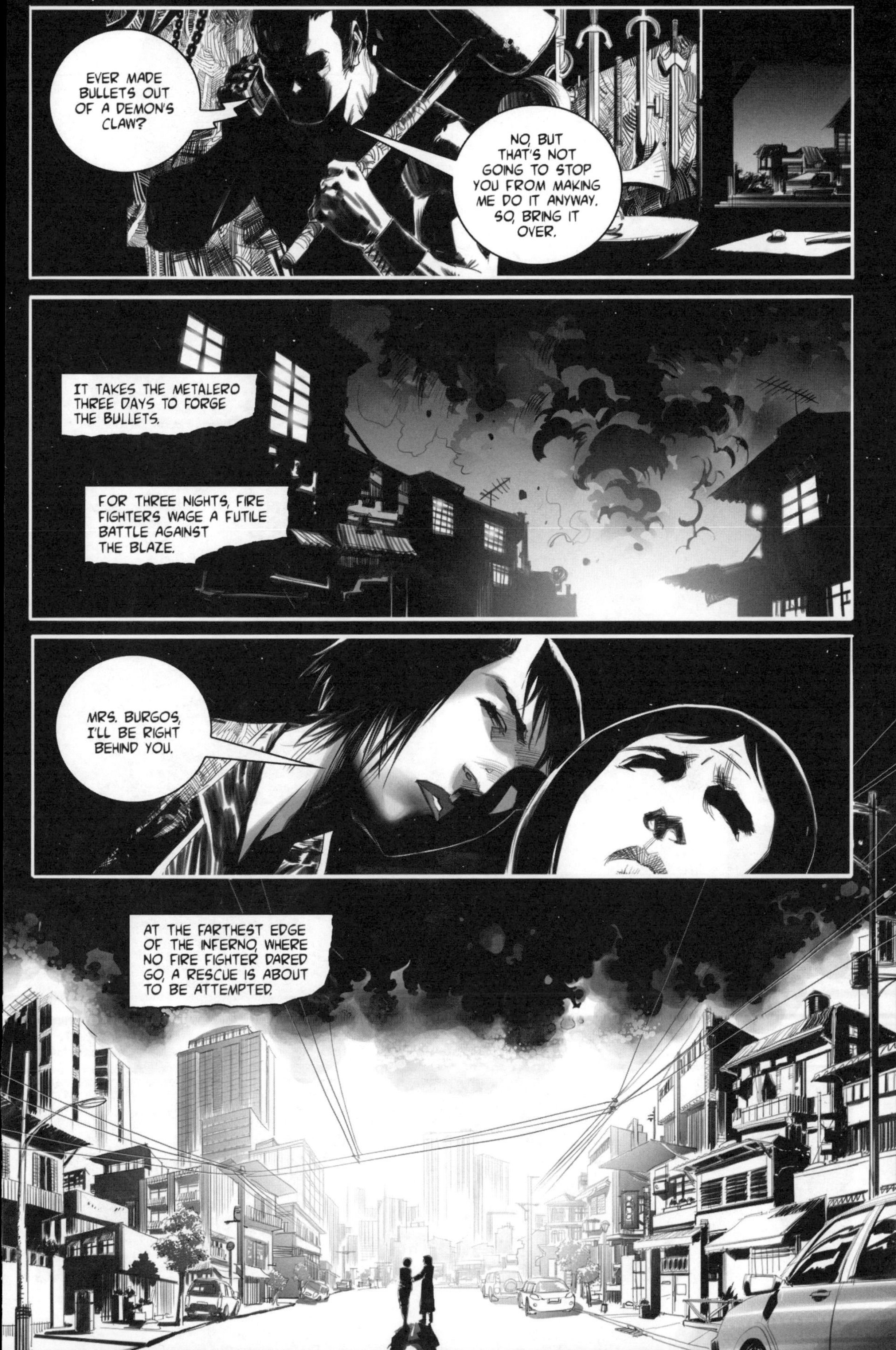
EVER MADE BULLETS OUT OF A DEMON'S CLAW?
NO, BUT THAT'S NOT GOING TO STOP YOU FROM MAKING ME DO IT ANYWAY. SO, BRING IT OVER.
IT TAKES THE METALERO THREE DAYS TO FORGE THE BULLETS.
FOR THREE NIGHTS, FIRE FIGHTERS WAGE A FUTILE BATTLE AGAINST THE BLAZE.
MRS. BURGOS, I'LL BE RIGHT BEHIND YOU.
AT THE FARTHEST EDGE OF THE INFERNO, WHERE NO FIRE FIGHTER DARED GO, A RESCUE IS ABOUT TO BE ATTEMPTED.

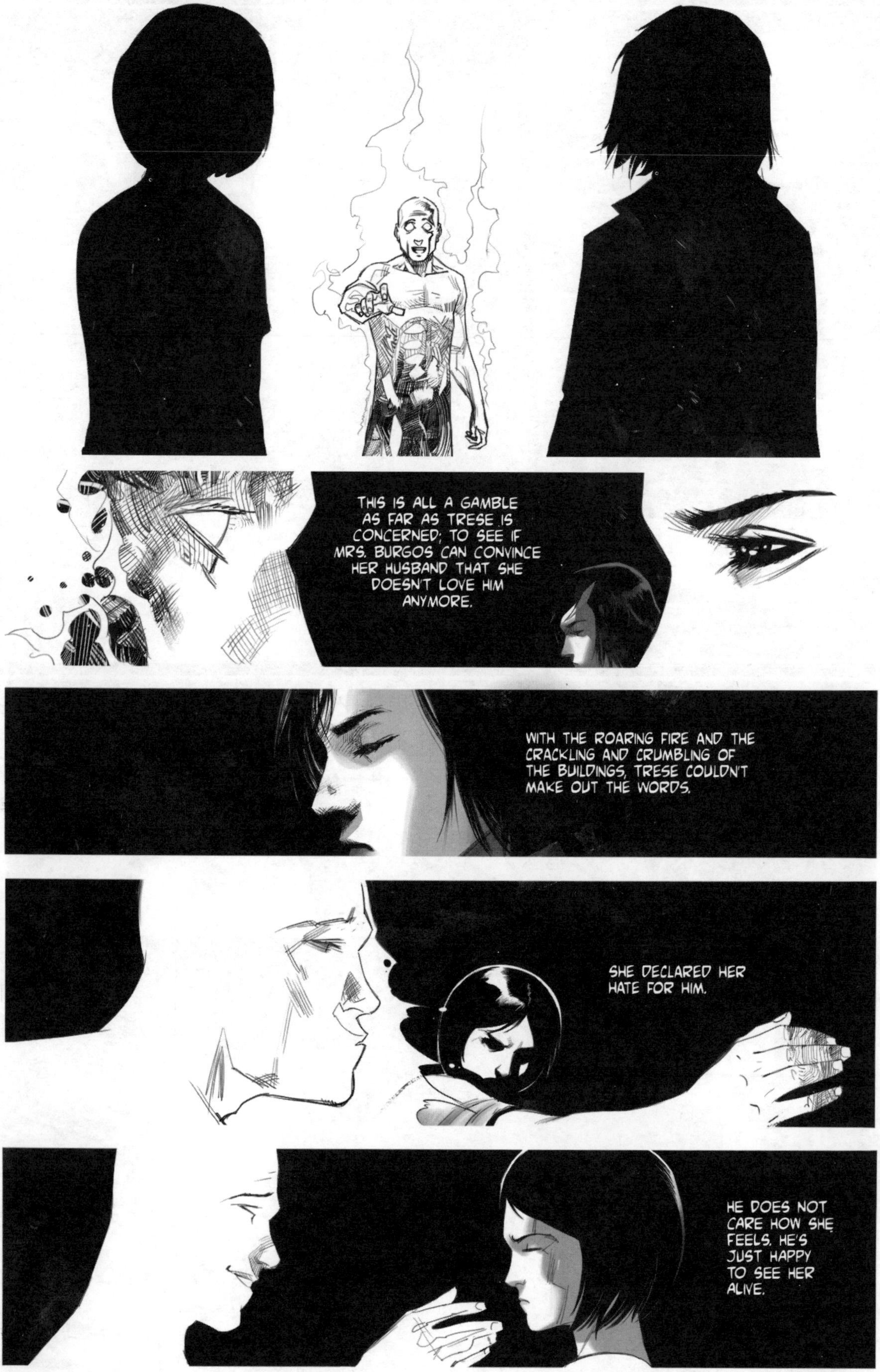
THIS IS ALL A GAMBLE AS FAR AS TRESE IS CONCERNED; TO SEE IF MRS. BURGOS CAN CONVINCE HER HUSBAND THAT SHE DOESN'T LOVE HIM ANYMORE.
WITH THE ROARING FIRE AND THE CRACKLING AND CRUMBLING OF THE BUILDINGS, TRESE COULDN'T MAKE OUT THE WORDS.
SHE DECLARED HER HATE FOR HIM.
HE DOES NOT CARE HOW SHE FEELS. HE'S JUST HAPPY TO SEE HER ALIVE.

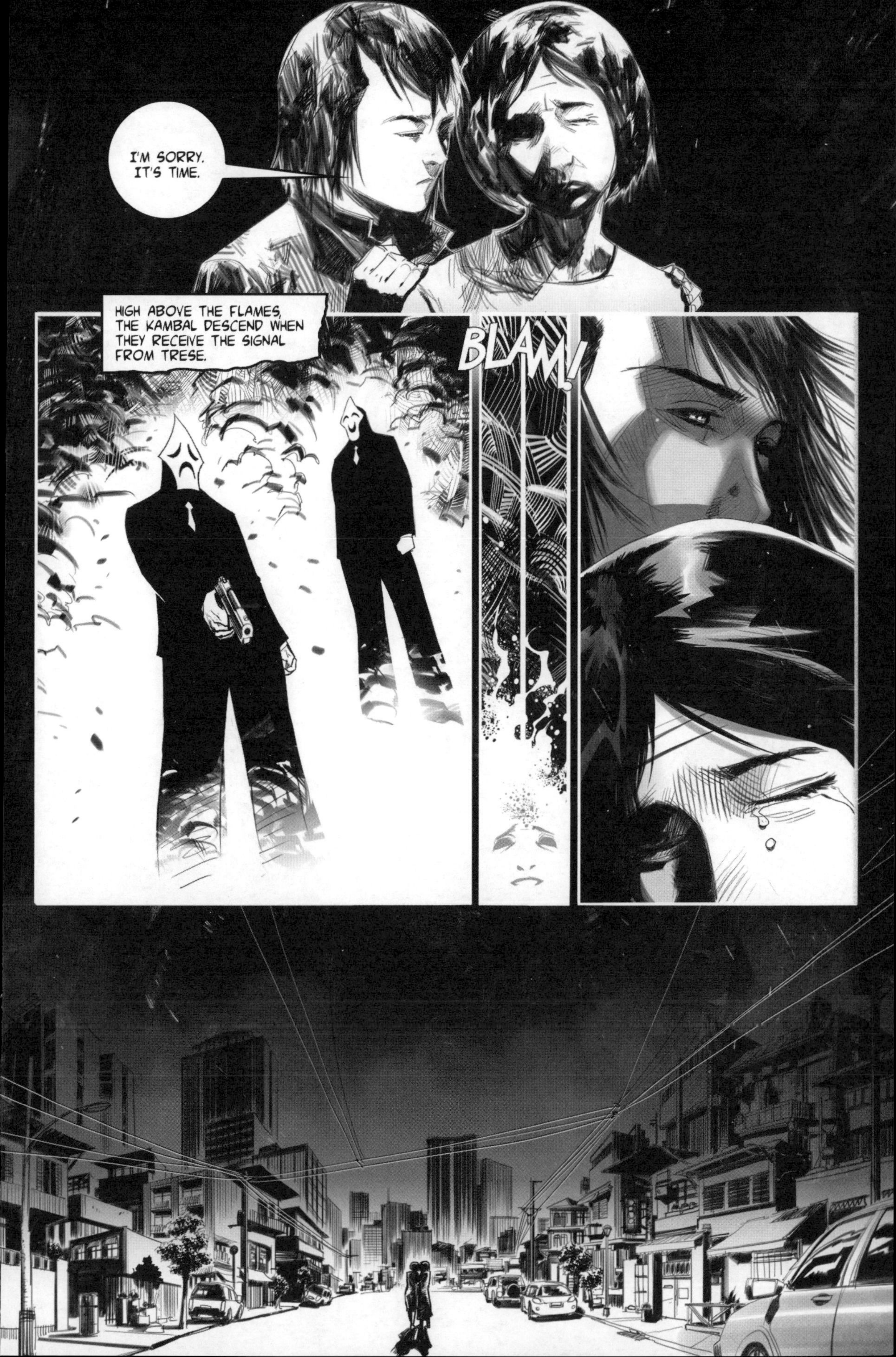

I'M SORRY.
IT'S TIME.
HIGH ABOVE THE FLAMES, THE KAMBAL DESCEND WHEN THEY RECEIVE THE SIGNAL FROM TRESE.
BLAM!

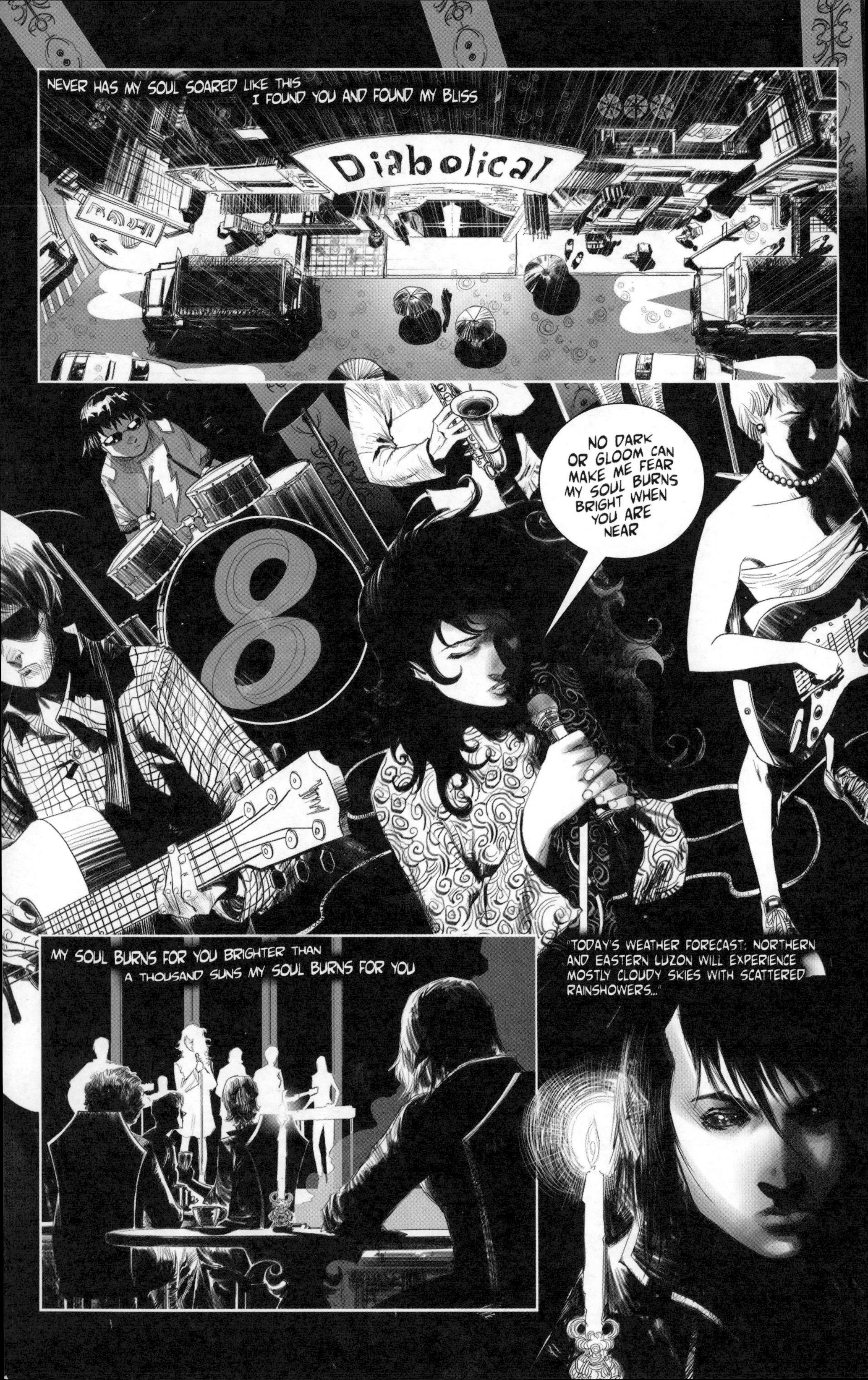
NEVER HAS MY SOUL SOARED LIKE THIS
I FOUND YOU AND FOUND MY BLISS
Diabolical
NO DARK OR GLOOM CAN MAKE ME FEAR MY SOUL BURNS BRIGHT WHEN YOU ARE NEAR
8
MY SOUL BURNS FOR YOU BRIGHTER THAN
A THOUSAND SUNS MY SOUL BURNS FOR YOU
"TODAY'S WEATHER FORECAST: NORTHERN AND EASTERN LUZON WILL EXPERIENCE MOSTLY CLOUDY SKIES WITH SCATTERED RAINSHOWERS..."

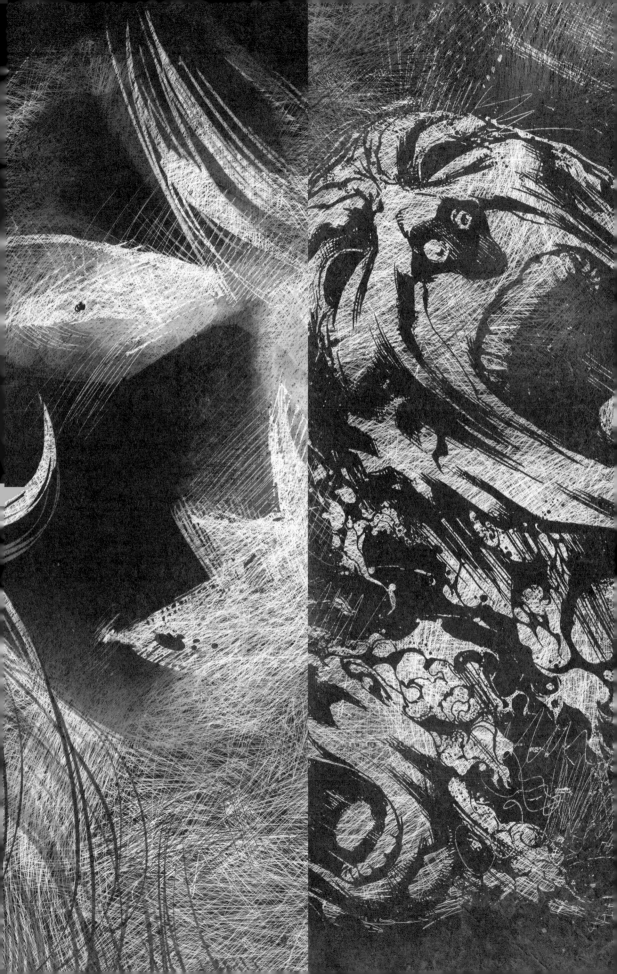

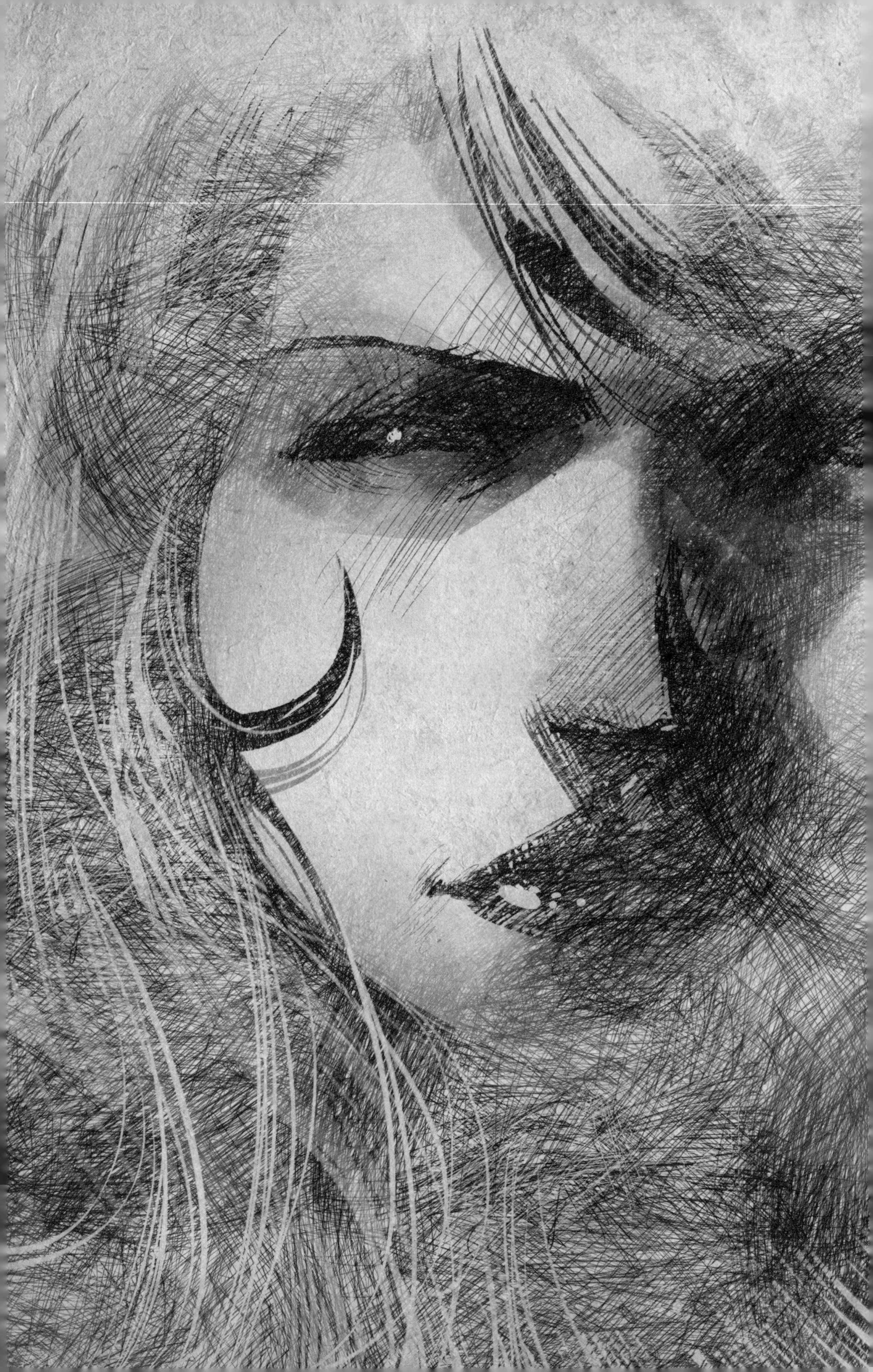

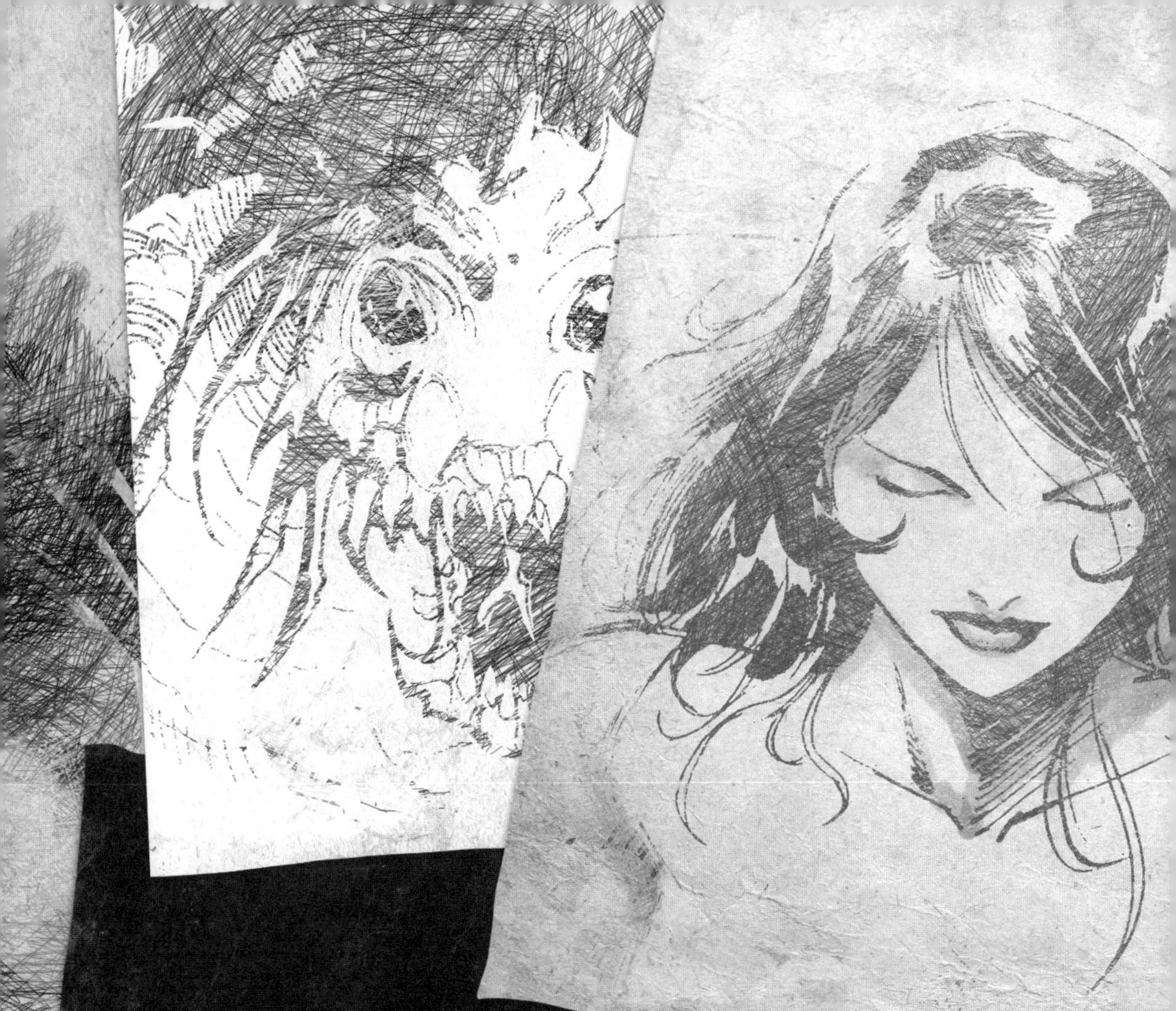

FROM THE JOURNAL OF PROF. ALEXANDER TRESE

September 29

The Oriol

The Oriol are the spawn of Assu Ang, one of the notorious kingpins of the underworld. This water demon is usually found in lakes and springs. It lures unsuspecting men into the water by assuming the form of a beautiful enchantress.

It will either convince the man to give up his soul for her or she will take it by force, transforming into her true form, which can either resemble a snake or a centipede, and it will tear into the man's body to wrench out his soul.

The last Oriol we encountered had set up a brothel in Makati, which was shut down with the help of Captain German and his squad.

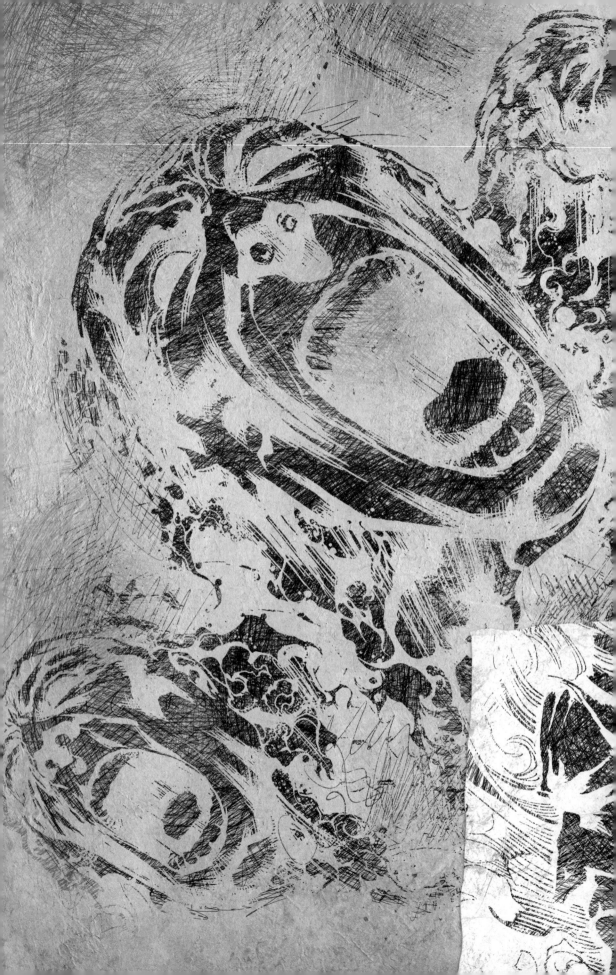

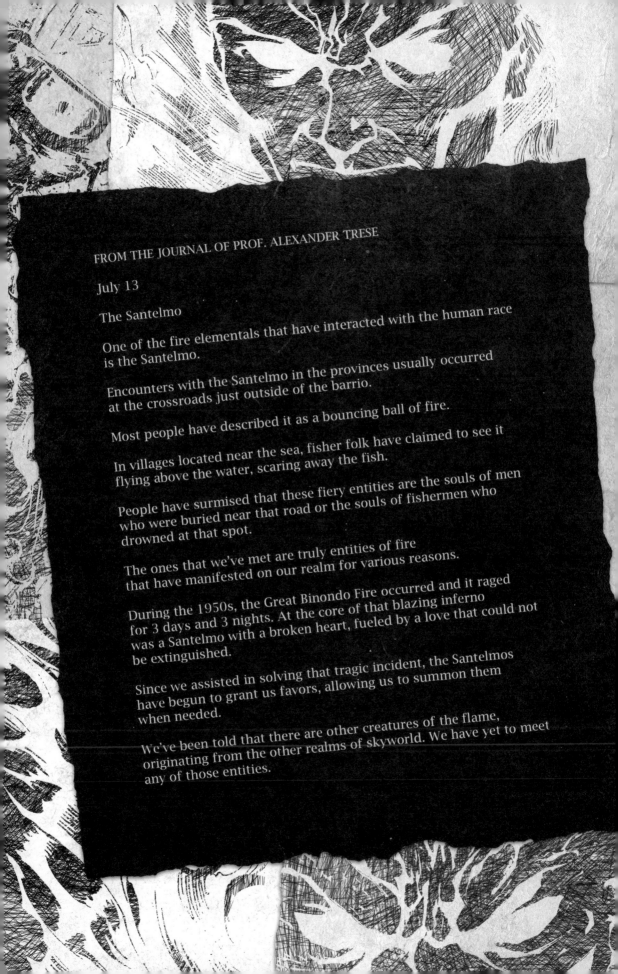

FROM THE JOURNAL OF PROF. ALEXANDER TRESE

July 13

The Santelmo

One of the fire elementals that have interacted with the human race is the Santelmo.

Encounters with the Santelmo in the provinces usually occurred at the crossroads just outside of the barrio.

Most people have described it as a bouncing ball of fire.

In villages located near the sea, fisher folk have claimed to see it flying above the water, scaring away the fish.

People have surmised that these fiery entities are the souls of men who were buried near that road or the souls of fishermen who drowned at that spot.

The ones that we've met are truly entities of fire that have manifested on our realm for various reasons.

During the 1950s, the Great Binondo Fire occurred and it raged for 3 days and 3 nights. At the core of that blazing inferno was a Santelmo with a broken heart, fueled by a love that could not be extinguished.

Since we assisted in solving that tragic incident, the Santelmos have begun to grant us favors, allowing us to summon them when needed.

We've been told that there are other creatures of the flame, originating from the other realms of skyworld. We have yet to meet any of those entities.

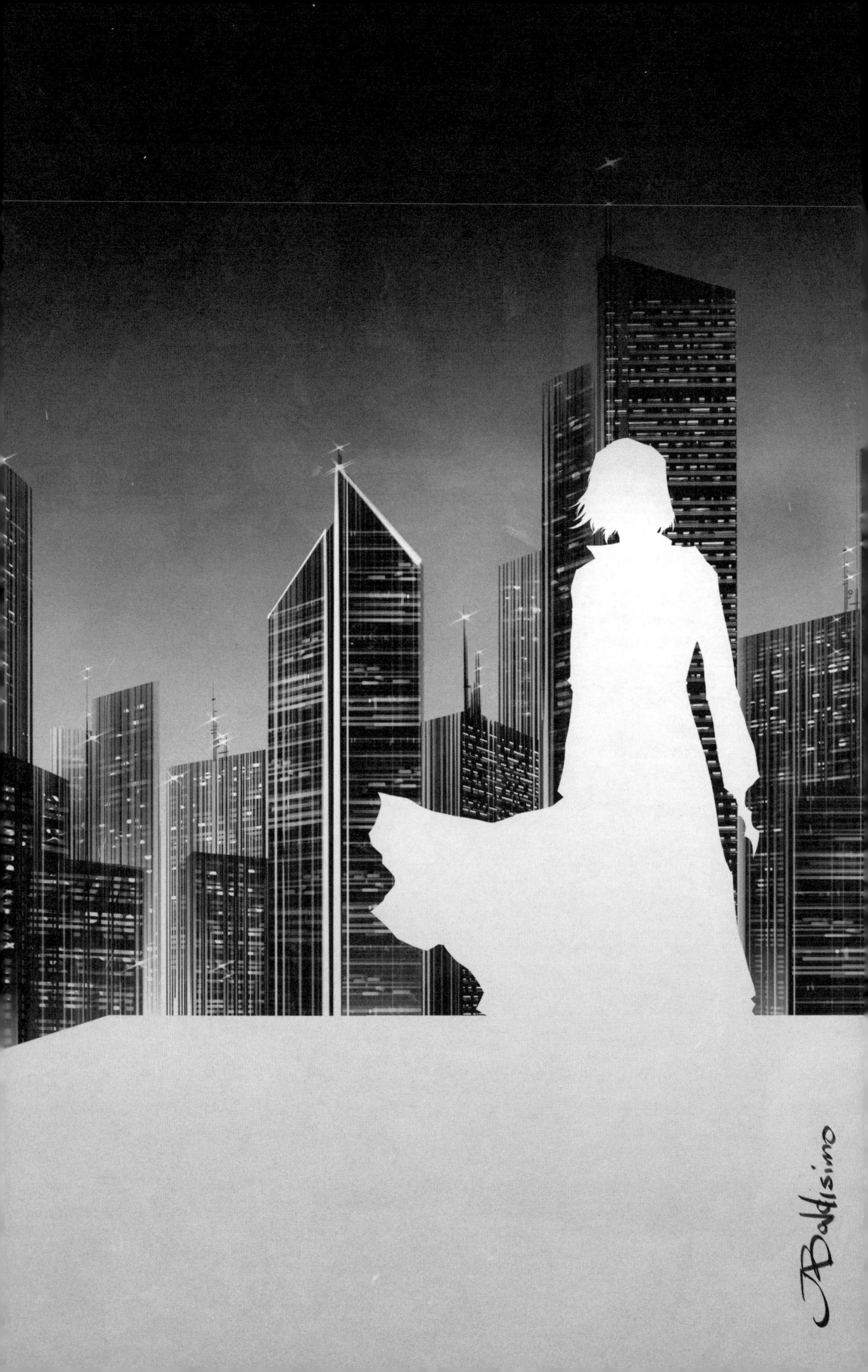
Baldisimo

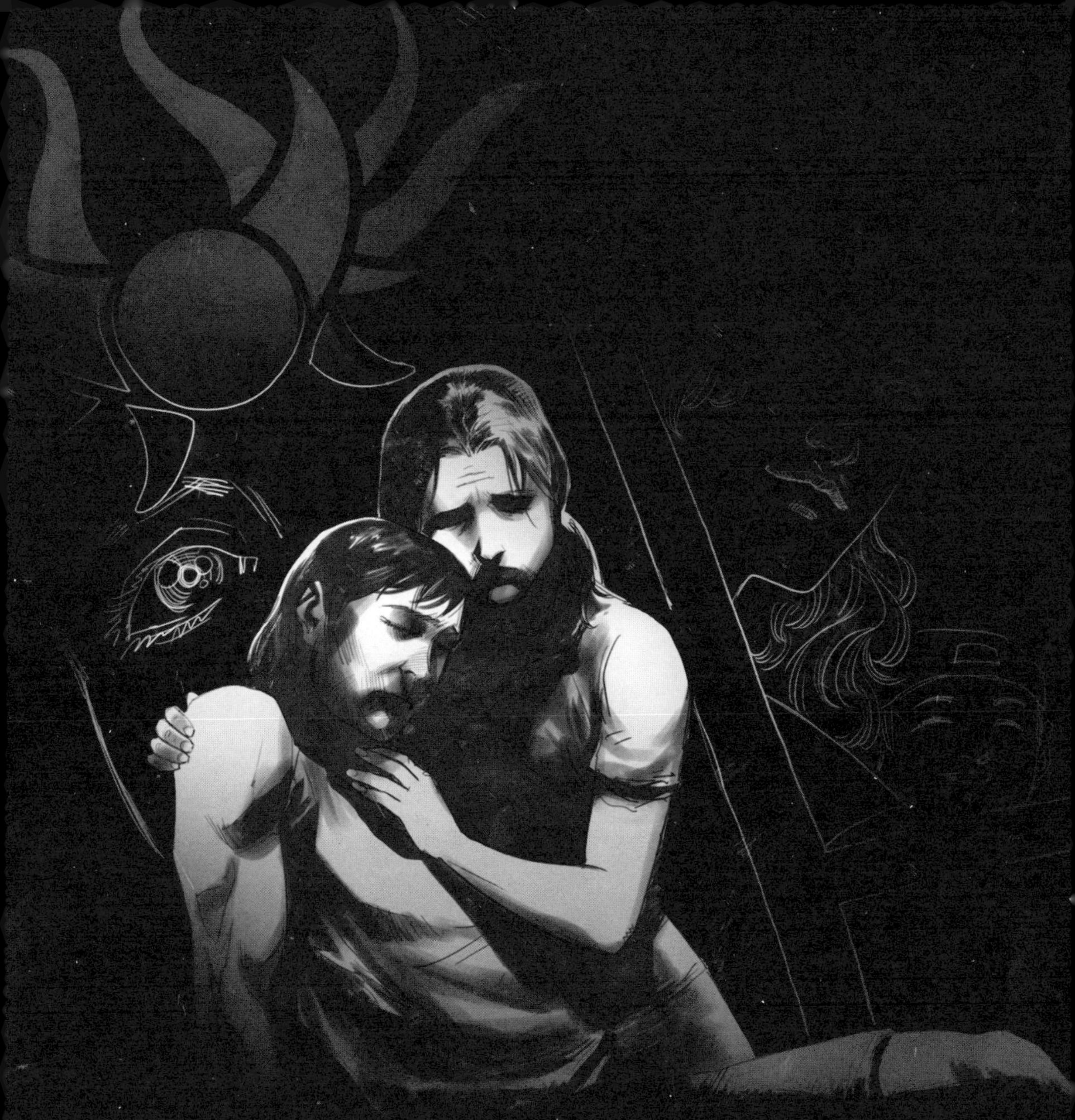

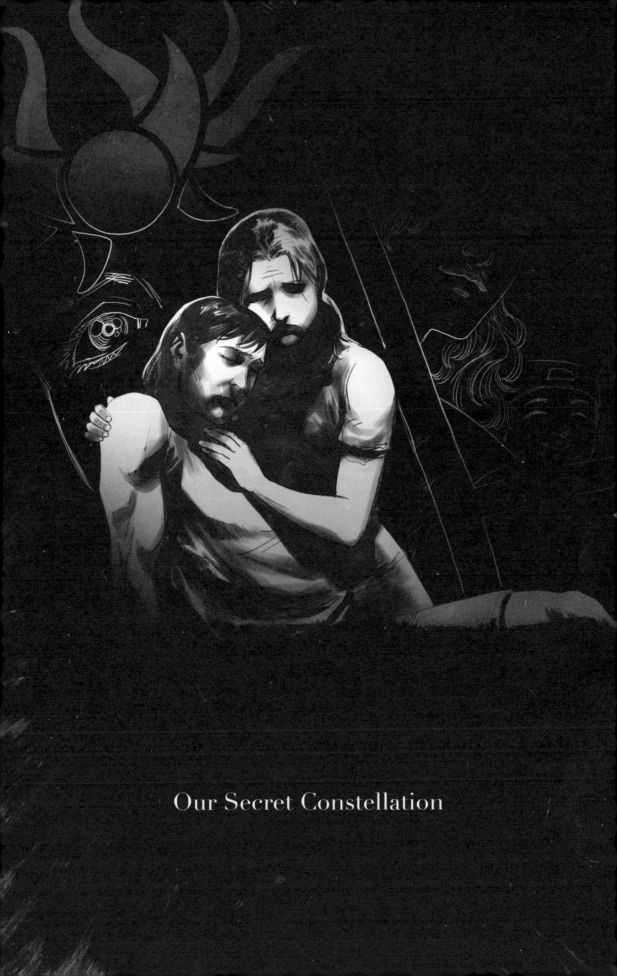

Our Secret Constellation

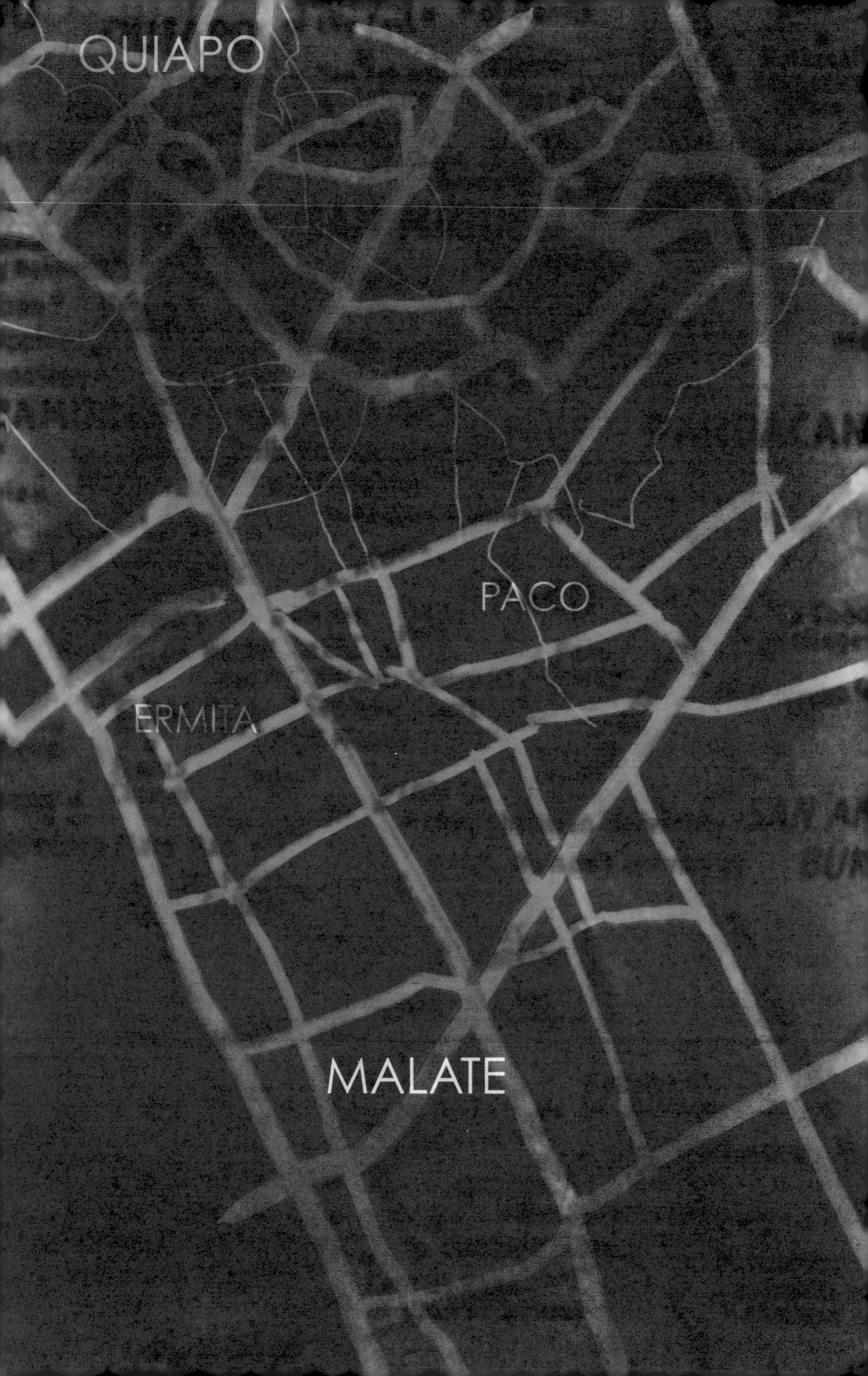
QUIAPO
PACO
ERMITA
MALATE

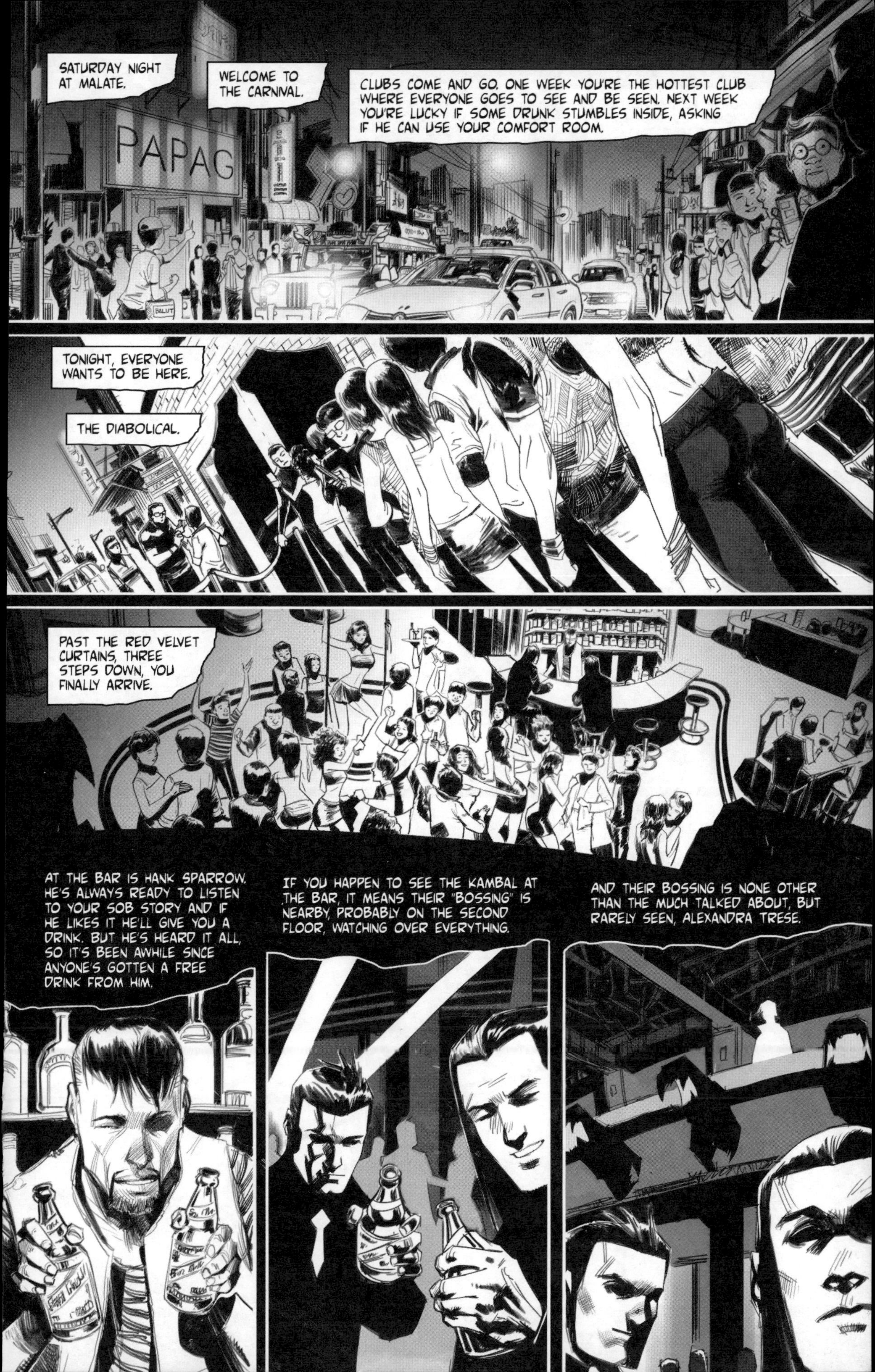
SATURDAY NIGHT AT MALATE.
WELCOME TO THE CARNIVAL.
CLUBS COME AND GO. ONE WEEK YOU'RE THE HOTTEST CLUB WHERE EVERYONE GOES TO SEE AND BE SEEN. NEXT WEEK YOU'RE LUCKY IF SOME DRUNK STUMBLES INSIDE, ASKING IF HE CAN USE YOUR COMFORT ROOM.
PAPAG
BALUT
TONIGHT, EVERYONE WANTS TO BE HERE.
THE DIABOLICAL.
PAST THE RED VELVET CURTAINS, THREE STEPS DOWN, YOU FINALLY ARRIVE.
AT THE BAR IS HANK SPARROW. HE'S ALWAYS READY TO LISTEN TO YOUR SOB STORY AND IF HE LIKES IT HE'LL GIVE YOU A DRINK. BUT HE'S HEARD IT ALL, SO IT'S BEEN AWHILE SINCE ANYONE'S GOTTEN A FREE DRINK FROM HIM.
IF YOU HAPPEN TO SEE THE KAMBAL AT THE BAR, IT MEANS THEIR "BOSSING" IS NEARBY, PROBABLY ON THE SECOND FLOOR, WATCHING OVER EVERYTHING.
AND THEIR BOSSING IS NONE OTHER THAN THE MUCH TALKED ABOUT, BUT RARELY SEEN, ALEXANDRA TRESE.

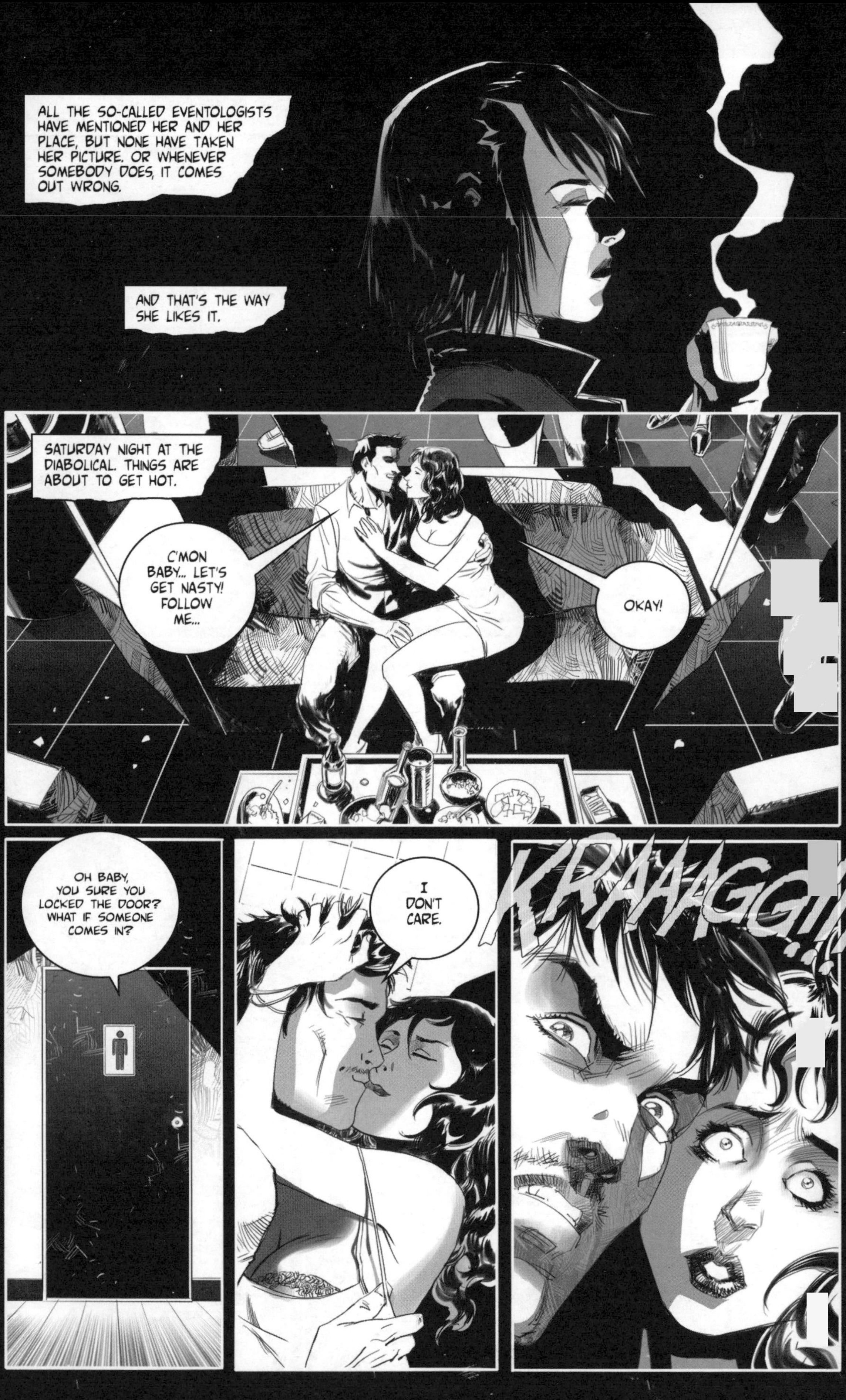
ALL THE SO-CALLED EVENTOLOGISTS HAVE MENTIONED HER AND HER PLACE, BUT NONE HAVE TAKEN HER PICTURE. OR WHENEVER SOMEBODY DOES, IT COMES OUT WRONG.
AND THAT'S THE WAY SHE LIKES IT.
SATURDAY NIGHT AT THE DIABOLICAL. THINGS ARE ABOUT TO GET HOT.
C'MON BABY... LET'S GET NASTY! FOLLOW ME...
OKAY!
OH BABY, YOU SURE YOU LOCKED THE DOOR? WHAT IF SOMEONE COMES IN?
I DON'T CARE.
KRAAAGG!!!

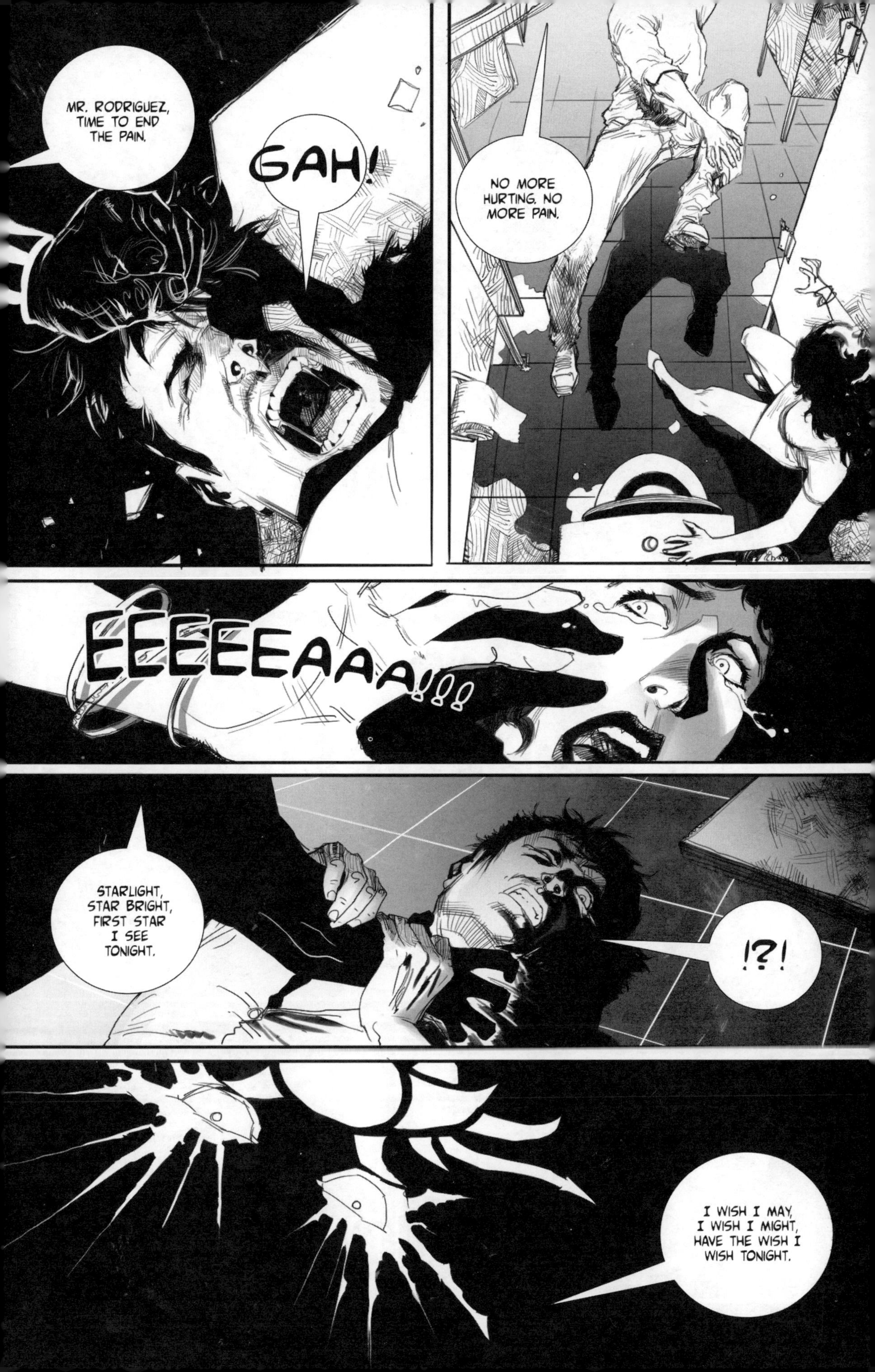

MR. RODRIGUEZ, TIME TO END THE PAIN.
GAH!
NO MORE HURTING. NO MORE PAIN.
EEEEEAAAA!!!
STARLIGHT, STAR BRIGHT, FIRST STAR I SEE TONIGHT.
!?!
I WISH I MAY, I WISH I MIGHT, HAVE THE WISH I WISH TONIGHT.

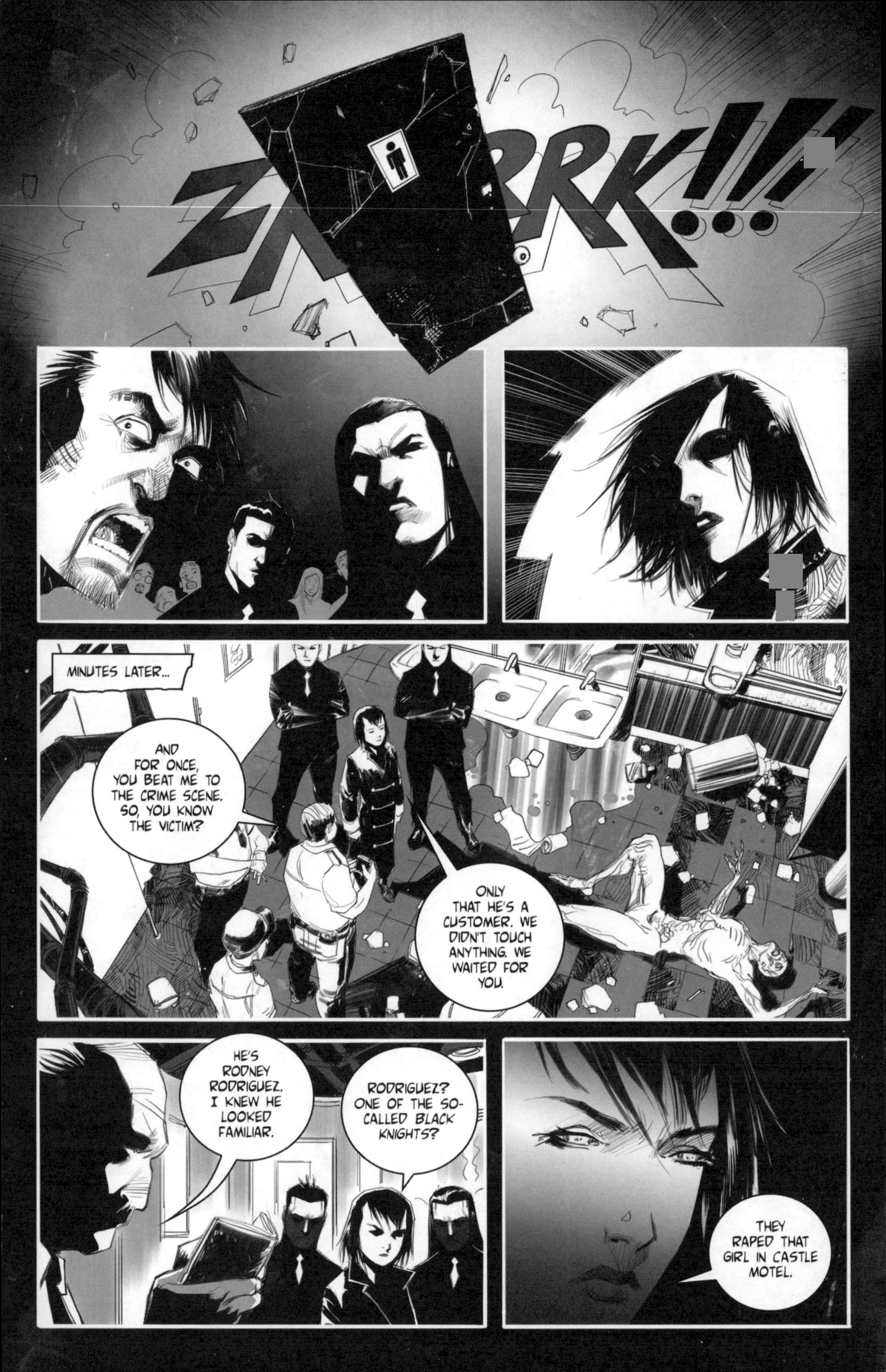
MINUTES LATER...
AND FOR ONCE, YOU BEAT ME TO THE CRIME SCENE. SO, YOU KNOW THE VICTIM?
ONLY THAT HE'S A CUSTOMER. WE DIDN'T TOUCH ANYTHING. WE WAITED FOR YOU.
HE'S RODNEY RODRIGUEZ. I KNEW HE LOOKED FAMILIAR.
RODRIGUEZ? ONE OF THE SO-CALLED BLACK KNIGHTS?
THEY RAPED THAT GIRL IN CASTLE MOTEL.

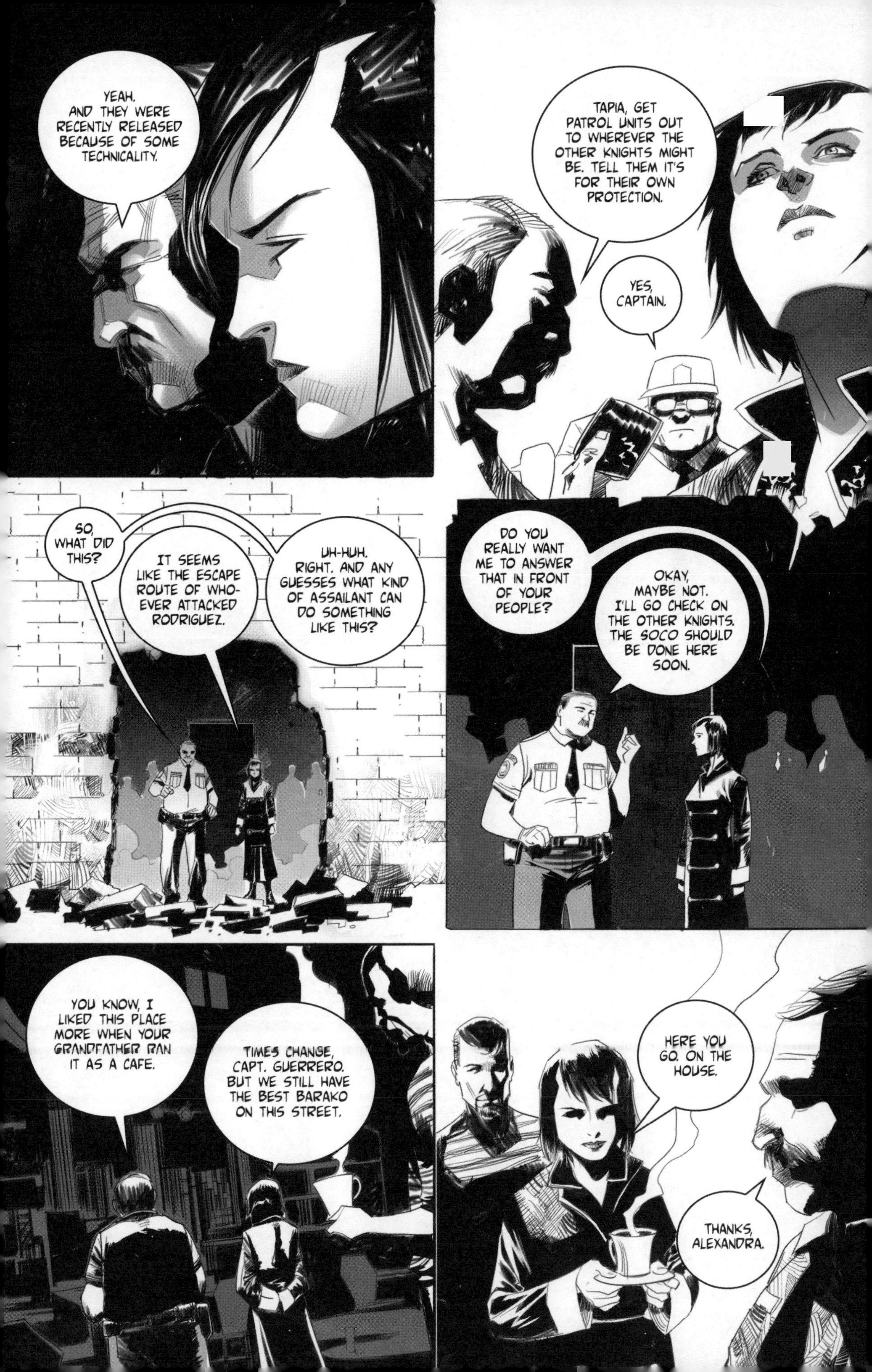
YEAH. AND THEY WERE RECENTLY RELEASED BECAUSE OF SOME TECHNICALITY.
TAPIA, GET PATROL UNITS OUT TO WHEREVER THE OTHER KNIGHTS MIGHT BE. TELL THEM IT'S FOR THEIR OWN PROTECTION.
YES, CAPTAIN.
SO, WHAT DID THIS?
IT SEEMS LIKE THE ESCAPE ROUTE OF WHO-EVER ATTACKED RODRIGUEZ.
UH-HUH. RIGHT. AND ANY GUESSES WHAT KIND OF ASSAILANT CAN DO SOMETHING LIKE THIS?
DO YOU REALLY WANT ME TO ANSWER THAT IN FRONT OF YOUR PEOPLE?
OKAY, MAYBE NOT. I'LL GO CHECK ON THE OTHER KNIGHTS. THE SOCO SHOULD BE DONE HERE SOON.
YOU KNOW, I LIKED THIS PLACE MORE WHEN YOUR GRANDFATHER RAN IT AS A CAFE.
TIMES CHANGE, CAPT. GUERRERO. BUT WE STILL HAVE THE BEST BARAKO ON THIS STREET.
HERE YOU GO. ON THE HOUSE.
THANKS, ALEXANDRA.

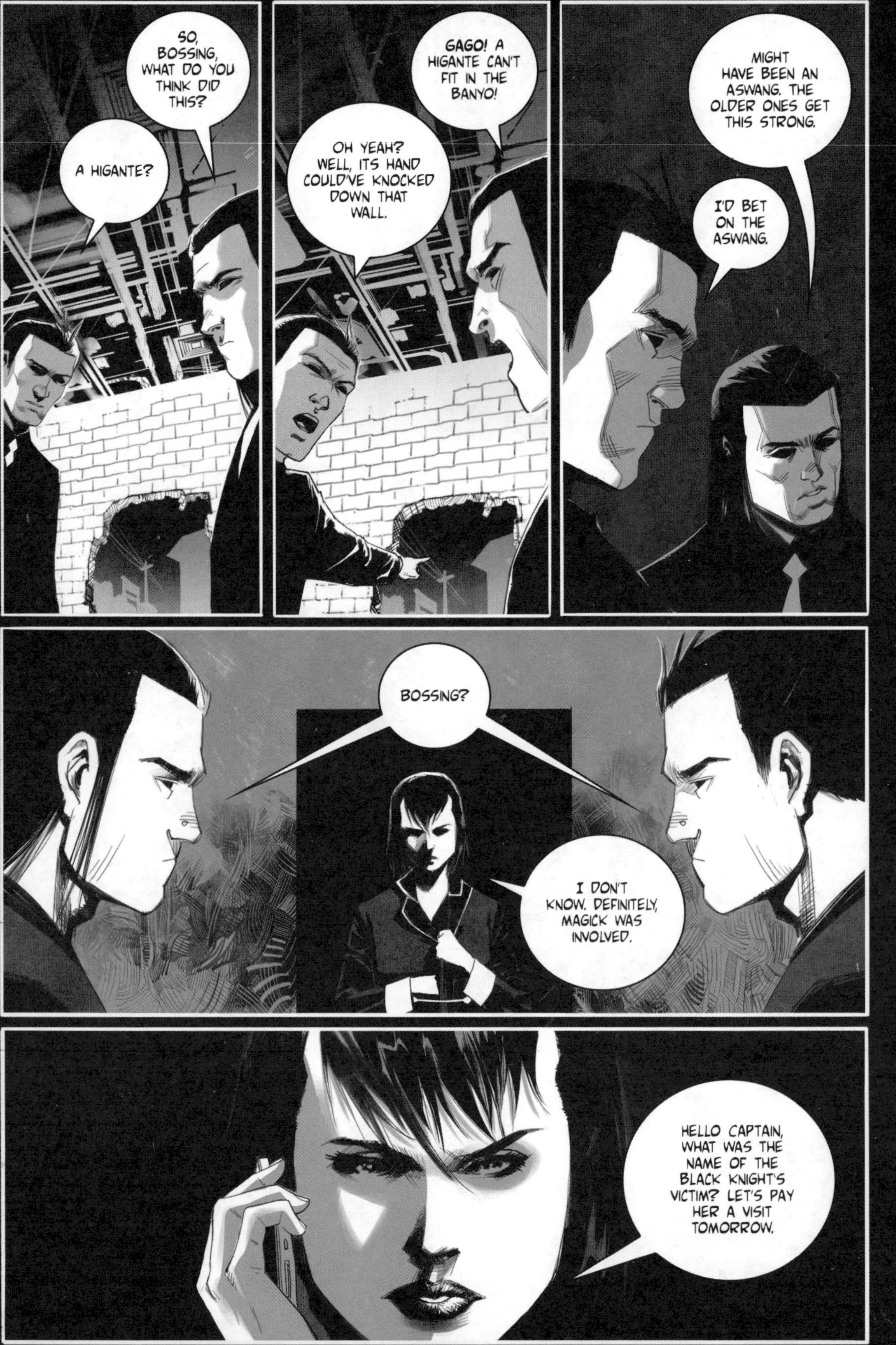
SO, BOSSING, WHAT DO YOU THINK DID THIS?
A HIGANTE?
GAGO! A HIGANTE CAN'T FIT IN THE BANYO!
OH YEAH? WELL, ITS HAND COULD'VE KNOCKED DOWN THAT WALL.
MIGHT HAVE BEEN AN ASWANG. THE OLDER ONES GET THIS STRONG.
I'D BET ON THE ASWANG.
BOSSING?
I DON'T KNOW. DEFINITELY, MAGICK WAS INVOLVED.
HELLO CAPTAIN, WHAT WAS THE NAME OF THE BLACK KNIGHT'S VICTIM? LET'S PAY HER A VISIT TOMORROW.

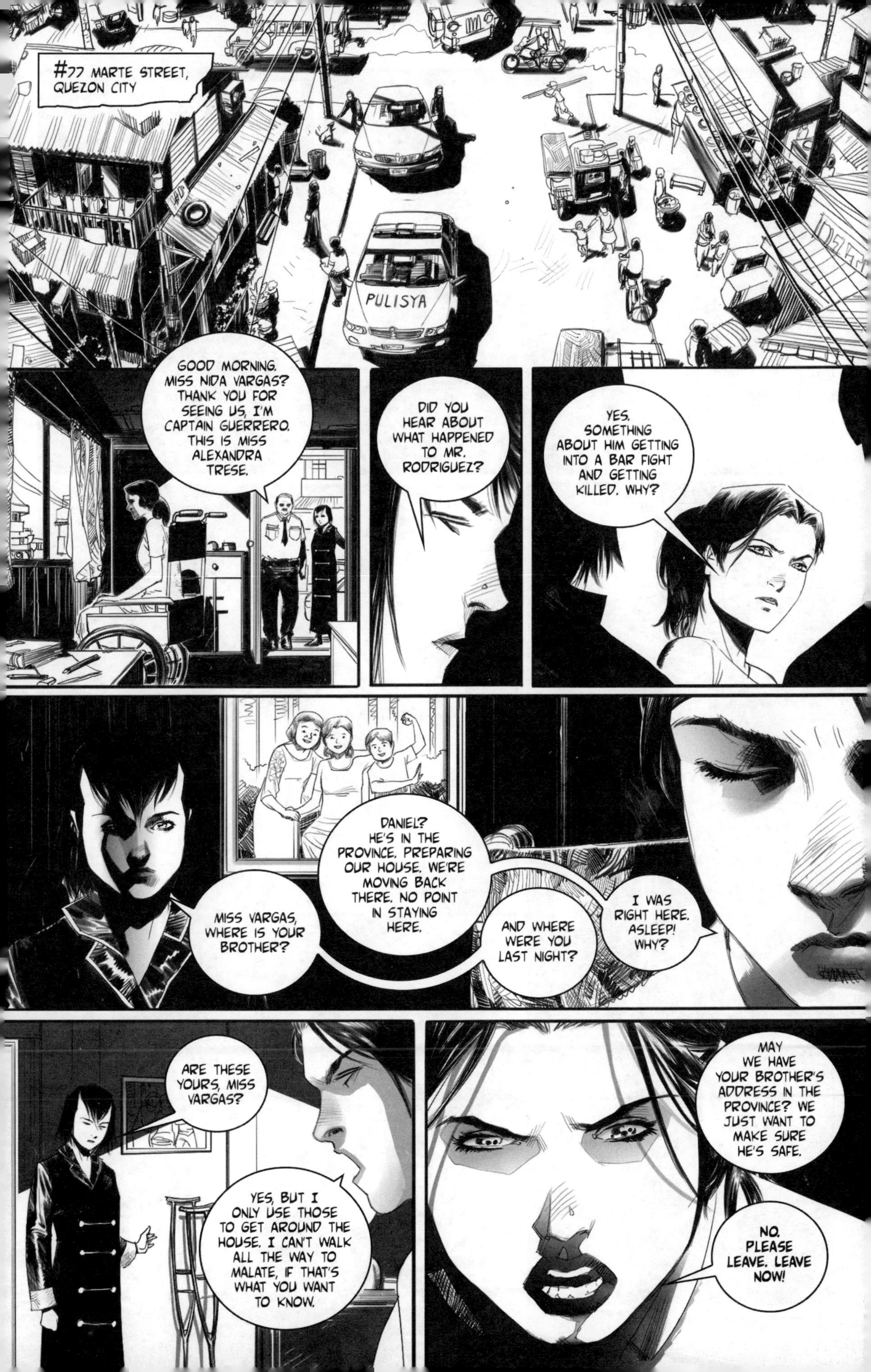

#77 MARTE STREET, QUEZON CITY
PULISYA
GOOD MORNING. MISS NIDA VARGAS? THANK YOU FOR SEEING US, I'M CAPTAIN GUERRERO. THIS IS MISS ALEXANDRA TRESE.
DID YOU HEAR ABOUT WHAT HAPPENED TO MR. RODRIGUEZ?
YES. SOMETHING ABOUT HIM GETTING INTO A BAR FIGHT AND GETTING KILLED. WHY?
MISS VARGAS, WHERE IS YOUR BROTHER?
DANIEL? HE'S IN THE PROVINCE, PREPARING OUR HOUSE. WE'RE MOVING BACK THERE. NO POINT IN STAYING HERE.
AND WHERE WERE YOU LAST NIGHT?
I WAS RIGHT HERE. ASLEEP! WHY?
ARE THESE YOURS, MISS VARGAS?
YES, BUT I ONLY USE THOSE TO GET AROUND THE HOUSE. I CAN'T WALK ALL THE WAY TO MALATE, IF THAT'S WHAT YOU WANT TO KNOW.
MAY WE HAVE YOUR BROTHER'S ADDRESS IN THE PROVINCE? WE JUST WANT TO MAKE SURE HE'S SAFE.
NO. PLEASE LEAVE. LEAVE NOW!

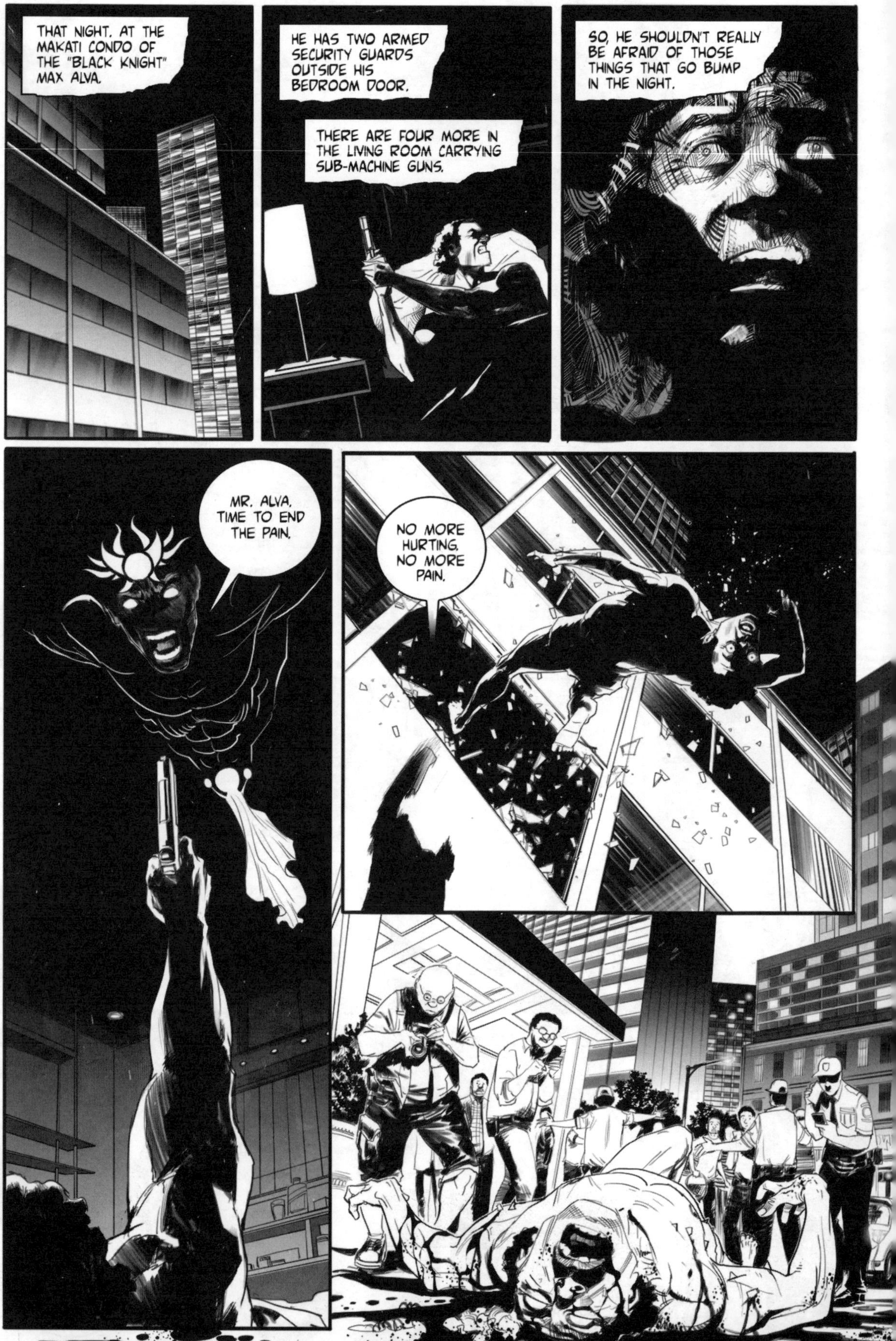
THAT NIGHT, AT THE MAKATI CONDO OF THE "BLACK KNIGHT" MAX ALVA.
HE HAS TWO ARMED SECURITY GUARDS OUTSIDE HIS BEDROOM DOOR.
THERE ARE FOUR MORE IN THE LIVING ROOM CARRYING SUB-MACHINE GUNS.
SO, HE SHOULDN'T REALLY BE AFRAID OF THOSE THINGS THAT GO BUMP IN THE NIGHT.
MR. ALVA, TIME TO END THE PAIN.
NO MORE HURTING, NO MORE PAIN.

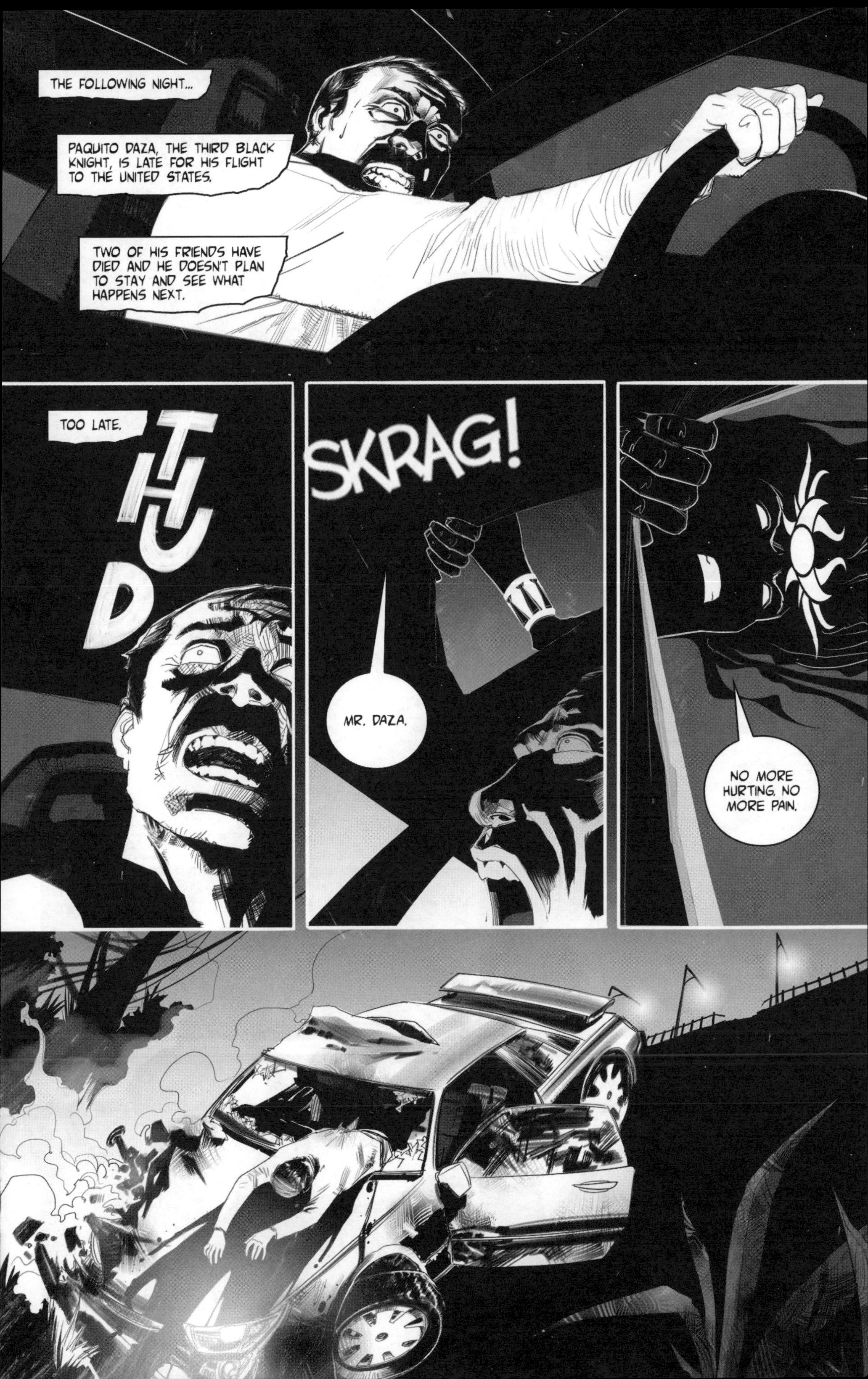
THE FOLLOWING NIGHT...
PAQUITO DAZA, THE THIRD BLACK KNIGHT, IS LATE FOR HIS FLIGHT TO THE UNITED STATES.
TWO OF HIS FRIENDS HAVE DIED AND HE DOESN'T PLAN TO STAY AND SEE WHAT HAPPENS NEXT.
TOO LATE.
THUD
SKRAG!
MR. DAZA.
NO MORE HURTING. NO MORE PAIN.

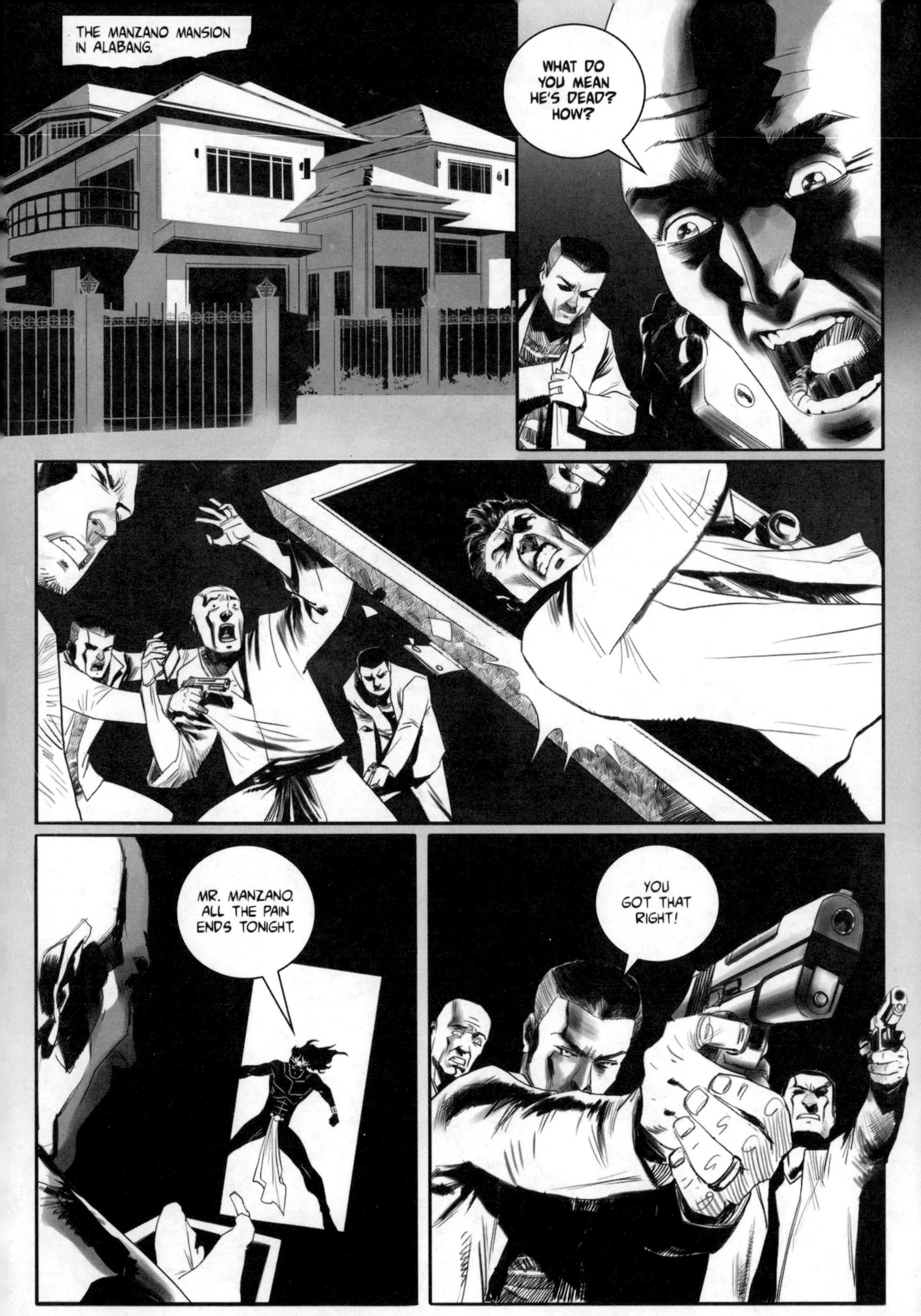
THE MANZANO MANSION IN ALABANG.
WHAT DO YOU MEAN HE'S DEAD? HOW?
MR. MANZANO. ALL THE PAIN ENDS TONIGHT.
YOU GOT THAT RIGHT!

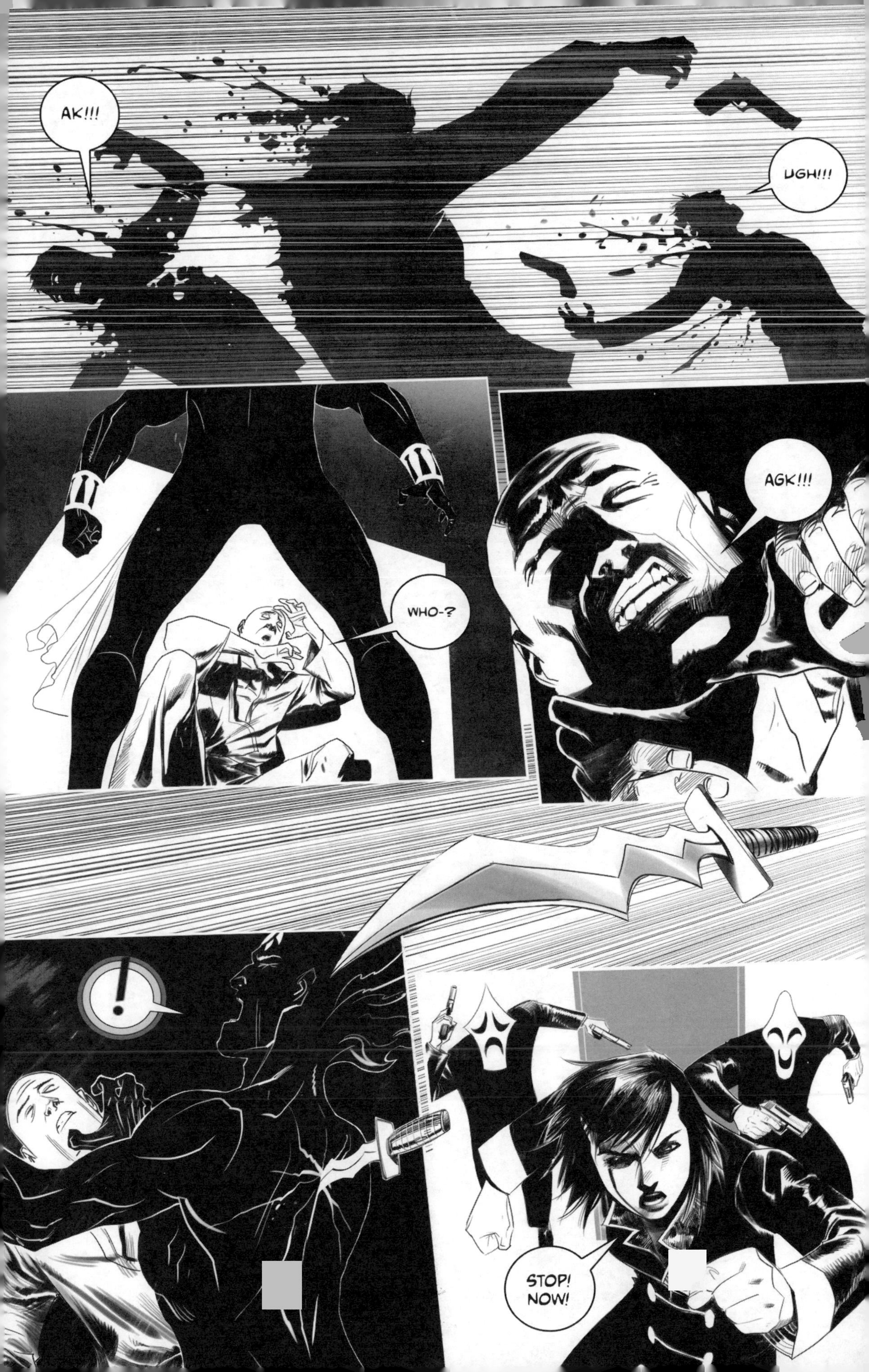

AK!!!
UGH!!!
WHO-?
AGK!!!
!
STOP! NOW!

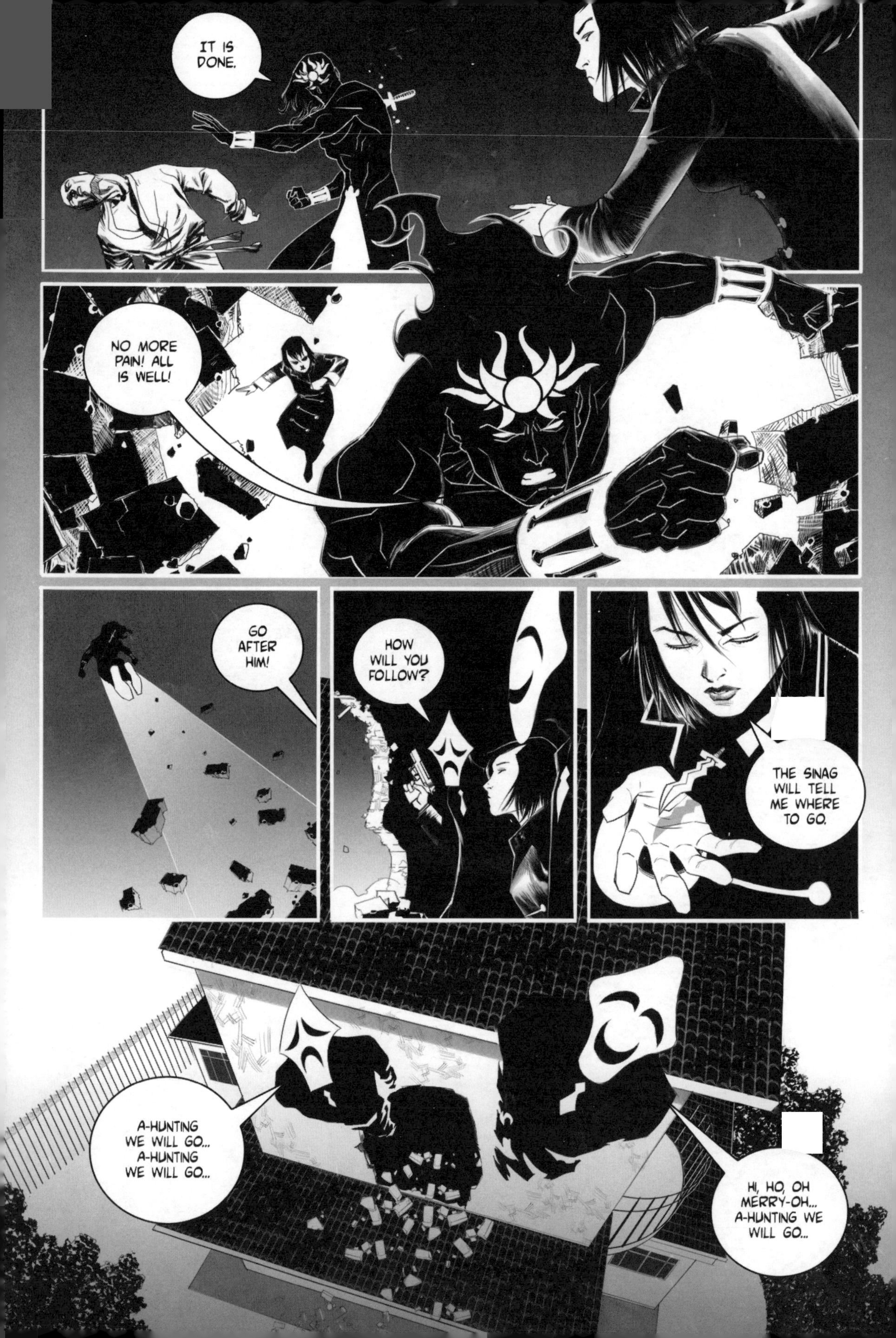
IT IS DONE.
NO MORE PAIN! ALL IS WELL!
GO AFTER HIM!
HOW WILL YOU FOLLOW?
THE SINAG WILL TELL ME WHERE TO GO.
A-HUNTING WE WILL GO... A-HUNTING WE WILL GO...
HI, HO, OH MERRY-OH... A-HUNTING WE WILL GO...

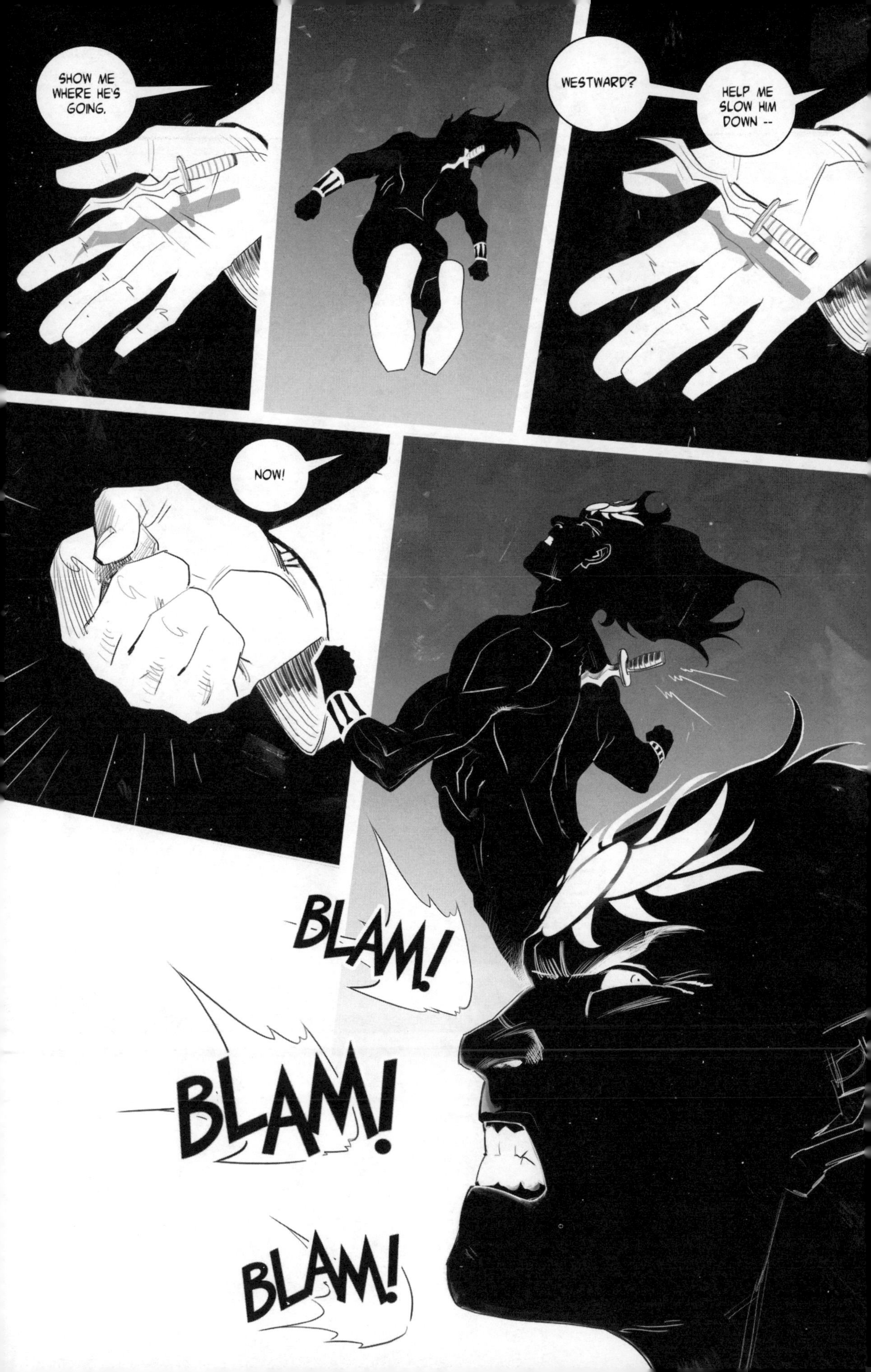
SHOW ME WHERE HE'S GOING.
WESTWARD?
HELP ME SLOW HIM DOWN --
NOW!
BLAM!
BLAM!
BLAM!

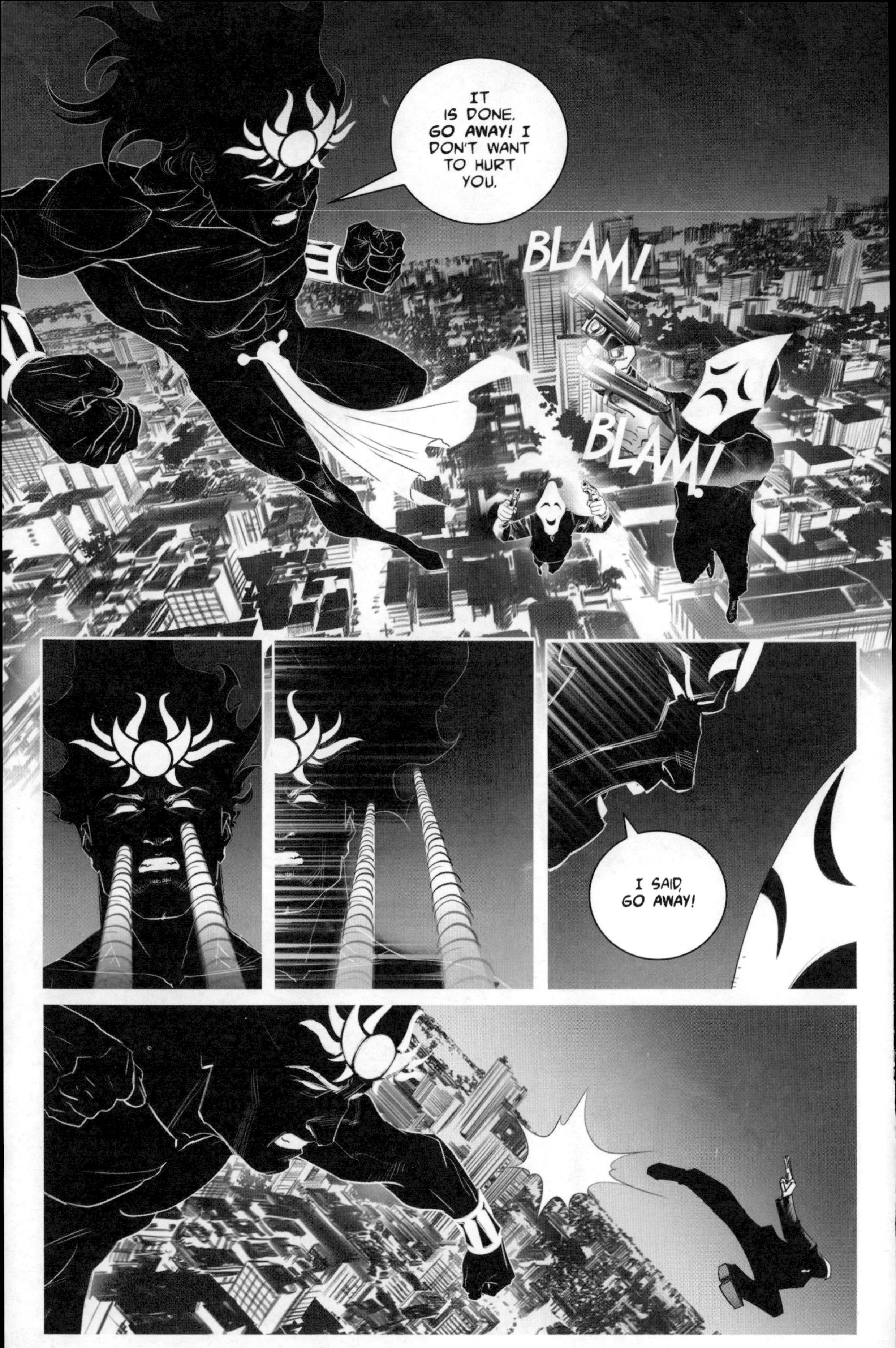
IT IS DONE. GO AWAY! I DON'T WANT TO HURT YOU.
BLAM!
BLAM!
I SAID, GO AWAY!

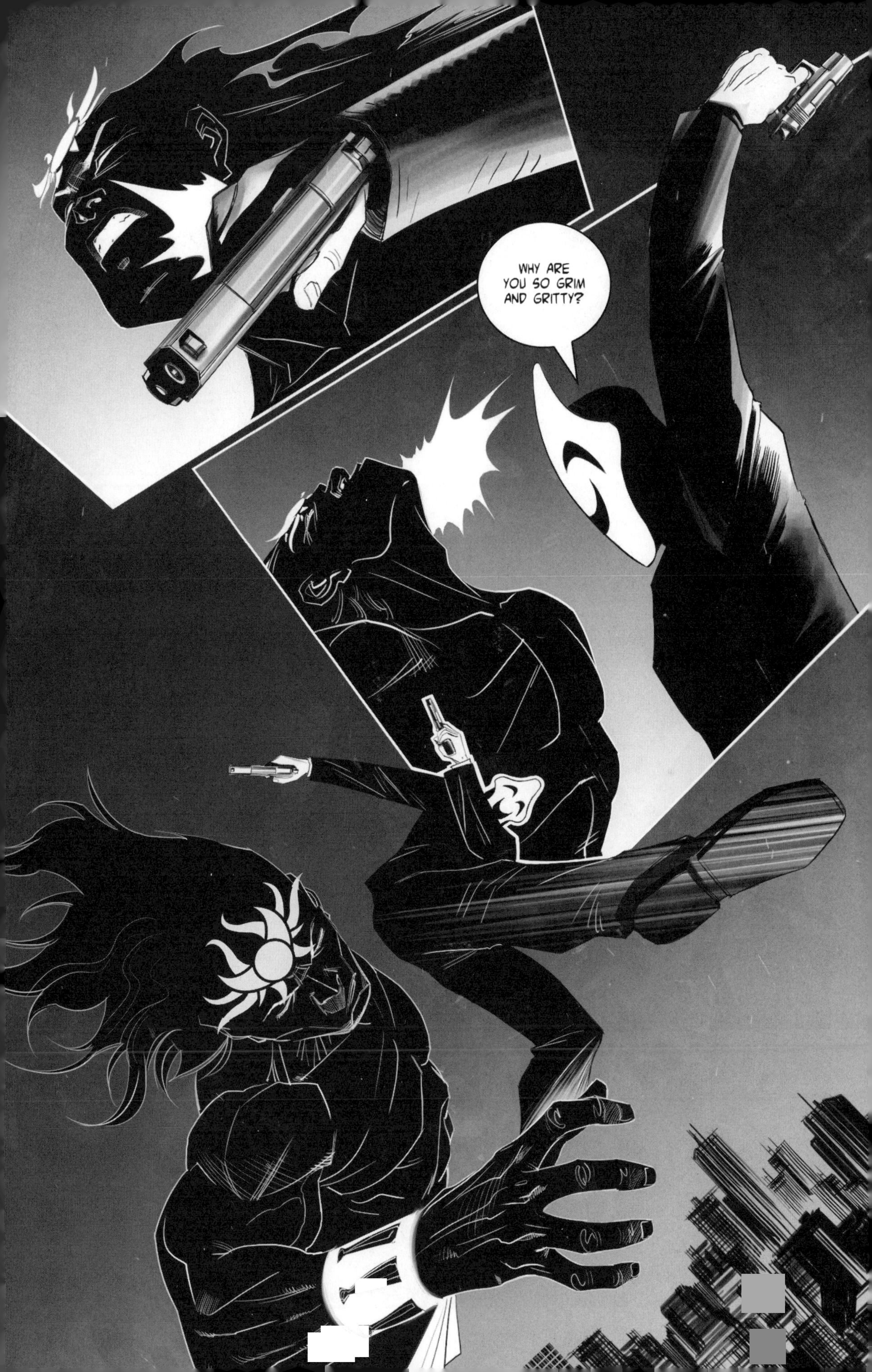
WHY ARE YOU SO GRIM AND GRITTY?

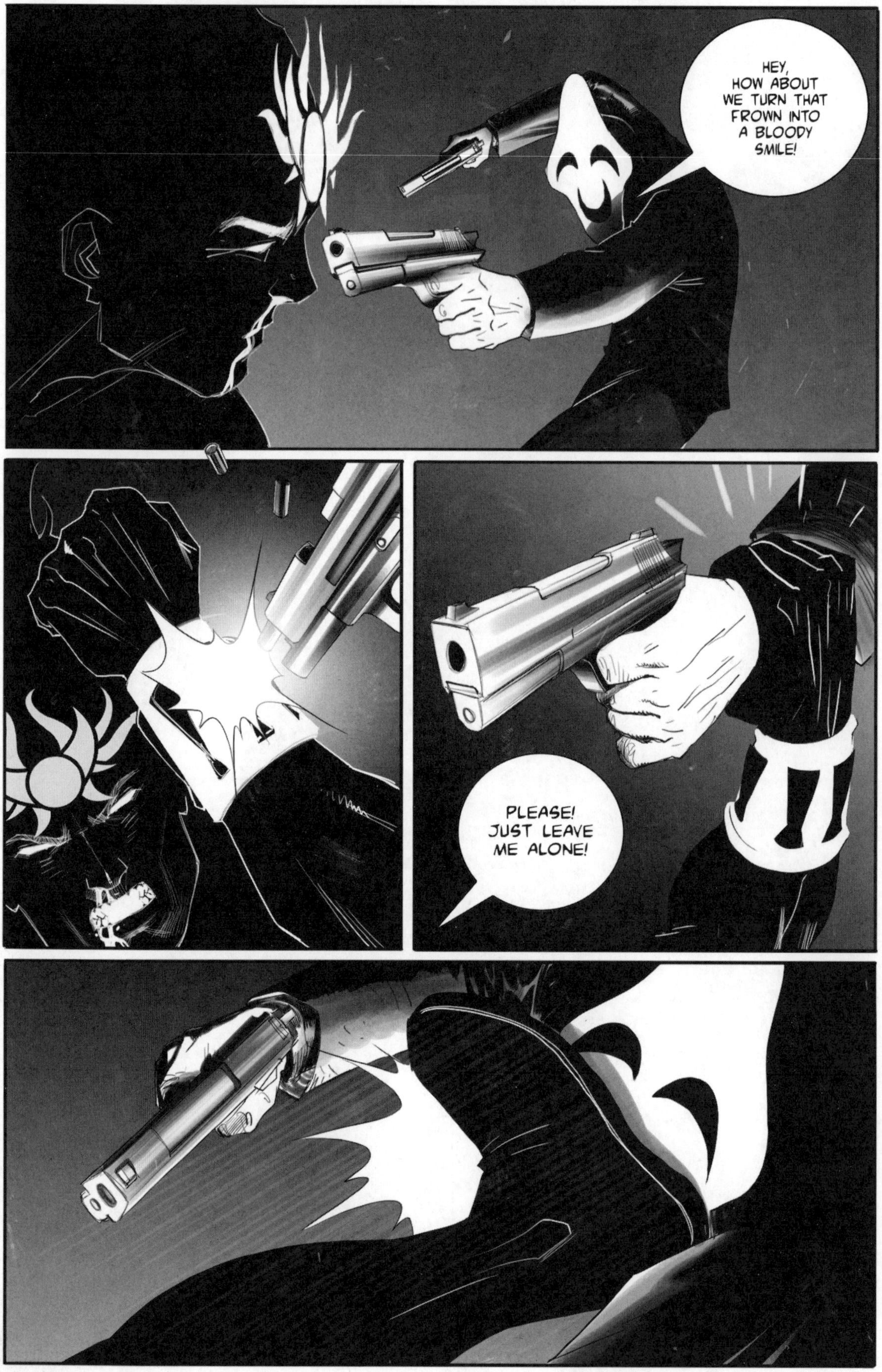
HEY, HOW ABOUT WE TURN THAT FROWN INTO A BLOODY SMILE!
PLEASE! JUST LEAVE ME ALONE!

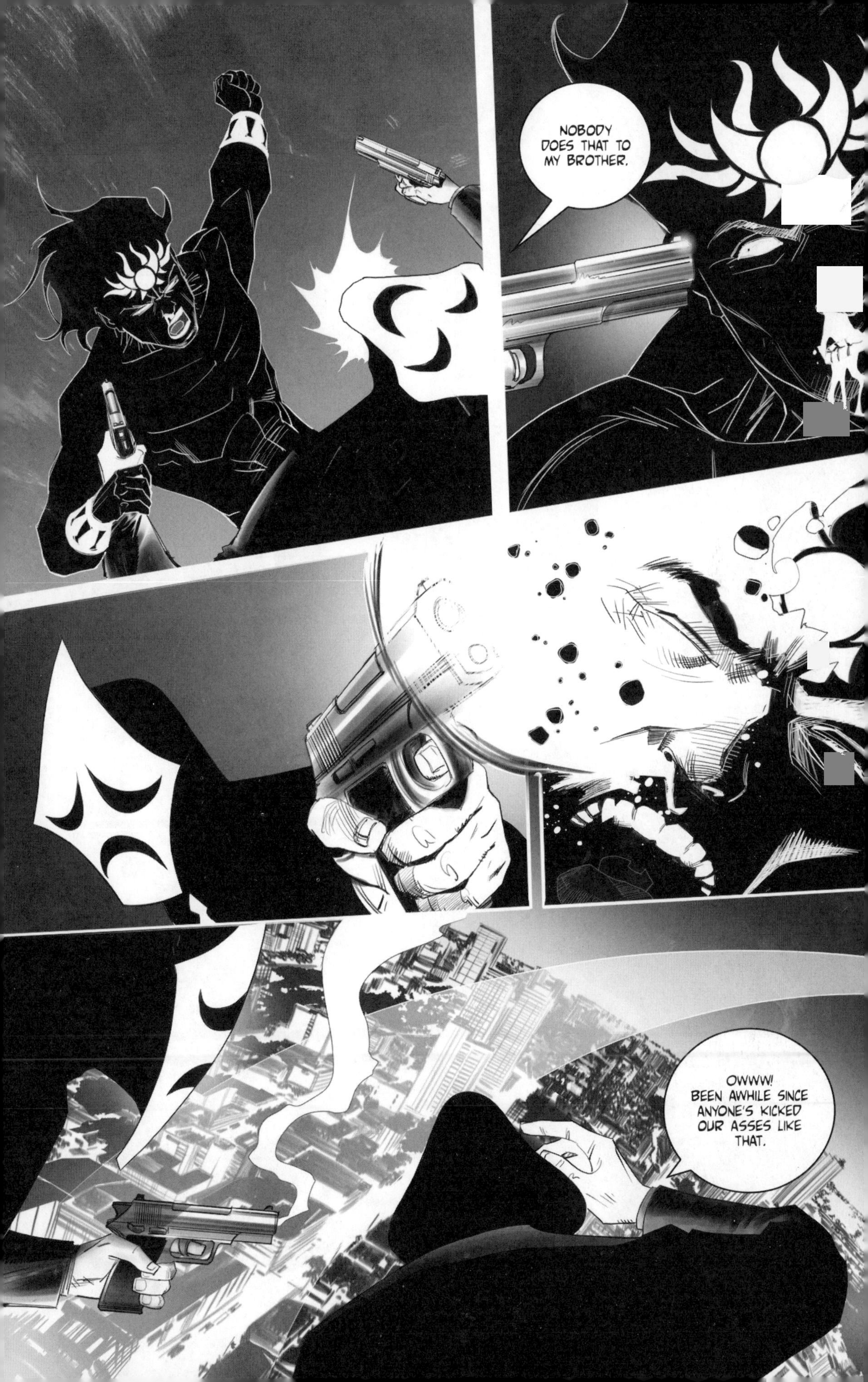
NOBODY DOES THAT TO MY BROTHER.
OWWW! BEEN AWHILE SINCE ANYONE'S KICKED OUR ASSES LIKE THAT.

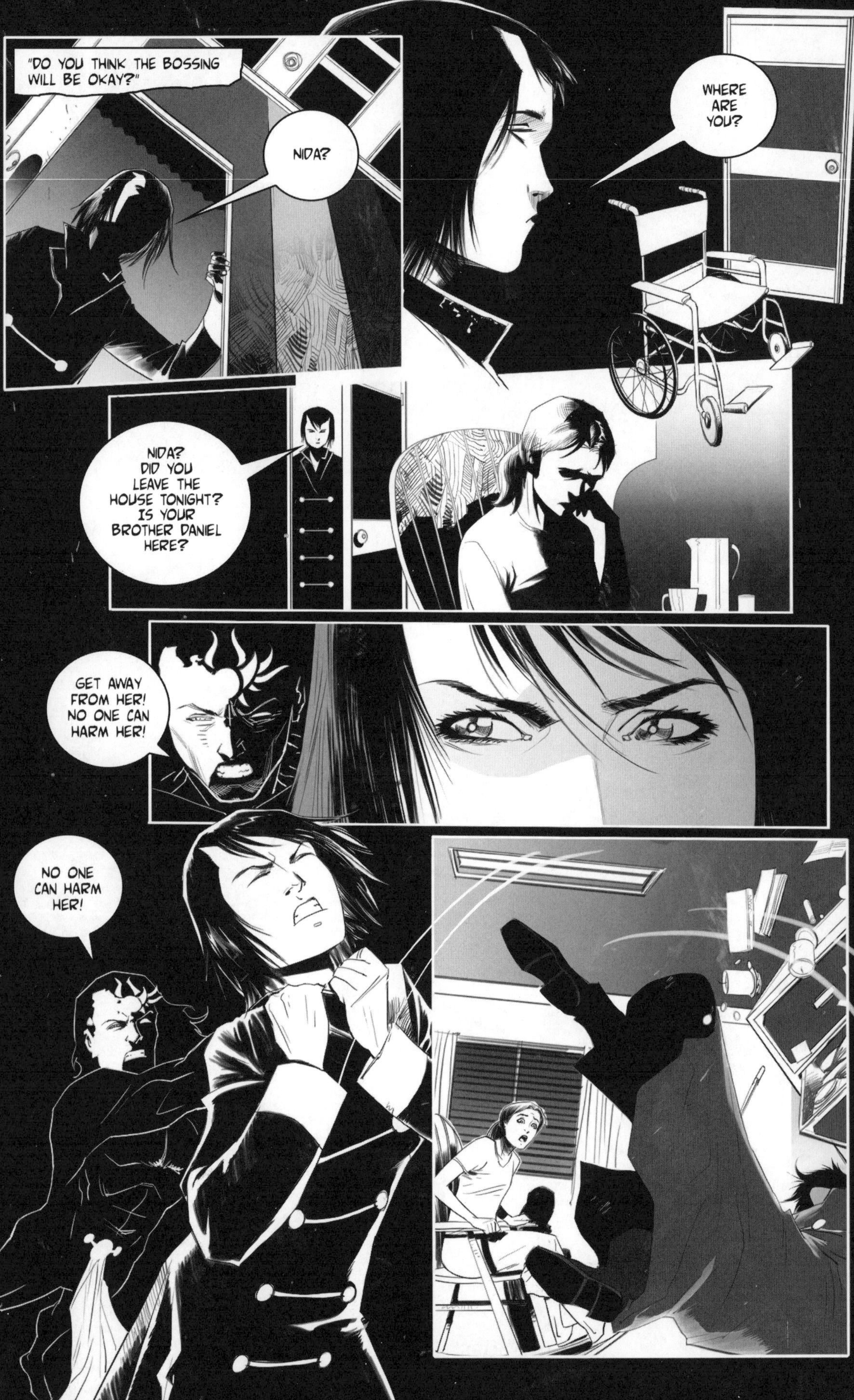

"DO YOU THINK THE BOSSING WILL BE OKAY?"
NIDA?
WHERE ARE YOU?
NIDA? DID YOU LEAVE THE HOUSE TONIGHT? IS YOUR BROTHER DANIEL HERE?
GET AWAY FROM HER! NO ONE CAN HARM HER!
NO ONE CAN HARM HER!

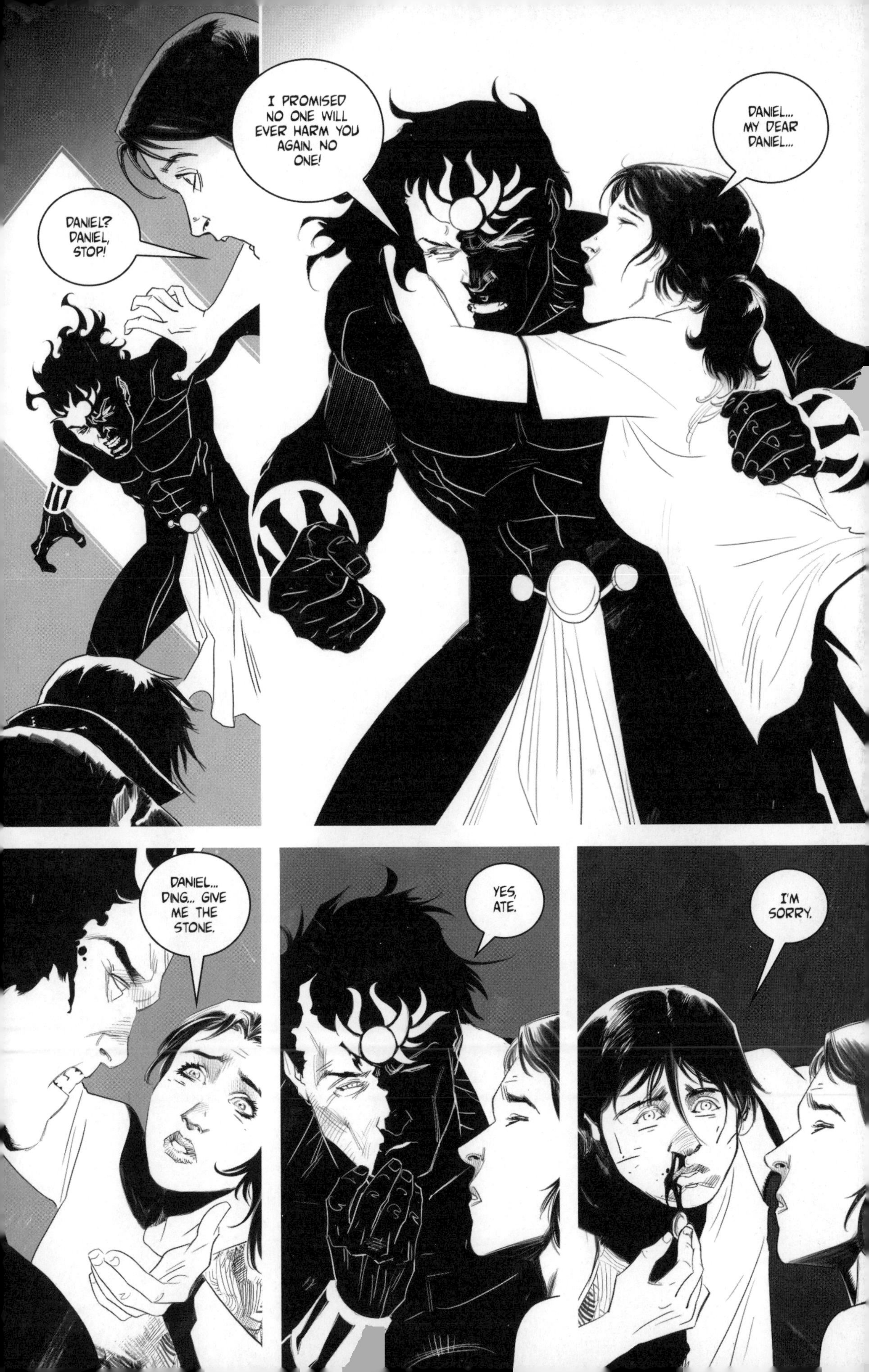
DANIEL? DANIEL, STOP!
I PROMISED NO ONE WILL EVER HARM YOU AGAIN. NO ONE!
DANIEL... MY DEAR DANIEL...
DANIEL... DING... GIVE ME THE STONE.
YES, ATE.
I'M SORRY.

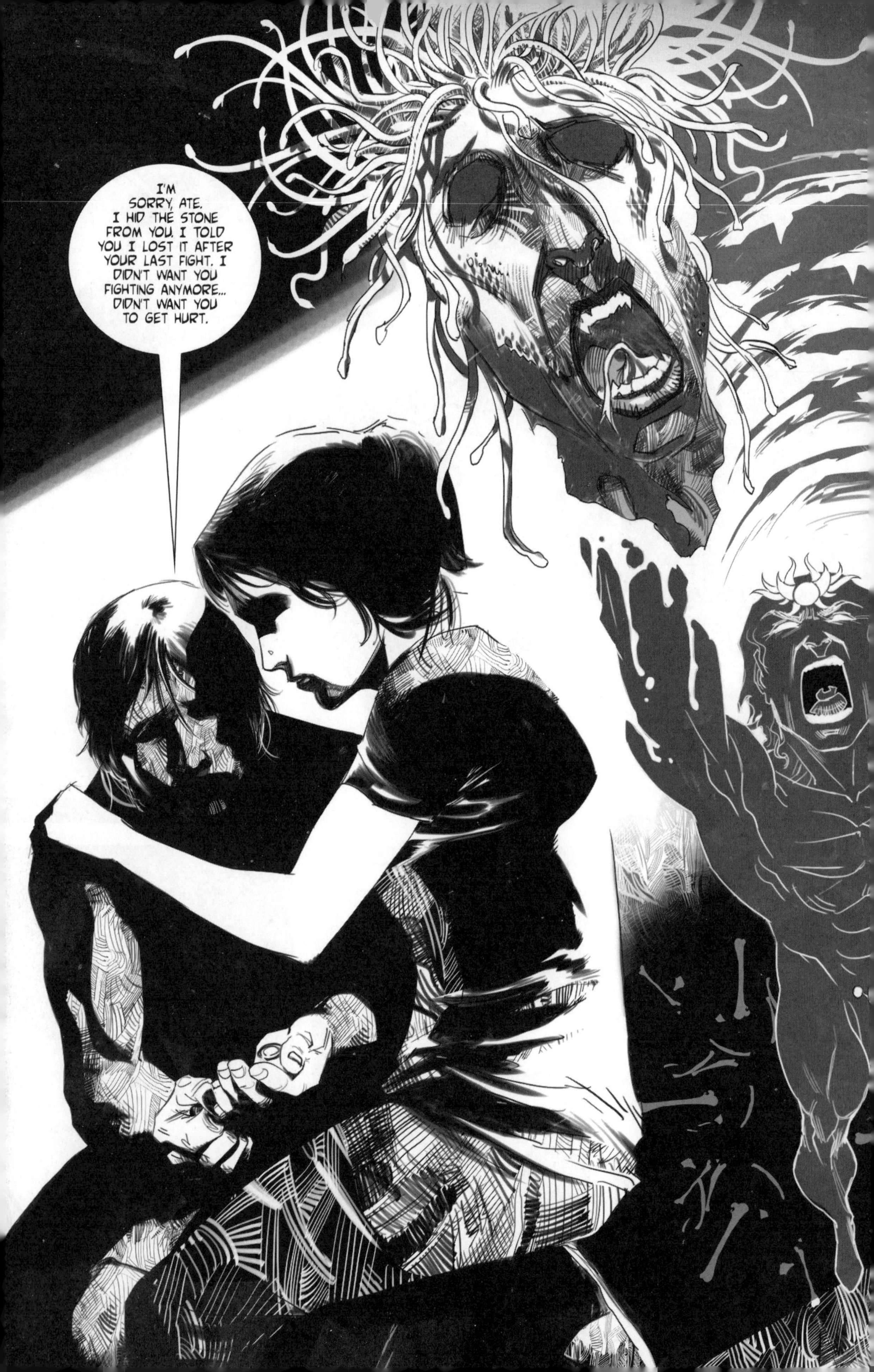
I'M SORRY, ATE. I HID THE STONE FROM YOU. I TOLD YOU I LOST IT AFTER YOUR LAST FIGHT. I DIDN'T WANT YOU FIGHTING ANYMORE... DIDN'T WANT YOU TO GET HURT.

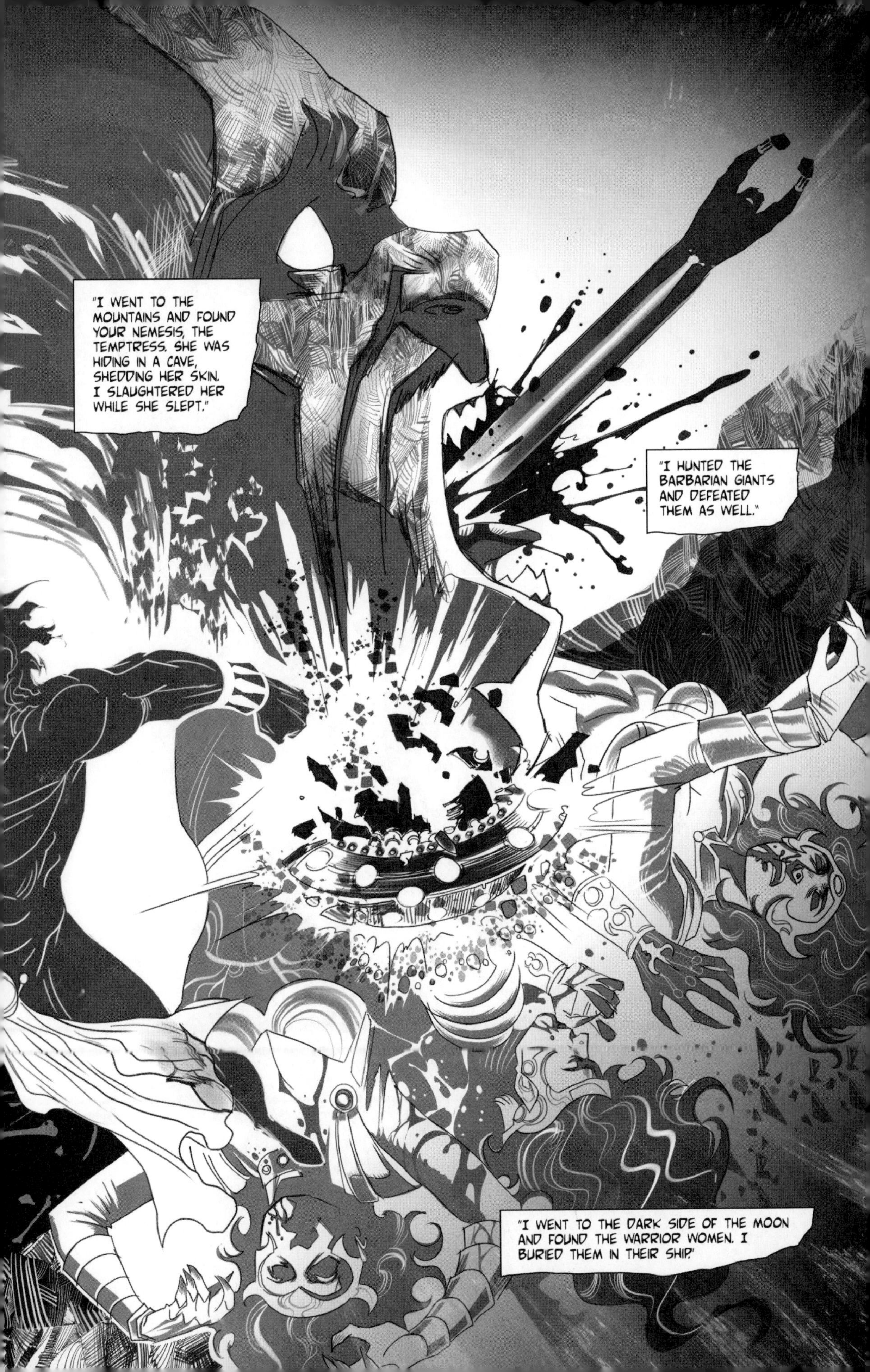
"I WENT TO THE MOUNTAINS AND FOUND YOUR NEMESIS, THE TEMPTRESS. SHE WAS HIDING IN A CAVE, SHEDDING HER SKIN. I SLAUGHTERED HER WHILE SHE SLEPT."
"I HUNTED THE BARBARIAN GIANTS AND DEFEATED THEM AS WELL."
"I WENT TO THE DARK SIDE OF THE MOON AND FOUND THE WARRIOR WOMEN. I BURIED THEM IN THEIR SHIP."

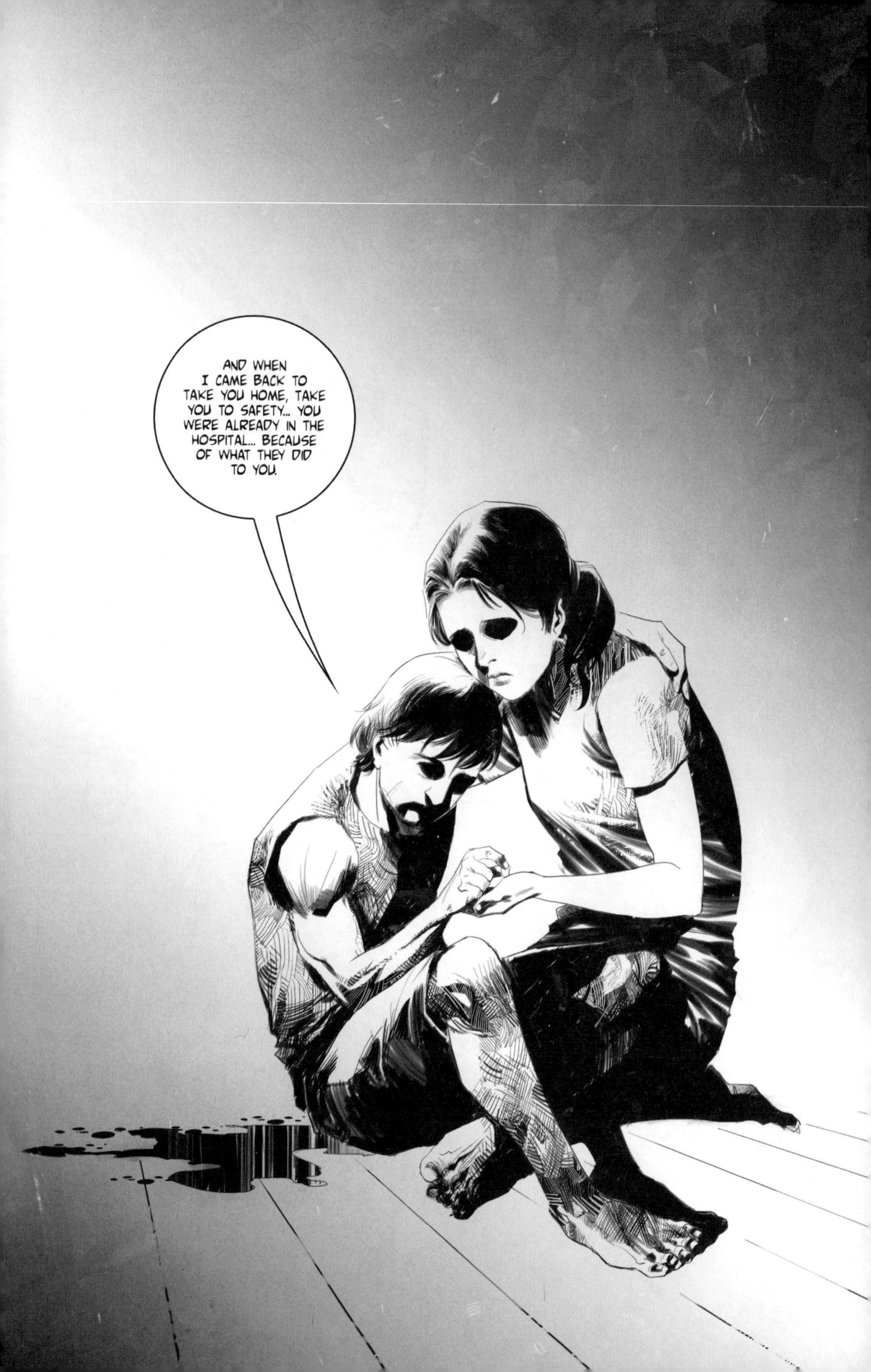
AND WHEN I CAME BACK TO TAKE YOU HOME, TAKE YOU TO SAFETY... YOU WERE ALREADY IN THE HOSPITAL... BECAUSE OF WHAT THEY DID TO YOU.

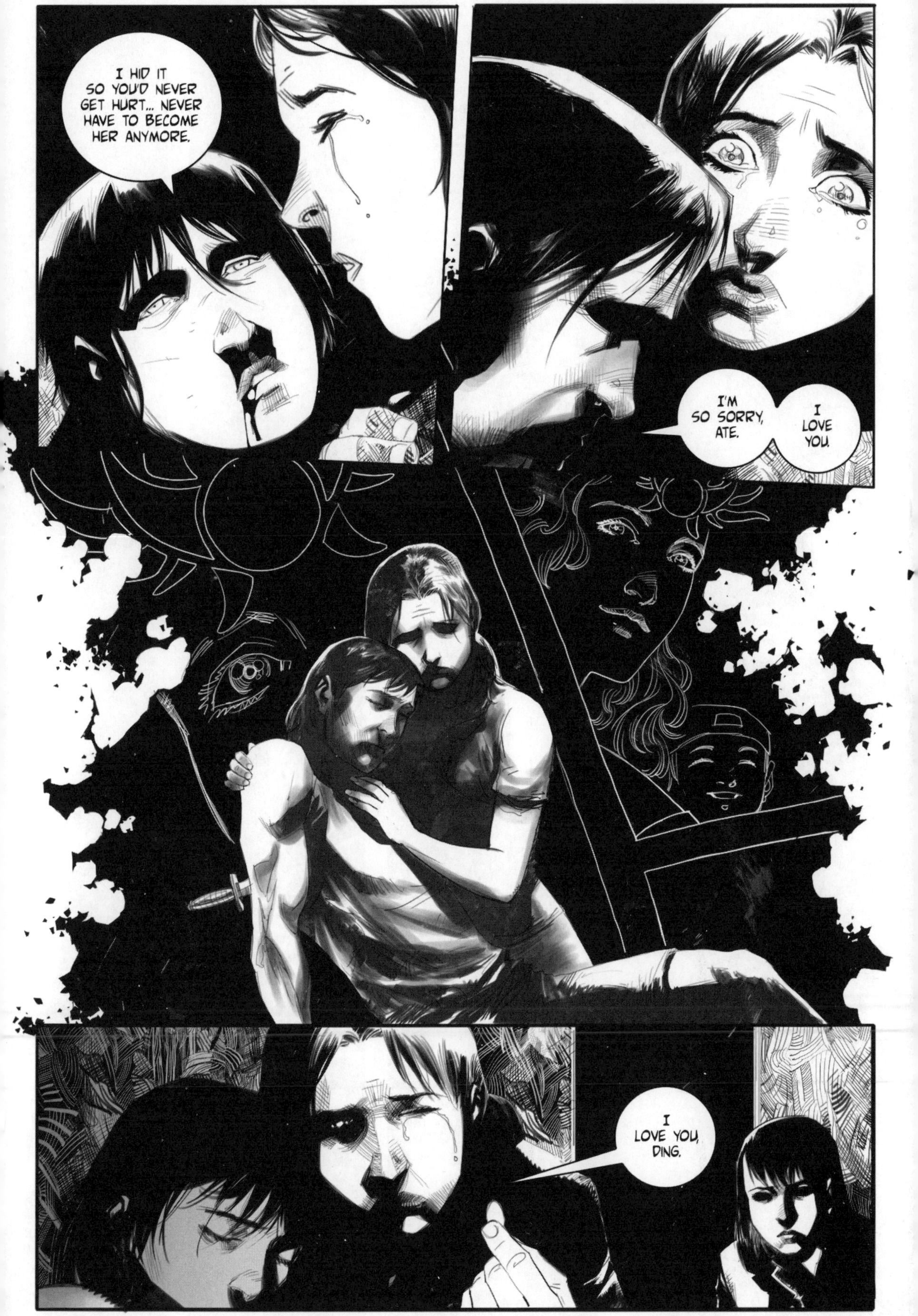

I HID IT SO YOU'D NEVER GET HURT... NEVER HAVE TO BECOME HER ANYMORE.
I'M SO SORRY, ATE.
I LOVE YOU.
I LOVE YOU, DING.

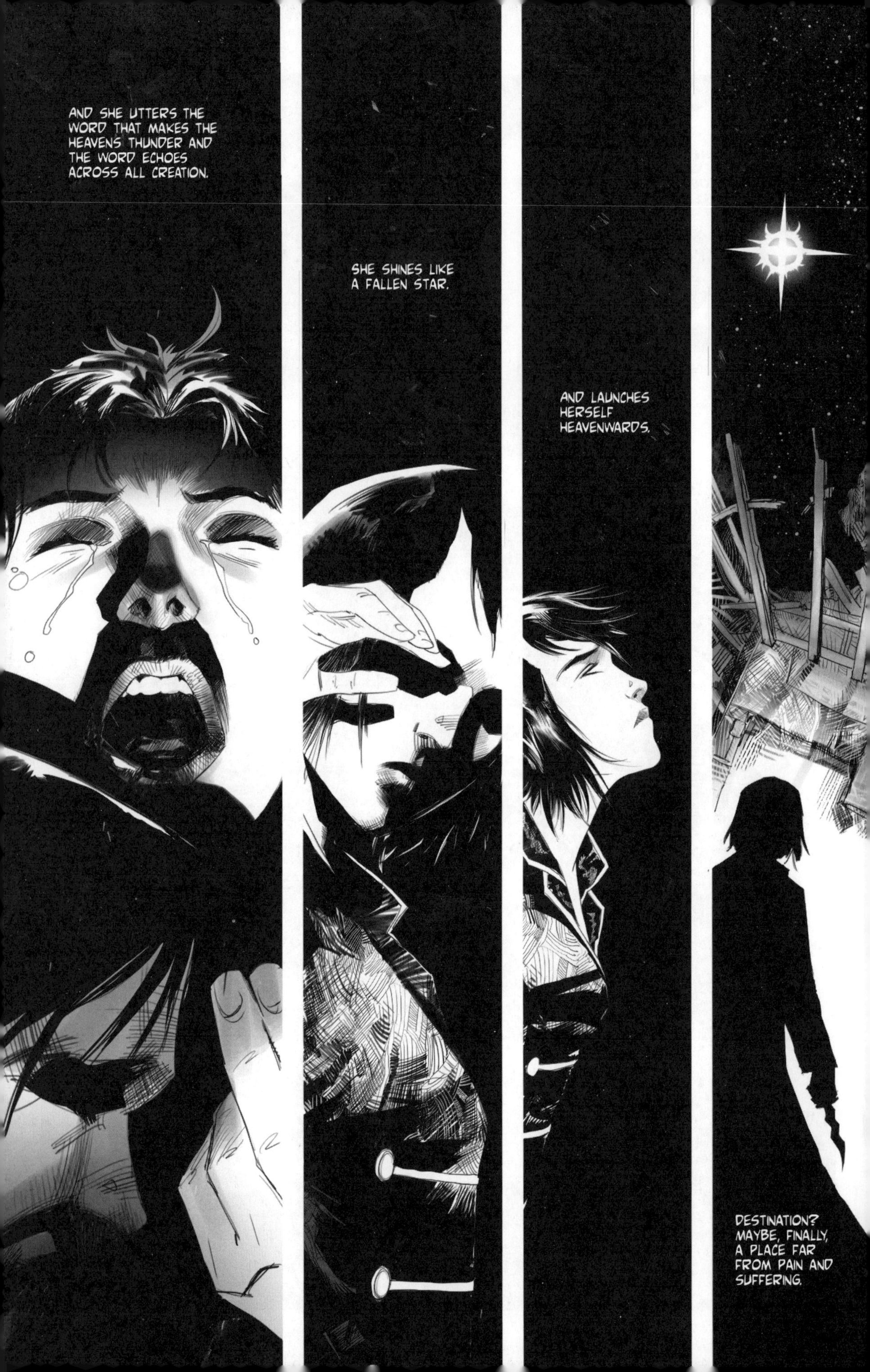
AND SHE UTTERS THE WORD THAT MAKES THE HEAVENS THUNDER AND THE WORD ECHOES ACROSS ALL CREATION.
SHE SHINES LIKE A FALLEN STAR.
AND LAUNCHES HERSELF HEAVENWARDS.
DESTINATION? MAYBE, FINALLY, A PLACE FAR FROM PAIN AND SUFFERING.

We dedicate this story to
Mars Ravelo and **Nestor Redondo**
who inspired us to fly high and seek better days.

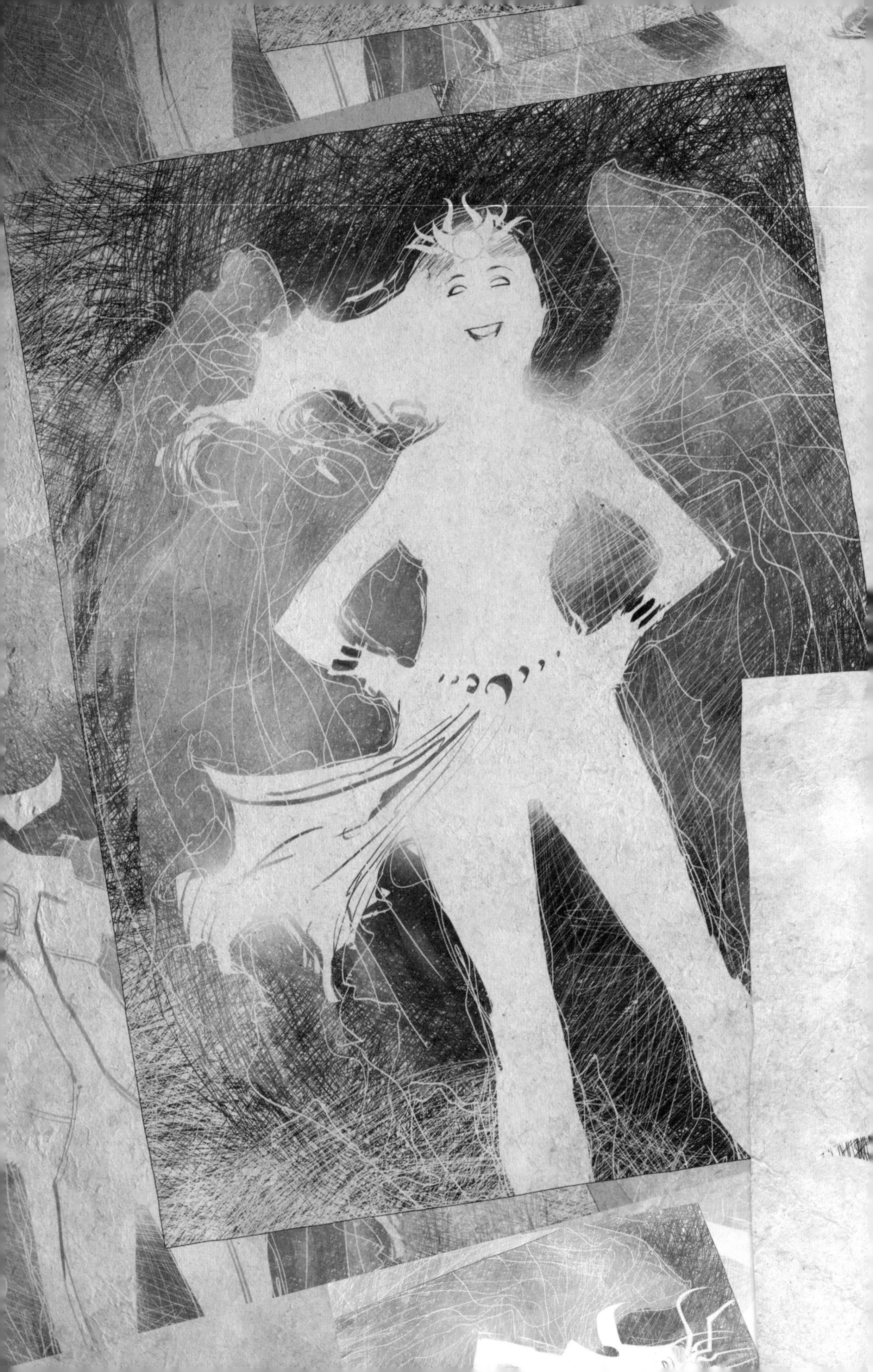

March 8

The Adarna Stone

In one of the highest levels of skyworld, there is a rock formation that floats above all and has been in existence ever since the universe began – so we have been told by the entities from the Wind Tribe and Star Tribe.

This sacred rock is called the Rock of Bathala. Every now and again, a piece from this holy stone falls on earth, granting great power to whoever finds it.

One such stone fell into the hands of a girl, which gave her a new form and the powers and abilities of Bathala's Adarna Warriors.

The people thought she was a super hero come to life. It didn't matter to her. She defended the country from all kinds of attacks from the underworld.

We discovered that she is usually accompanied by her younger brother when she goes on her adventures. Even though he was not gifted with a magical stone or any powers, this has not stopped him from always being there for his sister. The bravery and sense-of-duty of these siblings are highly admirable.

One can't help but wonder how many people have been granted with a shard of the Rock of Bathala. What happens when that power is misused?

AFTERWORD

"And when Budjette was six months old, he was possessed by the spirit of the old man who haunted our house!"

While other mothers would have cute memories about what their babies were doing during their early years, my mom told this ghost story – which I often heard as she'd recount the tale for relatives and friends.

As the story goes, we moved into this house where strange things started to happen – lights switching on and off by themselves, objects suddenly moving on their own, and voices being heard from empty rooms. All these incidents happened to the other people in the house and my mom didn't believe their wild stories.

One afternoon, after she had given me a bath, she gently placed me on the bed, turned around to get my clothes, and when she look at me again, half of my face had wrinkled up, like the skin of some ancient creature. My eye had turn grey and stared at her. She panicked and slapped my face and commanded the spirit to leave my body.

The thing on the bed didn't cry. It just started back at her, as if daring her to do it again.

She then dropped to her knees and started to pray the rosary.

And after what felt like an eternity of praying, my face returned to normal and I started to cry.

A séance was conducted in the house and the medium was able to communicate with the spirit, who turned out to be the old man who used to live in that house and insisted it was his home. The medium supposedly convinced the angry soul that it was time to move on and we were never bothered by the ghost again.

When I was around five or six years old, that was when my dad started to tell me stories about the aswang during bedtime. "You need to stay in bed because there's an aswang flying outside out window," which he'd say in a very matter-of-fact tone.

So, growing up with stories about ghosts in the house and aswang outside the house can either make one go crazy or you end up writing stories like TRESE.

To an outsider, Manila can sound like a city straight out of a magic realism novel or urban fantasy book – with our 300 year-old churches, mystical amulets that can bought from street corners, and newspaper headlines that scream in big, red fonts about the snake-men living under the mall and low-flying manananggal seen during the night of the full moon.

Add to that mix an unhealthy dose of American pop culture – from comic books like Batman, Hellblazer, Hellboy, Sandman and Planetary to TV shows like Karl Kolchak:The Nightstalker, The X-Files, and CSI, plus a dash of anime like Ghost in the Shell – and you have the ingredients for this comic book.

Of course, the spark that got this comic book started was a text message from Kajo Baldisimo sent in June 2005. At that time we were both working of ad agencies, handling very busy accounts, which meant that a normal work day would require late nights at the office. So, when he texted me, "Hey Budj! Let's do a comic book – a monthly comic book!" I laughed and said we wouldn't have the time to do such a thing. But he insisted and said if can give him a 20-page script every month, he can draw a page a day – using his one hour lunch break – so, by the end of 20 days he'd have all the art done and use the remaining 10 days to letter, revise some art, and do the cover.

So, I dug up an old script this didn't have an ending. The original draft of the script starred Anton Trese, who was investigating the death of the White Lady of Balete Drive.

The name "Anton Trese" was created by my friend Mark Gatela. Back in the mid-90s, we co-wrote a radio show about supernatural incidents set in Metro Manila and Anton Trese was the name of the narrator – a mash-up of Rod Serling, Robert Stack and the Cryptkeeper.

I sent Kajo a description of Anton Trese and a one-page fight scene. During his lunch break he drew the page and then sent it to me. Even though the artwork looked great, there was something about it that felt like it was just going to be your typical tough-guy fighting monsters. So, I texted Kajo, "What if we make Trese a woman?" And he replied, "That would be even more cool! She will be so bad-ass!" And before the day ended, he emailed me the first sketches of Alexandra Trese, which made me say, "Yup, that's her alright!"

And Kajo kept true to his promise and delivered issue after issue of TRESE from 2005 to 2006 and we released them in photocopied-ashcan format and sold them for less than a dollar at comic book shops and the local Komikon events.

In 2007, Nida Ramirez of Visprint Publishing accepted our pitch and we were able to compile our stories into a book format and that got us into bookstores.

In 2010, one of these books ended up in the hands of producer Tanya Yuson, who was looking for stories that can be adapted into a TV show or movie. Later on, we met her partner Shanty Harmayn, and for nearly a decade, they pitched TRESE to different studios around the world.

In 2018, we pitched TRESE to a US publisher and got rejected. Kajo insisted that we needed to find a way to get our book to a more global audience. So, he decided to redraw issue #1 and suggested we put it on Indiegogo. Around that same time, Tanya and Shanty's pitch to Netflix Anime got green-lit and our show was announced as part of the upcoming line-up of new anime series. Jay Oliva came on board as our show runner and executive producer.

Thanks to all that buzz about the anime series, Rich Young from Ablaze reached out and told us about their new publishing company. At that time, they already had a great line-up of graphic albums from Europe and manga from Japan. It felt like good company to be with and we'd be published by a company that brought new comic book stories to the North American market.

And that, gentle reader, is the not-so-short-not-so-secret-origin-story of why you're holding this book in your hands.

In 1994, when we released our first black-and-white, self-published comic book, we got interviewed and the reported asked, "Where do you see this book five years from now?" And with full confidence, we said that we'll probably be releasing new issues monthly and be distributed in the United States. (That didn't happen.)

I guess we missed our target by nearly three decades, but we finally got here.

Thank you very much for reading our book. We hope you've enjoyed our tour of the dark side of Metro Manila.

Please do come back to The Diabolical for another round of the strange and the unexplained.

Budjette Tan
Billund, Denmark
June 2020

Budjette would like to say thanks to: Nida Ramirez, VISPRINT crew, and Avenida Publishing; Tanya Yuson and Shanty Harmayn of BASE ENTERTAINMENT; Jay Oliva, Mihk Vergara, Zig Marasigan and the rest of Team TRESE ANIME; The Titos and Titas of Denmark; the guys and gals of The Brigade; the TRESE Chronicles contributors -- David Hontiveros, Marvin Malonzo, JB Tapia, Bow Guerrero; Hank "d'Bartender" Palenzuela and Karen Kunawicz; everyone in rowdy TRESE FB Group – whom I think are three steps ahead of me and have already guessed all my plot twists; all the comic books shops and book stores that have supported us through the years -- Comic Odyssey, Comic Quest, Druid's Keep, FILBARs, Fully Booked, Mt Cloud, National Bookstore, Pandayan, Secret HQ; the organizers of Komikon and Komiket, and of course, Rich Young and Team ABLAZE!

Kajo says thank you to all the avid Trese readers who supported us through the years, to Nida and the Visprint/Avenida team, to Tanya, Shanty, direk Jay and the rest of Base Entertainment, and now to Rich of Ablaze, for helping us share the story of Alexandra to the world. Also, to you, the new reader who's holding this book right now, for giving this world a glance.